Legal Writing:
Form and Function

Legal Writing:
Form and Function

Jane N. Richmond, Ph.D.

NATIONAL INSTITUTE FOR TRIAL ADVOCACY

© 2002 National Institute for Trial Advocacy
PRINTED IN THE UNITED STATES OF AMERICA
ALL RIGHTS RESERVED

Richmond, Jane N., *Legal Writing: Form and Function* (NITA, 2002).

ISBN 1-55681-696-0

Library of Congress Cataloging-in-Publication Data
Richmond, Jane N., 1944-
    Legal writing : form and function / Jane N. Richmond.
        p. cm.
    Includes index.
    ISBN 1-55681-696-0
        1. Legal composition. 2. Law--United States--Language. I. Title.
KF250 .R53 2001
808'.06634--dc21   2001044472

To Liz and Larry, who bring me so much joy

Summary of Contents

Glossary

A glossary at the back of this book will assist the reader with terms. See page 265.

Index

Contents

About the Author

Jane N. Richmond, Ph.D., is the Director of the Writing Program at Jones, Day, Reavis & Pogue, where she has taught writing to hundreds of lawyers since 1982. With a Ph.D. in English and more than thirty years' teaching experience, Richmond has a broad-based background that enables her to understand lawyers' writing weaknesses firsthand. To address these problems, she developed time-tested techniques, which are collected for the first time in *Legal Writing: Form and Function*.

Preface

Every lawyer can be a good writer. Consider the experience attorneys bring to their practice. They have an extensive education, including rigorous graduate study. Lawyers are extremely verbal and have developed strong reasoning skills. They have learned to trace one thread of argument or analysis without being distracted by other information. When attorneys start to practice, they are highly motivated and willing to work long hours to achieve success.

Law schools recognize the importance of their graduates' writing skills. In addition to the first-year course, many schools have established writing requirements for students in their second and third years. English professors or graduate students teach the principles of good writing in some law schools. Despite these efforts, some lawyers, even those at the top of their classes in prominent schools, begin to practice with gaps in their writing background.

Writing is an integral part of a lawyer's professional competence. Writing lies at the heart of a practice, and most attorneys write every day. Associates prepare legal memoranda. Litigators write to convince judges. Other documents record transactions. Behind the scenes, some lawyers draft arguments for others who will convince juries. Of course, most attorneys communicate with their clients in writing.

Legal Writing: Form and Function is designed for lawyers in all areas of practice and for aspiring attorneys. Samples in this book were drafted by practicing attorneys. Most materials come from writing related to practice, i.e., memoranda, briefs, and letters. A few examples were selected from office memoranda prepared by lawyers. Throughout *Legal Writing: Form and Function*, my goal is to help you identify gaps in your writing background, develop the skills to fill them, and write effectively with confidence.

CHAPTER ONE

～ *Style* ～

Legal writing can be direct, concise, engaging, and persuasive. If you apply the principles of good writing, you can express even the most complicated concepts clearly. Chapter 1 will illustrate these principles. Their special application to persuasive writing will be explained in chapter 2.

1.1 Sentence Structure

1.1.1 Dividing Long Sentences

Long, convoluted sentences make legal writing hard to understand. Clarity is especially important when you communicate complex legal matters. Readers cannot easily connect the ideas at the beginning of a long sentence with those at the end. Rather than start over, readers may skip to the next sentence, hoping that it will provide a context for earlier material.

As you revise, divide long sentences into shorter ones. First, look for conceptual and structural divisions in the material. If possible, create separate sentences and add a transition that expresses the relationship between them.

Sentence 1(a) is too long:

1(a) *Although the FHLBB Order exempts the conservator from obtaining director of FHLBB approval and thus Olson may have been correct in his view of his authority, to comply with § 548.2(k), Olson was obligated to determine that the agreement between Sunshine Savings and Capco was "burdensome" before he could renege on this previously approved contract.*

A clear break occurs after "authority." To divide the sentence, first delete "although" and convert the two dependent clauses to a compound sentence:

> *1(b)*   *The FHLBB Order exempts the conservator from obtaining director of FHLBB approval, and thus Olson may have been correct in his view of his authority.*

Then add "nevertheless" at the beginning of the second sentence:

> *1(c)*   <u>*Nevertheless*</u>*, to comply with § 548.2(k), Olson was obligated to determine that the agreement between Sunshine Savings and Capco was "burdensome" before he could renege on the previously approved contract.*

Exercise

Divide these long sentences.

A. We can negate this fact by establishing that Wesley and Newpact engaged in some type of fraud or collusion to make Anderson an unwilling signatory to the contract or by establishing that Anderson is not bound to the contract because Newpact is not a disclosed principal and because Wesley knew that Anderson did not intend to be bound by the contract.

B. The mistake cases arise in a setting where the contract has not been fully executed, and if the mistake excuses performance, the court has three options: it can do nothing; it can reform the agreement; or it can undo the agreement and return the parties to their previous status.

Answers

A. We can negate this fact by establishing that Wesley and Newpact engaged in some type of fraud or collusion to make Anderson an unwilling signatory to the contract.

   Alternatively, we can establish that Anderson is not bound to the contract because Newpact is not a disclosed principal and because Wesley knew that Anderson did not intend to be bound by the contract.

B. The mistake cases arise in a setting where the contract has not been fully executed.

   If the mistake excuses performance, the court has three options: do nothing, reform the agreement, or undo the agreement and return the parties to their previous status.

1.1.2 Long Sentences with Compound Predicates

Divide long sentences with compound predicates. A compound predicate consists of two or more verbs with the same subject. To revise these sentences, put a period after the first main clause, add a subject, and continue the second sentence.

When facts are complicated, use short sentences for clarity. With a compound predicate and many modifiers, sentence 1(a) is hard to read:

> 1(a)   *After Robert Miller sent the March 5 letter to Ms. Peterman, John Greene, CEO of Etco, knew he would need Ms. Peterman's approval under the Supervisory Agreement, and thus sent her the March 20 letter apologizing for the March 5 threat and stating that Etco was "studying the matter further."*

Three basic grammatical units make up this sentence. The first consists of the introductory adverbial clause, "after Robert Miller sent the March 5 letter to Ms. Peterman." The second unit is the main clause: "John Greene, CEO of Etco, knew he would need Ms. Peterman's approval under the Supervisory Agreement." The third unit contains: (1) the second main verb, "sent"; (2) its object, "letter"; (3) a prepositional phrase; and (4) two participial phrases.

Divide this sentence after "agreement" in line 3. The introductory elements and main clause will form the first sentence:

> 1(b)   *After Robert Miller sent the March 5 letter to Ms. Peterman, John Greene, CEO of Etco, knew that he would need Ms. Peterman's approval under the Supervisory Agreement.*

To convert the verb phrase into an independent clause, delete the conjunction and add a subject, "he":

> 1(c)   *Thus, he sent her the March 20 letter apologizing for the March 5 threat and stating that Etco was "studying the matter further."*

1.1.3   Long Sentences with Subordinate Clauses

Shorten long sentences with subordinate, or dependent, clauses. A subordinate clause contains a subject and verb but cannot stand alone as a sentence. Do not add dependent clauses before and after a main clause unless you first consider sentence length. In the example below, a lawyer created a long sentence by linking two subordinate clauses to a main clause:

> *1(a)   If the judge finds that the conflict meets the actual controversy require-ment, she probably would entertain the action, because a declaration that Newpact must indemnify Andrews would settle the dispute between Newpact and Andrews and also would clarify the rights and legal relations between the two parties.*

The sentence begins with a subordinate adverbial clause, "if the judge finds that the conflict meets the actual controversy requirement." An in-dependent clause, "she probably would entertain the action," follows. The lawyer should have ended here but added a long causal clause.

To improve this sentence, divide it and add transitions between sec-tions. You can maintain the causal element of the final dependent clause by inserting "for two reasons" at the end of the main clause:

> *1(b)   If the judge finds that the conflict meets the actual controversy requirement, she probably would entertain the action <u>for two reasons</u>.*

Next, draft a separate sentence to explain each reason:

> *1(c)   First, a declaration that Newpact must indemnify Andrews would settle the dispute between Newpact and Andrews.*

Delete "also" and add "second" at the beginning of sentence 1(d) to establish the relationship between the two reasons:

> *1(d)   Second, the declaration would clarify the rights and legal relationship between the two parties.*

1.1.4 Long Sentences with Two Independent Clauses

Use a semicolon between two short, closely related independent clauses joined without a conjunction. This structure sharply juxtaposes short clauses and stresses their relationship. But long clauses linked by a semicolon create a sprawling sentence:

1(a) *Therefore, in copyright cases, relation back to the date of registration creates no problem for the damages issue; relation back of a later-issued patent to the earlier filing date of the case, however, increases the defendants' exposure to damages in patent actions.*

To express the distinction more effectively, divide the sentence at the semicolon:

1(b) *Therefore, in copyright cases, relation back to the date of registration creates no problem for the damages issue. Relation back of a later-issued patent to the earlier filing date of the case, however, increases the defendants' exposure to damages in patent actions.*

Exercise

Divide this long sentence.

After briefly reviewing EAJA's legislative history, the court recognized that the Act does not authorize a fee award in favor of an acquitted criminal defendant; consequently, the court would not authorize such an award if during the course of his trial the defendant defeated a motion to quash a trial subpoena.

Answer

After briefly reviewing EAJA's legislative history, the court recognized that the Act does not authorize a fee award in favor of an acquitted criminal defendant.

Consequently, the court would not authorize such an award if during the course of his trial the defendant defeated a motion to quash a trial subpoena.

1.1.5 Long Sentences with Series

Do not insert a long series in a complicated sentence. Instead, look for grammatical divisions and create separate sentences.

An attorney used two series in the long sentence that follows:

> 1(a)　*In addition to the Master Schedule, Wicker should maintain a file, labeled <u>with the name and number of each purchaser</u>, on each such individual, including <u>all forms and correspondence received; and copies of all supplemental information, letters, records, and documents responding to inquiries from the purchaser</u>.*

You can separate this material into two parts: the recommendation to set up the files, and their contents:

> 1(b)　*In addition to the Master Schedule, Wicker should maintain a file, labeled with the name and number of each purchaser, on each such individual,*

> 1(c)　*including all forms and correspondence received; and copies of all supplemental information, letters, records, and documents responding to inquiries from the purchaser.*

Next, move the phrase describing the file labels from the first passage to the second. Without the first series, the main sentence is more direct:

> 1(d)　*In addition to the Master Schedule, Wicker should maintain a file on each <u>such individual</u>.*

Then clarify the referent for "such individual" by substituting "purchaser":

> 1(e)　*In addition to the Master Schedule, Wicker should maintain a file on each <u>purchaser</u>.*

Finally, combine the two series that describe the label and contents of each file. Insert the series in a new sentence:

> 1(f)　*Each file, labeled with <u>the name and number of the purchaser</u>, should include the following materials: <u>all forms and correspondence received; and copies of all supplemental information, letters,</u>*

records, and documents sent in response to inquiries from the purchaser.

Exercise

Divide this long sentence.

> Emory Club was a new construction site where LBH Roofing, a roofing subcontractor, was installing a Littleton Rubbercoat roofing system, the main components of which are: (1) the Rubbercoat membrane; (2) AP-7005 bonding adhesive manufactured by Aspen, Inc., but labeled and distributed by Littleton; and (3) BDC-90 polyisocyanurate insulation board manufactured by Nylomex, also labeled and distributed by Littleton.

Answer

> Emory Club was a new construction site where LBH Roofing, a roofing subcontractor, was installing a Littleton Rubbercoat roofing system.

> The main components of the roofing system are: (1) the Rubbercoat membrane; (2) AP-7005 bonding adhesive manufactured by Aspen, Inc., but labeled and distributed by Littleton; and (3) BDC-90 polyisocyanurate insulation board manufactured by Nylomex, also labeled and distributed by Littleton.

1.1.6 Long Sentences with a Quotation

Do not introduce a case, explain the circumstances, and outline the court's holding in the same sentence. With all this information, the sentence will be too long. After several lines, readers will have to stop, review previous material, and then make logical connections between clauses.

In sentence 1(a), a lawyer crammed too much into one sentence:

1(a) *In* United States v. Minarik, *875 F.2d 1186 (6th Cir. 1989), where the indictment alleged that defendant fraudulently concealed assets from the Internal Revenue Service and the indictment failed to allege that the defendant had a duty to disclose or even not to conceal assets, the court held that "[a] charge of conspiracy to defraud will not lie where there is no positive obstruction of a governmental program."*

This sentence contains four units of meaning: a prepositional phrase explaining the case name and citation, the "where" clause with two statements about the indictment, and the court's holding.

To revise this sentence, divide it into three shorter units. Combine the first two elements and delete "where":

> *1(b)* *In* United States v. Minarik, *875 F.2d 1186 (6th Cir. 1989), the indictment alleged that defendant fraudulently concealed assets from the Internal Revenue Service.*

Next, add a transition that expresses "addition" before the second statement about the indictment:

> *1(c)* <u>*Moreover*</u>*, the indictment failed to allege that the defendant had a duty to disclose or even not to conceal assets.*

The original independent clause stands effectively alone. By using the abbreviated case name before "court," you will link the new sentences conceptually:

> *1(d)* *The* Minarik *court held that "[a] charge of conspiracy to defraud will not lie where there is no positive obstruction of a governmental program."*

1.1.7 "Top-Heavy" Sentences

Use only short introductory structures before a main clause. A long clause or phrase creates a top-heavy sentence that is difficult to understand. The reader has no context for the long introductory element, and the main clause comes too late to anchor previous information.

In sentence 1(a), a lawyer included the case name and facts in a five-line introductory phrase with modifiers:

> *1(a)* *In* Acme Railroad Co. v. Conlin Chemical Corp., *where the plaintiff sought to recover for negligence, strict product liability, and breach of warranty in the design and manufacture of a tank car and wheel that allegedly caused a train derailment, the Fifth Circuit reversed the district court's summary judgment on the six-year limitation period.*

The sheer quantity of information in the introductory element makes the sentence top-heavy.

Divide this sentence to make it easier to read. First, delete "where" to convert the long introductory phrase to a sentence:

1(b) *In* Acme Railroad Co. v. Conlin Chemical Corp., *the plaintiff sought to recover for negligence, strict product liability, and breach of warranty in the design and manufacture of a tank car and wheel that allegedly caused a train derailment.*

The independent clause then stands alone:

1(c) *The Fifth Circuit reversed the district court's summary judgment on the six-year limitation period.*

Some top-heavy sentences begin with conjunctions like "while," "whereas," and "although." For example, an attorney used two long introductory clauses in sentence 2(a):

2(a) *While we cannot predict how the district court would address this issue, if that court rules in Southern's favor on either of the two pending motions, Granco can argue that Southern is entitled to an EAJA award.*

By dropping the conjunction "while," you convert the initial adverbial clause to an independent clause:

2(b) *We cannot predict how the district court for the Central District of California would address this issue.*

No division is needed between the second introductory clause and the main clause. To preserve the meaning expressed by "while," add a transition before the sentence:

2(c) <u>*But*</u> *if that court rules in Southern's favor on either of the two pending motions, Granco can argue that Southern is entitled to an EAJA award.*

"Although" introduces long introductory elements in sentence 3(a):

3(a) *Although several circuits require a defendant to meet its burden in the damages phase of Title VII cases with clear and convincing evidence, in*

Woolridge v. Marlene Indus. Corp., 875 F.2d 540 (6th Cir. 1989), the Sixth Circuit did not impose a clear and convincing proof requirement.

To revise this sentence, first delete "although" from the introductory clause:

> 3(b)   *Several circuits require a defendant to meet its burden in the damages phase of Title VII cases with clear and convincing evidence.*

Then add "yet" before the second main clause to maintain the relationship expressed by "although":

> 3(c)   <u>*Yet*</u> in Woolridge v. Marlene Indus. Corp., *875 F.2d 540 (6th Cir. 1989), the Sixth Circuit did not impose a clear and convincing proof requirement.*

Sentence 4(a) is top-heavy because the introductory clause contains a long series:

> 4(a)   *While parties rarely succeed on a special circumstance exception to an award of attorneys' fees in Ohio, California, Illinois, and Texas, a few courts have denied attorneys' fees based upon this exception.*

After dropping "while" from the introductory clause, you can express the same meaning with "however" after the subject in 4(c):

> 4(b)   *Parties rarely succeed on a special circumstance exception to an award of attorneys' fees in Ohio, California, Illinois, and Texas.*

> 4(c)   *A few courts, however, have denied attorneys' fees based upon this exception.*

CHAPTER ONE

Exercise

Revise these top-heavy sentences.

A. Although the Ohio General Assembly recently amended *Ohio Rev. Code* Chap. 5727 to remove interexchange carriers from the definition of "telephone company" in *Ohio Rev. Code* § 5727.01, this action provides only limited support for Teleco's argument that its personal property belongs in the more favored class of non-utility property.

B. In *United States v. Hickey,* 360 F.2d 127 (7th Cir. 1966), a case involving a conspiracy to defraud a federally insured savings and loan association through misapplication of its funds, the Seventh Circuit found that concealment was necessary to achieve the objective of the alleged conspiracy.

C. While *Leucadia, Dayco, Baker's Aid,* and some inadvertent waiver cases support the proposition that Simmons has not waived the attorney-client privilege with respect to the memoranda, this line of authority breaks with the traditional, strict theory where disclosure of privileged information waives the privilege regardless of the circumstances.

Answers

A. The Ohio General Assembly recently amended *Ohio Rev. Code* Chap. 5727 to remove interexchange carriers from the definition of "telephone company" in *Ohio Rev. Code* § 5727.01.

Yet this action provided only limited support for Teleco's argument that its personal property belongs in the more favored class of non-utility property.

• Delete "although" and add "yet" before the second sentence.

B. United States v. Hickey, 360 F.2d 127 (7th Cir. 1966) involved a conspiracy to defraud a federally insured savings and loan association through misapplication of its funds.

In *Hickey,* the Seventh Circuit found that concealment was necessary to achieve the objective of the alleged conspiracy.

• First, combine the two introductory elements in an independent clause. Add an "in" phrase before the main clause.

C. *Leucadia, Dayco, Baker's Aid,* and some inadvertent waiver cases support the proposition that Simmons has not waived the attorney-client privilege with respect to the memoranda.

But this line of authority breaks with the traditional, strict theory where disclosure of privileged information waives the privilege regardless of the circumstances.

• Delete "while" and begin the second sentence with "but."

1.1.8   Varying Your Sentence Structure

Vary the form of your sentences. As you revise, consider the effect of each structure in context. Experiment with different forms to ensure that every sentence expresses your intended meaning and holds the reader's attention. Overuse of one structure will bore the reader. Contrasting structures, on the other hand, will make your writing livelier and more persuasive.

Some basic sentence structures in English include:

<u>Simple sentence</u>: one subject and one or two verbs.

1. *Plaintiff signed an offer letter for employment with BOC Corporation.*

2. *Ms. Roberts purchased and sold commercial property in Miami last year.*

<u>Compound sentence</u>: two independent clauses joined by "and," "but," "or," "nor," "for," "so," or "yet."

3. *The creditor can extend new value to replenish the estate for the preferential transfer, but preferential payments do not carry forward.*

<u>Complex sentence with dependent clause first</u>: one subordinate clause and one main clause.

4. *When Mr. Gray resigned from BOC, he forfeited his right to the $5,000 transition payment.*

<u>Complex sentence with independent clause first</u>: one main clause and one subordinate clause.

5. *Plaintiff's claim will fail because he was an employee-at-will.*

You can use either the active or passive voice in these structures. For example, sentence 6 is a simple sentence with an active verb:

6. *An employer's legitimate decisions do not violate the reasonable person test.*

Sentence 7 is a compound sentence with a passive verb and an active verb:

> 7. *Ms. Walsh was subjected to sexual harassment by her supervisors, so she complained to the human resources manager.*

Exercise

Convert this sentence to four different structures. Add information as needed.

Elson Company owes $500,000 to Amco National Bank.

Answer

Possible structures:

Elson Company owes $500,000 to Fifth National Bank, which was founded by Thomas A. Mitchell in 1898. (Complex sentence with independent clause first)

Elson Company owes $500,000 to Amco National Bank, but Amco must repay the same amount to Transbank of Syracuse. (Compound sentence)

Although the board of directors attempted to clear all debts, Elson Company owes $500,000 to Amco National Bank. (Complex sentence with dependent clause first)

Elson Company owes $500,000 to Amco National Bank and plans to repay the debt by December 31. (Simple sentence with two verbs)

1.1.9 Revising Monotonous Sentence Structure

Using the same sentence structure over and over creates monotonous prose. To identify repetitive structures, read each paragraph aloud. Then analyze patterns, eliminate repetition, and add elements to create a graceful, balanced style.

Many readers will skip choppy passages like the fact section in 1(a):

> 1(a) *Ms. Parker defaulted on the contract. Central Financial sued Parker in state court in Cameron County, Texas. In its complaint, Central Financial sought a judgment for the amount due on the contract and for foreclosure of its security interest in the mobile home. Parker answered the complaint and denied every allegation. Central Financial subsequently*

filed a request for admissions. Parker did not respond. Central Financial filed a motion for summary judgment. The court granted the motion. Parker did not appeal and the judgment is final.

Before you revise a monotonous passage, analyze its style. In 1(a), every sentence begins with the subject and verb, and most sentences are short. Next, identify revisions that would improve the style, i.e., what elements of smooth prose are missing? To revise this passage, vary the length and beginnings of sentences. Then experiment with techniques for combining short sentences and adding introductory elements.

Note the improved prose in 1(b):

1(b)   *<u>When Ms. Parker defaulted on the contract</u>, Central Financial sued her in state court in Cameron County, Texas. In its complaint, Central Financial <u>then</u> sought a judgment for the amount due on the contract and for foreclosure of its security interest in the mobile home. <u>In her answer to the complaint</u>, Parker denied every allegation. Central Financial subsequently filed a request for admissions, <u>but</u> Parker did not respond. Central Financial <u>then</u> filed a motion for summary judgment. <u>After the court granted the motion</u>, Parker did not appeal. The judgment is final.*

In the revised passage, underlined terms show ways to vary sentence structure. For example, you can create an adverbial clause by adding "when" before "Ms. Parker defaulted on the contract" and combine the new clause with the next sentence. With revisions, "Parker answered the complaint" becomes "in her answer to the complaint," an introductory phrase. To clarify the chronology and break up the subject-verb pattern, insert adverbs like "then" and "subsequently" after subject nouns. Finally, combine short sentences with coordinating conjunctions, as in "Central Financial subsequently filed a request for admission, but Parker did not respond."

1.2 The Passive Voice

Use the passive voice in moderation. Overuse of the passive makes writing awkward, wordy, and indirect. In carefully chosen contexts, however, the passive voice can be effective.

1.2.1   Active vs. Passive

In an active sentence, the actor (or subject) performs the action stated by the verb. The verb must be transitive, i.e., able to take an object. An optional receiver (or object) may follow the verb. An active sentence has the following structure: actor (subject)-verb-receiver (object):

1.   *The attorney filed the brief.*

If you convert a sentence to its passive form, the receiver (or subject) of the action comes first. The verb consists of a form of "to be" and the past participle. The actor (which served as subject in the active version), introduced with the preposition "by," may follow the verb. A passive sentence with an actor has the following structure: receiver of the action (subject)-verb "to be" + past participle-"by" + actor:

2.   *The brief was filed by the attorney.*

The active voice is more concise and direct than the passive.

1.2.2   Disadvantages of the Passive Voice

A passive verb slows a sentence down and makes it indirect. In sentence 1(a), three passive verbs create a convoluted style:

1(a)   *Although this comparative labor cost data was furnished by Seton to U.A.W. Local 302, the concessions that were requested by Seton were rejected by the union.*

The long verb forms require seven words: "has been furnished," "were requested," and "were rejected." Moreover, repetition of "by" is awkward.

If you use the active voice, the sentence will be shorter and more direct:

1(b)   *Although Seton furnished this comparative labor cost data to U.A.W. Local 302, the union rejected the concessions that Seton requested.*

This change reduces the number of words from twenty-six to twenty, or by 23 percent. The reader does not have to struggle through all the helping verbs and repeated use of "by." In addition, the syntax is more logical; the audience can read and absorb the sentence quickly.

Vague passives create a weak introduction to quotations. A wordy passive precedes the quotation in sentence 2(a):

> 2(a)   It has been noted that "the overriding interest of a court in designating lead counsel is the vigorous protection of the rights of the plaintiff class."

If the source is important, convert the introduction to the active voice and name the case:

> 2(b)   The Smith v. Axco court noted that "the overriding interest of a court in designating lead counsel is the vigorous protection of the rights of the plaintiff class."

To place more emphasis on the quotation, delete the lead-in and add a cite after the sentence:

> 2(c)   "The overriding interest of a court in designating lead counsel is the vigorous protection of the rights of the plaintiff class." [Cite]

The passive voice also is indirect and wordy. In sentence 3(a), a lawyer used a passive verb to emphasize the plaintiff's delay:

> 3(a)   In September, over one and one-half years after the services at issue were rendered by Dr. Wood, the instant action against Med-Insured, Inc. was filed by her.

With long verbs, repetition of "by," and indirect syntax, the passive voice creates an awkward sentence. To be more persuasive, convert it to the active voice. This shortens the sentence from twenty-seven to twenty-three words, or 15 percent:

> 3(b)   In September, over one and one-half years after Dr. Wood rendered the services at issue, she filed the instant action against Med-Insured, Inc.

This revision also moves "Dr. Wood" and "she" into the subject position, stressing her role as creator of the delay.

The passive voice may weaken your introduction. Use active verbs to state legal issues and preview the contents of a legal memorandum. Writing in both these sections should be concise and direct. The wordy introduction in passage 1(a) contains five passive verbs:

1(a)   An analysis of the issues under Federal Rule 26 and applicable legal precedents is shown in this memo. First, whether disclosure of the substance of the interviews would be ordered by a federal court is discussed. Second, whether the identity of interviewees must be revealed to defendants by plaintiffs is analyzed.

The first sentence contains a passive verb, "is shown," and many unnecessary words. By moving "this memo" into the subject position and converting the noun "analysis" to its active verb form, you can make the sentence more direct:

1(b)   This memo analyzes two issues under Federal Rule 26 and applicable legal precedents.

Your choice between active and passive in issue statements will depend on your intended emphasis. In the second and third sentences, an indirect passive question is the subject. Both serve as subjects in a passive sentence:

1(c)   SUBJECT is discussed.

1(d)   SUBJECT is analyzed.

First, focus on each issue statement and determine whether you want to stress the result or the actor. The passive voice emphasizes the result:

1(e)   Whether disclosure of the substance of the interviews would be ordered by a federal court.

1(f)   Whether the identity of interviewees must be revealed to defendants by plaintiffs.

When you convert these issues to the active voice, you stress the actor. Compare the first passive question, "whether disclosure of the substance of the interviews would be ordered by a federal court," to the active version:

> 1(g)   Whether a federal court would order disclosure of the substance of the interviews.

You also can use the active voice in the second passive question:

> 1(h)   Whether plaintiffs must reveal the identity of interviewees to defendants.

Finally, to improve the overall passive structure, omit the verb phrases "is discussed" and "is analyzed." The verb "analyzes" in the lead-in expresses the same meaning. The two tabulated issues should follow. If you use the active voice for the two issues, the passage will be more concise:

> 1(i)   This memo analyzes two issues under Federal Rule 26 and applicable legal precedents:
>
> i.   Whether a federal court would order disclosure of the substance of the interviews.
>
> ii.   Whether plaintiffs must reveal the identity of interviewees to defendants.

You can state the issues more concisely without the traditional "whether" form. Convert these indirect questions to direct questions:

> i.   Would a federal court order disclosure of the substance of the interviews?
>
> ii.   Must plaintiffs reveal the identity of interviewees to defendants?

These revisions cut the number of words in the passage by 33 percent.

1.2.3　Advantages of the Passive Voice

The passive voice enables you to conceal the identity of the actor. For example, when you start with the passive sentence 1(a), you may omit the actor, as shown in 1(b):

1(a)　Plaintiff was injured by Ms. Snow's truck on October 1.

1(b)　Plaintiff was injured on October 1.

The new sentence consists of only the subject, verb, and modifiers. This deletion has advantages, especially if you do not know, or do not wish to reveal, the identity of the actor. For example, in sentence 2 a lawyer used a passive verb without the actor:

2.　Insider information was leaked at Acme Brokers, Inc. on June 26.

With this structure, you can state that an action occurred even if you do not know who performed it. At times, you may know the actor-agent but prefer to omit that information. If your clients leaked the insider information, you can use a passive verb without naming an actor.

The passive voice can emphasize an indirect role or result. For example, if you offered a client only general advice, you might use the passive voice, as shown in sentence 3(a):

3(a)　Last year, as part of the transition to the new rules, efforts were made with the Altan Insiders to have them review their prior transactions.

With the passive structure "efforts were made," you do not have to provide an actor. The vague noun "efforts" and general verb "were made" enable you to "cover yourself" since you do not have to state particular advice you offered.

If, on the other hand, you can point to specific guidance that you provided, use the active voice:

3(b)　Last year, as part of the transition to the new rules, Ms. Brown and Mr. Little advised the Altan Insiders to review their prior transactions.

This active version names actors and uses the verb "advised," in contrast with the passive "efforts were made." In this context, the active voice is more persuasive.

Exercise

A. Convert these passive sentences to their shorter active version. Make other revisions as needed.

1. Section 203(d) has been cited by other federal courts as tolling the running of the limitations period.

2. Corporate and governmental entities' claims of attorney-client privilege were not considered by the *Teleco* court.

3. The report is required to be furnished by White, Inc. to shareholders and the SEC.

B. Explain the potential effect of the passive voice in these sentences:

1. The senator was persuaded by lobbyists to vote against his convictions.

2. The plaintiff was assaulted at the corner of Third Avenue and Willow Street.

C. Analyze the effectiveness of the passive voice in this passage. Convert all verbs to the active voice, and note the effect of your revisions.

The directors were advised by the bank examiner to exercise more supervision over loans. In addition, the board members were encouraged by management to improve their knowledge of applicable laws. The examiner's written report was then discussed by the board members, and a copy was given to each director.

Answers

A. 1. Other federal courts have cited Section 203(d) as tolling the running of the limitations period.

2. The *Teleco* court did not consider corporate and governmental entities' claims of attorney-client privilege.

3. White, Inc. must furnish the report to shareholders and the SEC.

B. 1. The passive voice portrays the senator as a person whom others easily can sway.

2. The writer concedes that the assault occurred but conceals the actor's identity.

C. Overuse of the passive voice in "were advised," "was encouraged," "was discussed," and "was given" creates an awkward, wordy style. Convert the passive verbs to the active:

The bank examiner advised the directors to exercise more supervision over loans. In addition, management encouraged the board members to improve their knowledge of applicable laws. The board members then discussed the examiner's written report, and each director received a copy.

• In the active version, the prose is more concise and direct.

1.3 Awkwardness

Replace awkward structures with smoother forms. As you revise, analyze the cause of each convoluted clause or phrase. Did you separate major elements? Have you used multiple negatives? Extra words? Awkward syntax? Read your prose aloud to identify structures that need revision.

1.3.1   Separation of Major Elements by a Modifier

As a general rule, keep a sentence's major grammatical elements together. Do not separate them with long intervening clauses or phrases. With these interrupters, the reader must work hard to connect important grammatical units.

Avoid placing a long phrase or clause between a sentence's subject and verb. In sentence 1(a), a prepositional phrase separates these elements:

1(a)   *The employee, after consuming several alcoholic drinks at a holiday party given by her employer, Ross Company, at the Woodlawn Club in Buffalo on December 23, became visibly intoxicated and attempted to drive home.*

The subject, "employee," is separated from the verb, "became," by the long intervening phrase: "after consuming several alcoholic drinks at a holiday party given by her employer, Ross Company, at the Woodlawn Club in Buffalo on December 23." To revise this awkward structure, move the intervening phrase to the sentence's beginning:

1(b)   *After consuming several alcoholic drinks at a holiday party given by her employer, Ross Company, at the Woodlawn Club in Buffalo on December 23, the employee became visibly intoxicated and attempted to drive home.*

The subject and verb are together, but the long introductory phrase creates a top-heavy sentence. Next, divide it into shorter units:

1(c)   *The employee consumed several alcoholic drinks at a holiday party given by her employer, Ross Company, at the Woodlawn Club in Buffalo on December 23.*

1(d)   *After she became visibly intoxicated, she attempted to drive home.*

A long intervening modifier creates a disjointed effect below:

2(a)   *The United States court, because Alco's operations and most of its
       assets are located in Canada, likely will defer to the Canadian
       proceedings.*

This writer has separated the subject, "the United States court," from the
verb phrase, "likely will defer to the Canadian proceedings." The modifier is
a dependent adverbial clause, "because Alco's operations and most of its
assets are located in Canada."

To improve the structure, move the adverbial clause to the end of
the sentence. This revision links the major grammatical elements and
improves the sentence's flow:

2(b)   *The United States court likely will defer to the Canadian proceedings
       <u>because Alco's operations and most of its assets are located in
       Canada</u>.*

When a long clause or phrase interrupts major elements, convert it to
a separate sentence. Note the separation of object and complement
below:

3(a)   *In Faries v. Atlas Truck Body Mfg. Co., 797 F. 2d 619, (8th Cir. 1986),
       the court held a police officer's accident report, which contained the
       statement that "apparently [plaintiff] was driving at an excessive rate
       of speed, lost control on a curve, crossed over the center line, over-
       turned and slid under [the milk truck]," inadmissible because it was
       based on hearsay.*

With the long intervening "which" clause, the reader must struggle to connect the object, "report," with the complement, "inadmissible." Link
these elements and move the relative clause to a separate sentence:

3(b)   *In Faries v. Atlas Truck Body Mfg. Co., 797 F. 2d 619 (8th Cir. 1986),
       the court held a police officer's accident report inadmissible because
       it was based on hearsay.*

3(c)   *which contained the statement that "apparently [plaintiff] was
       driving at an excessive rate of speed, lost control on a curve, crossed
       over the center line, overturned and slid under [the milk truck]."*

Substitute "the report" for "which":

> *3(d)*   *The report stated that "apparently [plaintiff] was driving at an excessive rate of speed, lost control on a curve, crossed over the center line, overturned and slid under [the milk truck]."*

Exercise

Analyze the separation of major elements in these sentences. Identify those elements and the intervening structures. Revise as needed.

A. He stated that the Home Real Estate brochure, a copy of which was originally attached to the response by plaintiffs to Request for Production of Documents by Defendant Ann Reese and is attached as Exhibit B hereto, specified that the Subject Parcel was served by a well and septic system.

B. Judge Alexander, after first considering comment "j" of the Restatement of Torts § 402A, which requires a warning only when the manufacturer knows or should know that there is a special danger, stated that the rule of strict liability protects the injured party from the defective product.

C. If the recently enacted *Tenn. Code Ann.* § 66-24-101(23) and § 66-26-116, which provide that a security interest in rents is perfected when it is recorded, applied retroactively, the "transfer" would not be within the applicable time period and therefore would not be subject to avoidance.

Answers

A. Separated elements: subject, "brochure," and verb, "specified"

Intervening structure: relative clause, "which was originally attached to the response by plaintiffs to Request for Production of Documents by Defendant Ann Reese and is attached as Exhibit B hereto"

Revision: The Home Real Estate brochure specified that the Subject Parcel was served by a well and septic system. (A copy of this brochure was originally attached to the response by plaintiffs to Request for Production of Documents by Defendant Ann Reese and is attached as Exhibit B hereto.)

B. Separated elements: subject, "Judge Alexander," and verb, "stated"

Intervening structures: "after first considering comment 'j' of the Restatement of Torts § 402A, which requires a warning only when the manufacturer knows or should know that there is a special danger"

Revision: Judge Alexander first considered comment "j" of the Restatement of Torts § 402A, which requires a warning only when the manufacturer knows or should know that there is a special danger.

She then stated that the rule of strict liability protects the injured party from the defective product.

C. Separated elements: subject, "*Tenn. Code Ann.* § 66-24-101 (23) and § 66-26-116," and verb, "applied"

Intervening structure: "which provide that a security interest in rents is perfected when it is recorded"

Revision: The recently enacted *Tenn. Code Ann.* § 66-24-101 (23) and § 66-26-116 provide that a security interest in rents is perfected when it is recorded.

If these code sections applied retroactively, the "transfer" would not be within the applicable time period and therefore would not be subject to avoidance.

1.3.2   Multiple Negatives

Do not pile up multiple negatives in the same sentence. The human mind cannot absorb negatives as easily as positives. Each negative changes the direction of the argument. With many negatives, a sentence twists and turns in ways that even the most sophisticated reader finds difficult to follow. Negatives include forms such as "no," "not," and "never," as well as words that contain a negative element, e.g., "prevent," "hinder," and "however."

CHAPTER ONE

Multiple negatives make sentence 1(a) complicated and ambiguous:

> 1(a) *Not only does defendants' participation in a conspiracy not end when they stop taking action to advance it, but also their participation begins at the inception of the conspiracy even though they did not join it until later.*

This sentence contains six negatives: "not only," "not," "stops," "but," "even though," and "not." Two of these, "not only . . . but also," create an overall structure for adding clauses. Each part of this expression begins with a negative. When these appear with other negatives, the sense of "addition" is lost. To revise this convoluted sentence, first remove "not only" and "but." Then create shorter units:

> 1(b) *Defendants' participation in a conspiracy does not end when they stop taking action to advance it.*

Add "moreover" before the second sentence to preserve the meaning previously expressed by "not only . . . but":

> 1(c) *Moreover, their participation begins at the inception of the conspiracy even though they did not join it until later.*

The other negatives, which are essential to the sentence's meaning, do not create confusion.

Even short sentences with multiple negatives can be wordy and indirect. For example, sentence 2(a) contains an awkward lead-in with two negatives:

> 2(a) *There is no question but that Gremex currently uses the Marling Building as a warehouse.*

The negatives "no" and "but" are part of a wordy lead-in "there is no question but that." Delete this impersonal expression:

> 2(b) *Gremex currently uses the Marling Building as a warehouse.*

A similar lead-in with the first element of a "double" negative introduces 3(a):

> 3(a)   This does <u>not</u> mean that Vaxco will be <u>without</u> funds available for investment during the next two years.

This writer began with a long phrase that contains an ambiguous pronoun, "this." If you delete the lead-in and move "not" to the main clause, the sentence is shorter and more direct:

> 3(b)   Vaxco will <u>not</u> be <u>without</u> funds available for investment during the next two years.

This double negative structure is called *litotes*, an understatement for effect, in which something is expressed by negating its opposite. In some contexts, litotes can be effective because it communicates a more subtle meaning than a positive assertion. But the double negative in sentence 3(b) is wordy. To make the sentence more concise and affirmative, delete the negatives:

> 3(c)   Vaxco will have funds available for investment during the next two years.

Exercise

Eliminate confusing negatives in this sentence.

> Not only did the defendant not execute the sale before the deadline, but also he did not return the proceeds to Mr. Littleton within ten days.

Answer

> The defendant neither executed the sale before the deadline nor returned the proceeds to Mr. Littleton within ten days.

- With four negatives, this sentence is confusing. Delete "not only" and "but also," and express the other two negatives with "neither . . . nor."

1.3.3   Awkward Subject-Complement Match

When you use the subject-verb-complement structure, match the subject and complement carefully. Put parentheses around intervening words to analyze the subject-complement agreement.

A lawyer used a convoluted subject-complement match in sentence 1(a):

> *1(a)   Thus, <u>the only ways</u> that a Medical Mutual trustee may leave office are <u>to resign, cease to be a policyholder, or die</u>.*

First, put parentheses around intervening words, and isolate the subject, verb, and complement:

> *1(b)   Thus, the only ways (that a Medical Mutual trustee may leave office) are to resign, cease to be a policyholder, or die.*

The subject-verb-complement combination, "the only ways are . . . to + verb," is awkward and wordy.

To revise this sentence, change its overall structure to subject-verb-prepositional phrase. First, delete "the only ways that" and "are:"

> *1(c)   A Medical Mutual trustee may leave office . . . resign, cease to be a policyholder, or die.*

Next, change the infinitive phrases ("to" + verb) to gerunds, "-ing" forms that function as nouns:

> *1(d)   A Medical Mutual trustee may leave office . . . resigning, ceasing to be a policyholder, or dying.*

Finally, add "only" and "by" before the gerunds:

> *1(e)   Thus, a Medical Mutual trustee may leave office <u>only by</u> resigning, ceasing to be a policyholder, or dying.*

1.3.4 Structure of Definitions

Use parallel structure in definitions. The traditional form of a definition contains the verb "to be." To balance the subject and complement, define nouns with nouns, verbs with verbs, etc.

Note the awkward subject-complement match in sentence 1(a):

1(a)   *Slack filling is when a manufacturer makes a package much larger than the product to deceive the customer.*

The writer defined a noun, "slack filling," by using an adverbial clause, "when a manufacturer makes a package much larger . . . ":

1(b)   *Slack filling is <u>when a manufacturer makes a package much larger than the product to deceive the customer</u>.*

To preserve the definition form, change the adverbial phrase to a noun phrase:

1(c)   *Slack filling is <u>a manufacturer's enlargement</u> of a package, beyond the size of the product, to deceive the customer.*

If you prefer to use the adverbial phrase, substitute "occurs" for "is":

1(d)   *Slack filling <u>occurs</u> when a manufacturer makes a package much larger than the product to deceive the customer.*

Exercise

Correct the parallelism problem in this definition.

> Under the New Source Performance Standard, a modification is where any physical or operational change to an existing facility increases the emission rate to the atmosphere of any pollutant to which a standard applies.

Answer

> Under the New Source Performance Standard, a modification is any physical or operational change to an existing facility that increases the emission rate to the atmosphere of any pollutant to which a standard applies.

- The writer matched a noun subject with an adverbial "where" clause. Convert the "where" clause to a noun phrase.

1.3.5 Awkward Syntax

Do not startle your reader with an awkward switch in syntax (word order). You can vary sentence structure without abrupt syntactical changes. To correct problems in syntax, restore normal word order and delete extra words.

In sentence 1(a), a lawyer began with the complement:

1(a)   Also <u>inapplicable is</u> the <u>declaration</u> against interest exception.

The adjective "inapplicable" and its modifier precede the verb and subject. The long phrase "also inapplicable" creates an awkward beginning for the sentence. Instead, use subject-verb-complement order:

1(b)   The <u>declaration</u> against interest exception <u>is</u> also <u>inapplicable</u>.

Placing the direct object before the verb also creates an awkward sentence, as shown in 2(a):

2(a)   Ms. Scott cannot recover on the theory of negligence. <u>This she cannot do</u> because it was not reasonably foreseeable that Atco would substantially modify the control buttons.

In "this she cannot do," the writer reversed the normal subject-verb-object word order. To revise this clause, move the object to its normal position after the verb:

2(b)   Ms. Scott cannot recover on the theory of negligence. <u>She cannot do this</u> because it was not reasonably foreseeable that Atco would substantially modify the control buttons.

Then eliminate the repetition of subject and verb, and combine the clauses:

2(c)   Ms. Scott may not recover on the theory of negligence because it was not reasonably foreseeable that Atco would substantially modify the control buttons.

Inverted syntax in sentence 3(a) creates ambiguity:

3(a)   Charco alleges _in both this litigation and the arbitration claims_ based on ABC's misappropriation of trade secrets and confidential information.

The writer has inserted a long prepositional phrase between the verb, "alleges," and the object, "claims." Readers expect the intervening phrase, "in both this litigation and the arbitration," to fall at the beginning or end of the sentence. As written, "arbitration" seems to modify "claims." With that interpretation, however, "alleges" has no object. Restore the subject-verb-object sequence by moving the "in" phrase to the sentence's beginning:

3(b)   _In both this litigation and the arbitration_, Charco alleges claims based on ABC's misappropriation of trade secrets and confidential information.

Exercise

Revise inverted syntax in these sentences.

A. Also relevant is the defendant's motive.

B. Please forward to me your e-mail address.

Answers

A. The defendant's motive is also relevant.

•   Restore subject-verb-complement order.

B. Please forward your e-mail address to me.

•   Restore verb-object order.

1.4 Verbosity

1.4.1 Deleting Extra Words

Use a clear, direct style in all legal writing. Extra words add clutter and can obscure your message. As you revise, cut every superfluous word.

CHAPTER ONE

Many verbose phrases appear so frequently in legal writing that they may sound natural. Shorten wordy phrases when you can do so without changing their meaning:

1. his being dismissed—*his dismissal*

2. effected the purchase—*purchased* or *bought*

3. to bring suit against—*to sue*

4. to be in breach of—*to breach*

5. in the event that—*if*

6. in order to satisfy—*to satisfy*

7. to have a dispute—*to dispute*

8. the occurrence of a default—*a default*

9. those who succeed us—*our successors*

10. may choose to terminate—*may terminate* or *may end*

11. in the absence of—*without*

12. a small number of—*few*

13. may impair the possibility of success—*may limit the success*

14. is in contrast with—*contrasts with*

15. a large number of—*many*

16. in the exercise of its discretion—*at its discretion*

Review each sentence to eliminate unnecessary repetition. Note repetition of the verb "establish" in sentence 1(a):

> *1(a)*   *The contract's provisions <u>establish when the liquidator must give notice and establish which party should receive notice</u>.*

You can tighten this sentence by deleting "establish" before the "which" clause:

> *1(b)*   *The contract's provisions <u>establish when the liquidator must give notice and which party should receive notice</u>.*

Repetition of "to have" is awkward in sentence 2(a):

> 2(a) *Every bankruptcy law that this country <u>has had has</u> recognized the right of setoff.*

To shorten this sentence, paraphrase the relative clause "that this country has had." You can communicate the same meaning with the shorter phrase "in United States history":

> 2(b) *Every bankruptcy law <u>in United States history</u> has recognized the right of setoff.*

If you convert the phrase "in United States history" to an adjective before "bankruptcy law," the sentence will be even more concise:

> 2(c) *Every <u>United States</u> bankruptcy law has recognized the right of setoff.*

An associate concluded a research assignment with the wordy sentence in 3(a):

> 3(a) *A more formal memorandum, including source citations and more extensive analysis, can be prepared later, if such proves necessary or desirable.*

To revise this sentence, focus first on the wordy adverbial clause, "if such proves necessary or desirable." "Such proves" sounds pretentious in this context. Also, the writer doesn't need both "necessary" and "desirable." Use "necessary," which has a more professional tone. You can shorten or eliminate this turgid clause:

> 3(b) *A more formal memorandum, including source citations and more extensive analysis, can be prepared later, <u>if necessary</u>.*

> 3(c) *A more formal memorandum, including source citations and more extensive analysis, can be prepared later.*

If you assume that the reader is familiar with legal memorandum format, you also can delete the "including" phrase:

> 3(d) *A more formal memorandum can be prepared later.*

Moreover, if you assume that assigning lawyers understand their role in directing the writing process, you could delete the entire sentence.

Exercise

Eliminate extra words in these sentences.

A. Neither case involves a trustee of an *inter vivos* trust, and neither involves an indemnity agreement.

B. The cases are as they are and, as will be seen, present several arguments that support Mr. Joseph's right to damages.

Answers

A. Neither case involves a trustee of an *inter vivos* trust or an indemnity agreement.

B. The cases present several arguments that support Mr. Joseph's right to damages.

1.4.2 Redundancy

Do not say the same thing twice. Distinguish between redundancy and forceful repetition for effect. Redundancy weakens prose and adds clutter. As you revise, consider the definition of each word and check to see if another phrase repeats that meaning. Then eliminate terms that are implicit in other definitions.

Note the word-level redundancy in these phrases:

1. blur together

2. the reason is because

3. final conclusion

4. representative illustrative examples

5. whether or not

6. especially unique

7. very minimal

Some redundancy involves longer groups of words:

8.   *This discussion is <u>not exhaustive</u>; <u>additional elements may be lacking</u>.*

Obviously, this writer needed only the first clause, since the second one repeats the definition of "not exhaustive." Look for redundancy even in transitions:

9.   *<u>In addition</u>, we <u>also</u> included four boxes of due diligence materials that DEM submitted.*

Use either "in addition" or "also," but not both.

1.4.3   Impersonal Expressions

You can cut two types of impersonal expressions without changing the meaning of a sentence. First, look for structures that contain "it," the verb "to be," and an adjective. In addition, try to trim "there" and the verb "to be" from your sentences.

A lawyer began sentence 1(a) below with a wordy impersonal impression:

1(a)   *<u>It is possible that</u> the commission may impose other sanctions.*

Delete "it is possible that." The helping verb "may" expresses the same meaning:

1(b)   *The commission <u>may</u> impose other sanctions.*

"There" and "to be" add unnecessary words to sentence 2(a):

2(a)   *<u>There is</u> disagreement among the courts about the effect of Brulotte misuse.*

To revise this sentence, first delete "there is." Then convert the long noun "disagreement" to its verb form, "disagree." Begin with the subject and delete extra words:

> 2(b)   *Courts disagree about the effect of* Brulotte *misuse.*

Exercise

Eliminate extra words in these sentences.

A. There is substantial Pennsylvania precedent supporting Portco's claim.

B. It is this language that implies that a telecommunications carrier could install and maintain its service equipment without a municipality's consent.

C. There are two separate agreements that govern the Ambassador program.

Answers

A. Substantial Pennsylvania precedent supports Portco's claim.

• Cut "there is" and change "supporting" to the present tense.

B. This language implies that a telecommunications carrier could install and maintain its service equipment without a municipality's consent.

• Trim "it is" and "that."

C. Two separate agreements govern the Ambassador program.

• Delete "there are " and "that."

1.4.4   "The Fact That"

As you revise, look for expressions you can shorten with no loss of meaning. For example, the phrase "the fact that" is unnecessary in most contexts. Replace the first four words below, "notwithstanding the fact that," with "although":

> 1(a)   <u>*Notwithstanding the fact that*</u> *Seton furnished U.A.W. Local 107 with this comparative labor cost data, the union rejected Seton's concessions.*

The verbose introductory phrase weakens sentence 1(a). By using one adverb instead of a long prepositional phrase, you focus attention on the parties' actions.

1(b) *Although Seton furnished U.A.W. Local 107 with this comparative labor cost data, the union rejected Seton's concessions.*

In some contexts, you can replace the phrase "the fact that" with a noun form. This phrase serves as the subject of sentence 2(a):

2(a) *The fact that Mr. Layman left the accident scene complicated his defense.*

Substitute the noun phrase "Mr. Layman's leaving" for "the fact that Mr. Layman left." This change shortens the sentence by three words, or 25 percent:

2(b) *Mr. Layman's leaving the accident scene complicated his defense.*

In certain contexts, you can use "the fact that" to make your writing more persuasive. Litigators often insert that phrase to stress a statement's truth. For example, in sentence 3(a) the writer wanted to emphasize that a ninety-year-old franchise ordinance was no longer valid:

3(a) *The fact that Franchise Ordinance #321 is obsolete makes it impossible to perform.*

Of course, you can delete the first three words and shorten the sentence, as shown in 3(b):

3(b) *Franchise Ordinance #321 is obsolete and thus impossible to perform.*

In the original version, however, the extra words stress the fact that the ordinance is anachronistic. When used sparingly and in carefully chosen contexts, this phrase can strengthen an argument.

Exercise

Identify extra words in these sentences. Revise as needed.

A. Because of the fact that plaintiff was not promoted to the position of security supervisor, he sued Camp-Co in Dade County court.

B. The attorney asserted the fact that Ms. Conan was not able to perform the essential functions of a delivery driver when she returned to work.

Answers

A. Extra words: "of the fact that"

   Revision: Because plaintiff was not promoted to the position of security supervisor, he sued Camp-Co in Dade County court.

B. Extra words: "the fact"

   Revision: The attorney asserted that Ms. Conan was not able to perform the essential functions of a delivery driver when she returned to work.

1.4.5 "Hidden" Verbs

Uncover verbs "hidden" in long noun forms. These multisyllabic nouns represent abstractions and end in suffixes like "-ence," "-ance," "-tion," "-sion," and "-ment." As you revise, look for the verbs in long nouns. Since verbs express action, they are more powerful than nouns. Moreover, you can usually delete extra words when you use the verb form.

The noun "determination" contains a hidden verb in sentence 1(a):

1(a) *Before filing a financing statement, the secured party must make the <u>determination</u> of which state's law governs filing.*

If you extract the verb "determine" from "determination," you also can cut "make the" and "of":

1(b) *Before filing a financing statement, the secured party must <u>determine</u> which state's law governs filing.*

Some shorter nouns also contain hidden verbs:

2(b) *The <u>reasoning</u> used by both courts was that the employment agreement required the NYSE to arbitrate disputes.*

LEGAL WRITING

Shorten "the reasoning used by both courts was" to "both courts reasoned":

> 2(c) Both courts *reasoned* that the employment agreement required the NYSE to arbitrate disputes.

With this change, you cut 23 percent of the words from the sentence.

Exercise

Uncover hidden verbs in these noun forms.

A. be in conformity with
B. occupation of the premises
C. did not express hesitancy in leaving
D. make reference to
E. be in agreement with
F. contains a discussion of
G. make amendments to
H. effected reorganization
I. creation of incentives
J. seek the imposition of
K. make inquiries
L. give a description

Answers
A. conform
B. occupy the premises
C. did not leave
D. refer to
E. agree with
F. discusses
G. amend
H. reorganized
I. create incentives
J. impose
K. inquire
L. describe

1.4.6   Overworked Introductory Phrases

Avoid verbose and overused introductory phrases. For example, the redundant phrase "at this point in time" weakens sentence 1(a):

> 1(a)   *At this point in time, Little Company subcontracts 50 percent of its work from general contractors.*

Shorten this phrase to "at this point" or "at this time," or insert "currently" before the verb. In some contexts, you can delete "at this point in time" with no loss of meaning because the present tense verb communicates a current condition:

> 1(b)   *Little Company subcontracts 50 percent of its work from general contractors.*

"In the final analysis" creates a wordy beginning for sentence 2(a):

> 2(a)   *In the final analysis, proceeds of the policies paid to Johnson Associates, Inc. will be taxable to the Estate of Richard S. Tower.*

Although this trite phrase may sound authoritative, overuse has weakened it. First, determine your intended meaning. Do you mean "this is my last point"?

> 2(b)   *In conclusion, proceeds of the policies paid to Johnson Associates, Inc. will be taxable to the Estate of Richard S. Tower.*

Did you use "in the final analysis" to mean "in light of all these factors"?

> 2(c)   *Thus, proceeds of the policies paid to Johnson Associates, Inc. will be taxable to the Estate of Richard S. Tower.*

Are you summarizing?

> 2(d)   *In summary, proceeds of the policies paid to Johnson Associates, Inc. will be taxable to the Estate of Richard S. Tower.*

When no transition is necessary, omit the introductory phrase.

Exercise

Identify the overworked phrases in these sentences. Revise as needed.

A. In the final analysis, we are not sure how courts will interpret the relevant reporting requirements.

B. At this point in time, no federal regulations require the removal of asbestos after it has been discovered in a building.

Answers

A. Overworked phrase: "in the final analysis"

   Revision: In conclusion, we are not sure how courts will interpret the relevant reporting requirements.

B. Overworked phrase: "at this point in time"

   Revision: No federal regulations currently require the removal of asbestos after it has been discovered in a building.

1.4.7 "Throat Clearing"

Do not use "throat clearing," a wordy introduction, for emphasis. Throat clearing distracts the reader from the main idea and adds little meaning. Although clauses like "it should also be noted that" may appear to stress the importance of the next clause, they add clutter at the beginning of a sentence. Delete these wordy preambles; then explain why the statement is important.

Throat clearing delays the lawyer's central point in sentence 1(a):

1(a)   _Suffice it to say that_ the New York statute bars Plaintiffs' claims for strict liability and breach of warranty.

Delete "suffice it to say that" and begin with the main subject:

1(b)   The New York statute bars Plaintiffs' claims for strict liability and breach of warranty.

An impersonal directive to the reader introduces sentence 2(a):

2(a)   _It should be noted that_ construction of the cofferdam accounted for only 10.9 percent of Miller's work.

This impersonal expression, in which "it" has no antecedent, contains a passive verb without the actor-agent phrase, "by you." To improve the style, omit the throat clearing:

> 2(b) *Construction of the cofferdam accounted for only 10.9 percent of Miller's work.*

Similar lead-ins obscure the message in sentences 3(a) and 4(a). Begin with the main idea, as shown in the revisions in sentences 3(b) and 4(b) :

> 3(a) <u>*It is important to note that*</u> *a cofferdam is "a temporary structure for keeping water from entering an enclosed area while work is taking place."*

> 3(b) *A cofferdam is "a temporary structure for keeping water from entering an enclosed area while work is taking place."*

> 4(a) <u>*It is an inescapable conclusion that*</u> *MG&E is responsible for paying sales and use taxes on materials for erection of installations that retain their status as personal property.*

> 4(b) *MG&E is responsible for paying sales and use taxes on materials for erection of installations that retain their status as personal property.*

Some stylists suggest inserting an adverb such as "obviously" or "clearly" for emphasis before the verb in 3(b) and 4(b). Use these modifiers only after careful consideration of audience, context, and tone. Many judges believe that lawyers add "clearly" and "obviously" to disguise assertions that are neither clear nor obvious.

Exercise

Eliminate throat clearing in these sentences.

A. It should be understood that there is no doubt that the regulatory agency has jurisdiction over Webb Company's direct sales to specific customers.

B. It is obvious that the plaintiff is entitled to summary judgment.

C. It is clear that the direct language of Section 33–806(b) contrasts with the conditional language in Section 33–442.

D. Suffice it to say that Netco must perform a complete PSD review for each pollutant emitted in significant quantities.

E. It is obvious that adolescents can recall a capitalized four-word message flashed on a screen better than a standard type thirteen-word message.

Answers

A. Omit "it should be understood that" and "there is no doubt that."

B. Delete "it is obvious that." Some lawyers would add "obviously" before "is." Others believe that this adverb disguises a false statement.

C. Delete "it is clear that."

D. Delete "suffice it to say that." The verb "must" expresses urgency.

E. Cut "it is obvious that."

1.4.8 Converting "Of" and "By" Phrases to Possessives

Eliminate extra words by converting some "of" and "by" phrases to possessives. These revisions create a smooth, direct style. As you edit, check each "of" and "by" phrase, make the object possessive, and place it before the modified noun. Then determine whether your revision improves the sentence's flow.

Sentence 1(a) contains eight "of" or "by" phrases:

1(a)   The obligations _of Surco_ are conditioned on the delivery _by ABC_ _of certain documents_ _by December 31_ and receipt _by Emtex_ _of clean opinions_ validating the legal, tax, and accounting aspects _of the transaction_ _by February 1_.

To revise this sentence, first test each "of" and "by" phrase to see if you can convert it to a possessive. Note three obvious revisions in sentence 1(b):

1(b) *Surco's* obligations are conditioned on *ABC's* delivery of certain documents by December 31 and *Emtex's* receipt of clean opinions validating the legal, tax, and accounting aspects of the transaction by February 1.

"By December 31" and "by February 1" must retain the same form. While many lawyers would convert "of the transaction" to the possessive, others object to the long adjective chain in "the transaction's legal, tax, and accounting aspects." Finally, if you change "deliver" and "receipt" to "-ing" forms, you can drop "of" after both nouns. All these revisions create a smoother, more concise sentence:

1(c) *Surco's* obligations are conditioned on *ABC's delivering* certain documents by December 31 and *Emtex's receiving* clean opinions validating *the transaction's* legal, tax, and accounting aspects by February 1.

Exercise

Convert "of" and "by" phrases to possessives in these sentences.

A. The length of Warning A affected the ability of study participants to recall its message.

B. The physicians could receive indirect compensation through distributions by Bantam.

Answers

A. Warning A's length affected study participants' ability to recall its message.

• Convert both "of" phrases to possessives.

B. The physicians could receive indirect compensation through Bantam's distributions.

• Change "by Bantam" to "Bantam's."

1.4.9 Unnecessary Modifiers

When you need to cut extra words, look for unnecessary modifiers. In some contexts, you can delete adjectives and adverbs without sacrificing persuasive power. Even familiar phrases can be shortened:

1. have no bearing <u>whatsoever</u>—*have no bearing*

2. is <u>amply</u> warranted—*is warranted*

3. in its <u>sound</u> discretion—*in its discretion*

1.4.10 Extra Stepping

Do not describe all perceptual processes involved in preparing a legal memorandum. Instead, include only those steps essential to the reader's understanding. Delete processes implicit in legal analysis. These wordy, awkward descriptions interrupt logical development and add clutter to your main points.

A lawyer used extra stepping in sentence 1(a):

1(a)   *A review of the cited sources reveals this language to be consistent with* Kalish-Jarcho *and* Carinno-Civetta.

To revise this sentence, first analyze its structure. Identify the most significant part, i.e., the description of the language. The main subject and verb, "a review of the cited sources reveals," explain the attorney's research exercise that led to the conclusion about language. Omit this unnecessary description. Change the verb to the present tense and characterize the language in a simple, direct sentence:

1(b)   *This language is consistent with* Kalish-Jarcho *and* Carinno-Civetta.

The "preview" sentence 2(a) also contains extra stepping:

2(a)   *This analysis will focus on the three cases that the New Jersey Bar Ethics Hotline identifies as seminal cases and apply their rationale to the current situation. Those cases are* Dill v. Superior Court, Global Van Lines v. Superior Court, *and* Rosenfeld Construction Company, Inc. v. Superior Court.

This passage begins with a subject, verb, and preposition, "this analysis will focus on," that describe the reader's perceptual step. A second unnecessary phrase, "and apply their rationale to the current situation," refers to the application process essential in preparing a legal memorandum. Delete both those structures and characterize the cases:

> 2(b)   *The New Jersey Bar Ethics Hotline identifies three seminal cases:* Dill v. Superior Court, Global Van Lines v. Superior Court, *and* Rosenfeld Construction Company, Inc. v. Superior Court.

Do not explain that the analysis will focus on these cases. After beginning with the sentence above, you should discuss the cases and their application to your client's needs. The focus of the memo will be clear from its organization.

Some awkward descriptions of perceptual steps create grammatical problems. For example, in a memo concerning California law, an attorney began passage 3(a) with a dangling modifier:

> 3(a)   *To see how a court from another state would view losses in a real estate venture, a case decided by the Virginia Supreme Court is helpful. In* Rosillo v. Winters *[cite and discussion of facts].*

The introductory phrase, "to see how a court . . . " is a "dangler." The initial phrase should "link itself" to the subject of the main clause. Yet "case" is not the subject of "to see." To revise this sentence, first delete the phrase "from another state." In a memo regarding California law, for example, if you name the Virginia court, it will be clear that a court from another state is involved. The adjective "helpful" is also unnecessary. All information in a memo should be helpful. In your revision, focus on the question before the court:

> 3(b)   *The Virginia Supreme Court considered losses in a real estate venture in* Rosillo v. Winters *[cite and discussion of facts].*

Exercise

Eliminate the perceptual steps in these sentences.

A. Before an analysis of the position of a defaulting partner can begin, it is important to note that the Uniform Partnership Act states that a partner has the power to dissolve the partnership relationship at any time, with or without proper cause and without regard to any agreement concerning dissolution.

B. While some authorities consistently limit the attorney's scope of representation by using language nearly identical to that adopted by the *Willis* court, it is necessary to reexamine the cases that have strayed from this language and implied a broader duty to disclose.

Answers

A. The Uniform Partnership Act states that a partner has the power to dissolve the partnership relationship at any time, with or without proper cause and without regard to any agreement concerning dissolution.

•   Delete the introductory phrase and throat clearing at the beginning of the main clause.

B. While some authorities consistently limit the attorney's scope of representation by using language nearly identical to that adopted by the *Willis* court, other cases have implied a broader duty to disclose.

•   The clause "it is necessary to reexamine" focuses on the writer's perceptual steps. Begin by stating the courts' two views. Delete "have strayed from this language and" since this meaning is expressed in "implied a broader duty to disclose." Next, discuss the cases that have implied a broader duty to disclose.

1.5 Diction

1.5.1 Word Choice and Tone

Maintain a level of diction appropriate for your audience, context, tone, and goal. Before you draft, determine the most effective tone for each part of your document. Do not use unnecessarily pretentious language. On the other hand, avoid informal words and phrases that seem unprofessional. As you revise, identify words that are not appropriate in context. Replace them with diction consistent with your intended purpose and goal.

The verb phrase "expounded upon" sounds awkward in sentence 1(a):

1(a)   The district court <u>expounded upon</u> the public policy reasons for applying common law strict liability.

"Expounded upon" stands out as inflated diction. Use "explained" instead:

> *1(b)   The district court <u>explained</u> the public policy reasons for applying common law strict liability.*

Note the awkward noun subject in sentence 2(a):

> *2(a)   A <u>paucity</u> of Arizona cases addresses the recognition of specific claims that Bluco asserts.*

"Paucity," which means "fewness, small number," is unnecessarily formal. Replace "a paucity of" with "few," and match the verb to the new subject:

> *2(b)   <u>Few</u> Arizona cases address the recognition of specific claims that Bluco asserts.*

Language that is too informal detracts from the professional tone of legal writing. For example, when discussing a letter of commitment in a legal memorandum, a lawyer used the verb "promise":

> *3(a)   Participating facilities must <u>promise</u> not to use any contracts Black Company has with manufacturers as leverage to negotiate their own contracts with manufacturers.*

"Promise" has an informal, almost childish tone in this context. For more appropriate diction, substitute "agree":

> *3(b)   Participating facilities must <u>agree</u> not to use any contracts Black Company has with manufacturers as leverage to negotiate their own contracts with manufacturers.*

You also could shorten the verb phrase by deleting "agree" and " to":

> *3(c)   Participating facilities <u>must not use</u> any contracts Black Company has with manufacturers as leverage to negotiate their own contracts with manufacturers.*

Sarcasm is rarely successful in legal writing. Readers cannot hear the writer's intended voice tone and may perceive sarcasm as adolescent annoyance or sheer nastiness. In a legal memorandum, a lawyer used sarcasm to describe a drug study:

> 4(a)   *There can be no excuse for misreporting Wilson group's age, drug history, numbers, and results. <u>At least Dr. Merton got the cities right</u>. <u>Of course</u>, he went on to misreport the same data for the Greene group as well.*

You can avoid confusion about tone by objectively describing the report:

> 4(b)   *Dr. Merton misreported the age, drug history, numbers, and results for the Wilson and Greene groups.*

Then explain the implications of misreporting for your analysis.

Exercise

Identify diction and tone problems in these sentences. Revise as needed.

A. To be held contributorily liable, somewhere along the way, a manufacturer must directly infringe the other party's trademark rights.

B. Once again, Ms. Chaikin has churned out another piece of anti-pharmaceutical junk science.

C. A rarity of cases indicates that the Uniform Disposition of Unclaimed Property Act would apply to Medifex's overpayments.

Answers

A. Colloquial phrase: "somewhere along the way"

   <u>Revision</u>: To be held contributorily liable, a manufacturer must directly infringe the other party's trademark rights.

B. Sarcasm: "has churned out another piece of anti-pharmaceutical junk science"

   <u>Revision</u>: "Ms. Chaikin's report contains serious errors." Then explain their significance for your analysis.

C. Pretentious phrase: "a rarity of"

   <u>Revision</u>: Few cases indicate that the Uniform Disposition of Unclaimed Property Act would apply to Medifex's overpayments.

1.5.2   Legalese

Do not pepper your writing with unnecessary legal terms. As you revise, ask if you need each term of art, and paraphrase where possible. If you use superfluous esoteric language, you may alienate your audience. To address this pervasive problem, leaders of the Plain English movement encourage lawyers to draft prose free of unnecessary legal terms. Moreover, SEC rules require a clear, direct style.

Lawyers should distinguish between legal drafting, with its requirement for precision, and "flowing prose" in other legal writing. If you draft agreements, do not mix the formal language of legal drafting with the prose in letters, briefs, and memoranda. Before you draft agreements, put on your "legal drafting hat." Then take it off and put on your "flowing prose hat" when you begin other types of writing. As you edit, substitute plain English for all superfluous terms of art.

Note the legalese in sentence 1(a), which appeared in the opening paragraph of an opinion letter:

> 1(a)   In reaching the opinions _set forth herein_, we reviewed Trepco's file history, the original patent, and Interference No. 103,428.

While the constraints of legal drafting might require the phrase "set forth herein," the beginning of an opinion letter should be clear and direct. In the first paragraph, you should establish rapport with the reader. Create a professional tone that respects the reader's needs for clarity. In the sentence above, delete "set forth herein" and change "the" to "these":

> 1(b)   In reaching _these_ opinions, we reviewed Trepco's file history, the original patent, and Interference No. 103,428.

Legalese creeps into short letters, too. In a client cover letter for a closing binder, an attorney used "same" unnecessarily:

> 2(a)   The enclosed binder does not include filed copies of Documents 37 and 38 because we have not received _same_.

Replace this awkward legal term with the pronoun "them":

> 2(b)   *The enclosed binder does not include filed copies of Documents 37 and 38 because we have not received <u>them</u>.*

Avoid legalese even when you write for lawyers. "Wherein" is awkward in a string cite from a legal memorandum:

> 3(a)   *See* Anderson Memorial Hospital *[cite] (<u>wherein</u> the court granted a defense motion based on the "door-closing" statute to strike class action allegations of nonresidents in a proposed class of building owners).*

Save "wherein" for legal drafting. You could replace this adverb with "in which," but string cites should be concise. Instead, delete "wherein the court" and change "granted" to "granting":

> 3(b)   *See* Anderson Memorial Hospital *[cite] (granting a defense motion based on the "door-closing" statute to strike class action allegations of nonresidents in a proposed class of building owners).*

In the conclusion to a memorandum, do not use awkward terms like "aforementioned" or "foregoing":

> 4(a)   *As the <u>aforementioned</u> cases suggest, courts will enforce Pepflex's bylaws providing for the mandatory advancement of legal fees to its directors and officers.*

Delete "the" and replace "aforementioned" with "these," which will refer to the cases discussed above:

> 4(b)   *As <u>these</u> cases suggest, courts will enforce Pepflex's bylaws providing for the mandatory advancement of legal fees to its directors and officers.*

Exercise

Identify legalese in these sentences. Revise as needed.

A. Pursuant to our discussion, I have enclosed two (2) UCC-1 Financing Statements and the exhibits thereto.

B. Prior to filing a financing statement, the secured party must determine which state's law will govern the process.

C. For the foregoing reasons, Plaintiff must return all copies of the Blackstone report to Defendant or certify their destruction.

D. The design must contain a down-hole pipe system wherein the joints are slim.

Answers

A. Legalese: "pursuant to" and "thereto." Also, adding the number (2) after "two" is unnecessary in a client cover letter.

   <u>Revision</u>: As we discussed, I have enclosed two UCC-1 Financing Statements with exhibits.

B. Legalese: "prior to"

   <u>Revision</u>: Before filing a financing statement, the secured party must determine which state's law will govern the process.

C. Legalese: "the foregoing"

   <u>Revision</u>: For these reasons, Plaintiff must return all copies of the Blackstone report to Defendant or certify their destruction.

D. Legalese: "wherein"

   <u>Revision</u>: The design must contain a down-hole pipe system with slim joints.

1.5.3 "Such"

The adjective "such" has a different meaning in legal drafting than in expository prose. When used correctly in memos, briefs, and letters, "such" means "of that type" and refers in a general, abstract sense to the modifiers of an earlier noun or noun phrase. "Such" is especially useful when it replaces a long chain of descriptive words, as in "such components" for "di-ester quat components that degrade over time to a fatty acid."

In agreements, "such" refers to the modifiers of a previous specific noun. Think of "such" in this context as a substitute for "the," "this," "that," "these," or "those." For example, "such buildings" stands concisely for "the buildings at 100 and 101 Elm Street." Avoid this usage in other types of legal writing.

Sentence 1 illustrates the correct use of "such" in expository prose:

1.   *Insolvency cannot be avoided by <u>a contribution to capital or discharge of intercompany debt that occurs shortly before the liquidation</u>. The IRS will ignore <u>such</u> a contribution or discharge.*

The attorney employs the phrase "such a contribution or discharge" to avoid repeating the long phrase, "a contribution to capital or discharge of intercompany debt that occurs shortly before the liquidation." The writer refers to that noun phrase in a general, abstract sense, not to a specific contribution or discharge. With "such," you can avoid repeating the earlier phrase or adding "of that type."

"Such a transaction" correctly refers to a longer phrase,"a settlement from South Lake's assets," in sentence 2:

2.   *Without bankruptcy court approval, LMI cannot accept <u>a settlement from South Lake's assets</u>, because <u>such</u> a transaction would constitute an improper post-petition transfer to LMI.*

"Such" means "of this type" and does not relate to a specific settlement. The dependent clause is concise and clear.

Do not use "such" unnecessarily to refer to a specific noun:

3(a)   *Mr. Bennett asserted that because of <u>the sale of the California Division #2</u>, Atco currently has no mechanism for purchasing hybrid broccoli. Furthermore, <u>such</u> sale may have restricted Atco's options and abilities to conduct field trials.*

The lawyer writes about only one specific sale; "such" does not refer to a noun used in an abstract sense. Use "this," not "such," to identify the sale:

3(b)   *Mr. Bennett asserted that because of <u>the sale of the California Division #2</u>, Atco currently has no mechanism for purchasing hybrid broccoli. Furthermore, <u>this</u> sale may have restricted Atco's options and abilities to conduct field trials.*

In legal memoranda, "such" used incorrectly creates dense prose:

4(a)   *Both the PACA statute and the regulations require the unpaid seller <u>to file Form 347a, stating an intent to preserve trust benefits with the debtor merchant and the United States Secretary of Agriculture</u>. Such measures are analogous to filing to perfect a security interest under secured transactions law.*

"Such" designates two specific measures, i.e., filing requirements in the previous sentence. For clarity, use "these" instead:

4(b)   *Both the PACA statute and the regulations require the unpaid seller <u>to file Form 347a, stating an intent to preserve trust benefits with the debtor merchant and the United States Secretary of Agriculture</u>. These measures are analogous to filing to perfect a security interest under secured transactions law.*

Finally, do not use "such" as a noun. For most readers, this usage is awkward and confusing:

5(a)   *The parties disagreed about First Community Orchestra's financial information and disclosure of <u>such</u>.*

This writer has inserted "such" into a noun slot, object of the preposition "of." "Such" stands for "financial information." To avoid repetition, delete "of such" and add "its" before "disclosure":

5(b)   *The parties disagreed about First Community Orchestra's financial information and <u>its</u> disclosure.*

Exercise

Determine whether "such" is used correctly in these passages. Revise as needed.

A. Appleton conceded that commercializing the Superlative Pest Control A.1 program would create problems. Thus, the committee agreed to give such program a low funding priority.

B. Either party may cease its business and still not breach its contractual obligations under such.

C. All rights to any benefits under the Maxwell Insurance contract belong solely to the employer, and Maxwell will pay such contract's proceeds to the employer only.

D. Atco released a May 1 report on the values of the nine programs under consideration. Ms. Whitman believed that Atco inflated these values by 100 percent. Marginal notes in her copy of such report indicate that the Atco model did not include research and development expenditures.

E. Although Webster Seed Companies had an existing distribution network throughout the relevant wheat growing area, such companies had no experience selling wheat.

F. I will briefly analyze the facts that Ms. Black advanced to support her claim, the legal basis of such claim, and its consequences for Sci-Co Labs.

Answers

A. Incorrect. "Such" refers to a specific noun phrase, "the Superlative Pest Control A.1 program." Use "this."

   Revision: Appleton conceded that commercializing the Superlative Pest Control A.1 program would create problems. Thus, the committee agreed to give this program a low funding priority.

B. Incorrect. "Such" serves as noun object of the preposition "under" and stands for the contract. This noun is implied in the adjective "contractual." Delete "under such," since the adjective communicates the same meaning.

   Revision: Either party may cease its business and still not breach its contractual obligations.

C. Incorrect. "Such" refers to a specific noun phrase, "the Maxwell Insurance contract." Use "the."

   Revision: All rights to any benefits under the Maxwell Insurance contract belong solely to the employer, and Maxwell will pay the contract's proceeds to the employer only.

D. Incorrect. "Such" refers to a specific noun phrase, "a May 1 report on the values of the nine programs under consideration." Use "the."

   Revision: Atco released a May 1 report on the values of the nine programs under consideration. Ms. Whitman believed that Atco inflated these values by 100 percent. Marginal notes in her copy of the report indicate that the Atco model did not include research and development expenditures.

E. Incorrect. "Such" refers to a specific noun phrase, "Webster Seed Companies." Use "they."

   Revision: Although Webster Seed Companies had an existing distribution network throughout the relevant wheat growing area, they had no experience selling wheat.

F. Incorrect. "Such" refers to a specific noun, "her claim." To avoid repetition, delete "the" and "of such claim," and add the pronoun "its" before "legal basis."

   Revision: I will briefly analyze the facts that Ms. Black advanced to support her claim, its legal basis, and its consequences for Sci-Co Labs.

1.5.4 Colloquial Adverbs

Colloquial adverbs create a jarring tone in legal writing. When speakers find a new, informal usage for a familiar adverb, it may become acceptable in some contexts. But these modifiers have a casual tone that does not fit in lawyers' writing.

According to its first definition, "hopefully" means "in a hopeful manner," as in "The defendant looked up hopefully when the judge began to speak." This usage rarely appears in legal writing.

Yet "hopefully" has taken on a new meaning in conversation and informal writing. The new colloquial definition is "it is to be hoped that." Many lawyers have adopted this usage:

> 1(a)   *I will complete your tax return early, hopefully by April 1.*

To be precise and correct, do not use "hopefully" in this way. Instead, convert the adverb to its verb form:

> 1(b)   *I hope to complete your tax return by April 1.*

A second colloquial usage, adding the suffix "-wise" to nouns, is also awkward in legal writing. On the evening news, the meteorologist may chat about conditions "weather-wise," "temperature-wise," or "rain-wise." Yet when used by lawyers, these colloquial adverbs create an informal and abrupt tone:

> 2(a)   *Ms. Collins, a partner in the New York office, will assess Compton's liabilities tax-wise.*

You can convert some adverbs of this type to an adjective that precedes the modified noun:

> 2(b)   *Ms. Collins, a partner in the New York office, will assess Compton's tax liabilities.*

In other contexts, a prepositional phrase can replace the adverb:

> 3(a)   *In his July 1 fax, the CEO of Axco Corp. listed seven concerns budget-wise.*

> 3(b)   *In his July 1 fax, the CEO of Axco Corp. listed seven concerns about the budget.*

Exercise

Identify the colloquial adverbs in these sentences. Revise as needed.

A. Mr. Johnson drafted questions about the corporation credit-wise.

B. This discussion hopefully will be helpful as you consider setting up a trust for Anne and Robert.

Answers

A. Colloquial adverb: "credit-wise"

Revision: Mr. Johnson drafted questions about the corporation's credit.

B. Colloquial adverb: "hopefully"

Revision: I hope this discussion will be helpful as you consider setting up a trust for Anne and Robert.

1.6 Word Arrangement

1.6.1 Parallel Structure

Use the same grammatical structure for all the elements of a series, comparison, or contrast. Match nouns with nouns, verbs with verbs, prepositional phrases with prepositional phrases, independent clauses with independent clauses, etc. Parallelism creates balanced structures and rhythmic prose.

A lawyer used two different grammatical structures for elements of a series:

> 1(a) *If corporate privileges are forfeited, the corporation is (1) denied the right to sue or defend in a state court, and (2) each director or officer of the corporation is liable for a debt of the corporation as provided in section 171.255.*

The first element, "denied the right to sue or defend in a state court," consists of a verb phrase with object, infinitive, and modifiers. But for the second element, the lawyer used an independent clause, or complete sentence. This clause does not follow from the lead-in to the series.

To correct a problem in parallel structure, change all the series' elements to the same grammatical form. Test each potential structure to determine which creates the smoothest series and expresses the ideas most precisely. For example, in sentence 1(a), you cannot convert both elements to verb phrases because they have different subjects. Instead, shorten the lead-in and use the independent clause form:

1(b)   *If corporate privileges are forfeited, (1) the corporation is denied the right to sue or defend in a state court, and (2) each director or officer of the corporation is liable for a debt of the corporation as provided in section 171.255.*

Lack of parallelism may confuse your reader, especially in a long series. Three different grammatical structures appear in series 2(a):

2(a)   *The five-pronged test requires the following elements:*

i.   *The complete and specific disclosure of potential conflicts of interest by Webco;*

ii.   *Consideration created by mutual waivers;*

iii.   *Negotiated transaction with both Greene and Webco represented by counsel;*

iv.   *Webco and Greene are both sophisticated; and*

v.   *Greene did not lack bargaining power.*

The first two elements consist of noun phrases, i.e., "disclosure" and "consideration" plus modifiers. The verb "negotiated," with object and modifiers, comprises the third element. Independent clauses fill the last two slots in the series.

To revise this series, experiment with different grammatical structures. Since noun phrase and verb phrase forms do not fit all five elements, convert them to independent clauses:

2(b)   *The five-pronged test requires the following elements:*

i.   *Webco completely and specifically disclosed potential conflicts of interest;*

ii.   *Mutual waivers created consideration;*

iii.   *Counsel represented both Greene and Webco when they negotiated the transaction;*

iv.   *Webco and Greene are both sophisticated; and*

v.   *Greene did not lack bargaining power.*

Exercise

Identify parallelism errors in these sentences. Revise as needed.

A. The Happleman device does not infringe because it is not used for high pressure applications, is not a mechanical pipe-to-fitting connection, does not have a flanged end, nor does it have extra fastener holes and does not include an adapter.

B. The company sells housewares, school supplies, runs a chain of nursery schools, and produces children's television programs.

Answers

A. The lawyer used four verb phrases and one independent clause in this series.

Revision: The Happleman device does not infringe because it:
i.   Is not used for high pressure applications;
ii. Is not a mechanical pipe-to-fitting connection;
iii. Does not have flanged end;
iv. Does not have extra fastener holes; and
v.   Does not include an adapter.

• Convert the fourth element to a verb phrase and tabulate the series for easy reading.

B. The writer used one noun phrase and three verb phrases with objects in this series.

Revision: The company sells housewares and school supplies, runs a chain of nursery schools, and produces children's television programs.

• Combine the first and second elements with "and."

1.6.2   Parallel Clauses

When you use parallel clauses, do not cram them into a long, complicated sentence. Instead, add transitions and create separate sentences.

To state the requirements for admitting evidence of noxious ingredients, a litigator used the long parallel clauses in sentence 1(a):

1(a)   Not only must plaintiff demonstrate an independent causal nexus between the ingredient and the injury, but of equal importance is a showing that the ingredient, as a part of the whole, was present in sufficient proportion to make the entire product harmful.

First, look for thought divisions in this long sentence. If you drop "not only," you create a new independent clause:

1(b)   *Plaintiff must demonstrate an independent causal nexus between the ingredient and the injury.*

Next, eliminate the awkward beginning of the second clause, "of equal importance is a showing." Add a smoother introduction to the "that" clause:

1(c)   *It is equally important for the plaintiff to show that the ingredient, as a part of a whole, was present in sufficient proportion to make the entire product harmful.*

You can begin more concisely without the "equally important" judgment:

1(d)   *The plaintiff also must show that the ingredient, as a part of a whole, was present in sufficient proportion to make the entire product harmful.*

The transitions "just as . . . so too" introduce long parallel clauses in sentence 2(a):

2(a)   *Just as the plaintiff in Oakes could not recast the manufacturer as an insurer of its product, so too Premco cannot argue that a small amount of residual pesticide transforms an entire product into an unreasonably dangerous instrumentality.*

To make this parallel clearer, drop the "just as . . . so too" and create two sentences. Begin the second sentence with "similarly":

2(b)   *The plaintiff in Oakes could not recast the manufacturer as an insurer of its product.*

2(c)   *Similarly, Premco cannot argue that a small amount of residual pesticide transforms an entire product into an unreasonably dangerous instrumentality.*

Exercise

Revise this sentence.

> Just as the mescaline in *Rittenhouse* and "additional chemicals and special paper" in *Lamke* did not necessarily cause the party's injuries, so too minute amounts of pesticides in the #2 fertilizer would not establish Merton's liability.

Answer

1. The mescaline in *Rittenhouse* and "additional chemicals and special paper" in *Lamke* did not necessarily cause the party's injuries.

2. Similarly, minute amounts of pesticides in the #2 fertilizer would not establish Merton's liability.

- Cut "just as" and "so too." Then divide the sentence, and add "similarly" and a comma before the second clause.

1.6.3   Parallelism with "As Such"

Use the phrase "as such" to link terms that are grammatically and conceptually parallel. "As such" is not a synonym for "consequently."

In passage 1, a lawyer used "as such" correctly. "As such" connects two parallel terms, a noun phrase and a pronoun:

> 1.   *Mr. Burnett served as an <u>employee assistant</u>, who helped to load and unload trucks. <u>As such</u>, <u>he</u> would be entitled to overtime pay under the wage and hour provisions of FSLA.*

The noun phrase "employee assistant" is the obvious referent for "such" and balances the pronoun "he." You understand that "as an employee assistant," Mr. Burnett is entitled to overtime pay under the FSLA regulations.

Do not use "as such" to express a cause-and-effect relationship:

> 2.   *The employment agreement conditioned the payment of commissions upon the successful completion of certain stages of the project. <u>As such</u>, Avco's commission payment record reflects that commissions were customarily awarded on an installment basis over the life of the project.*

"Avco's commission payment record" is not linked conceptually to any noun phrase in the first sentence. Use "thus" or a similar connective.

Exercise

Determine whether "as such" is used correctly in these sentences. Revise as needed.

A. Chemlo and its affiliates are Subchapter S corporations. As such, their shareholders are taxed on corporate level income even if that income is distributed to them.

B. The tax commissioner found that ISM Corporation is the "consumer" of the cleaning supplies and equipment. As such, ISM will be liable for use tax under § 5741.02.

Answers

A. Incorrect. "Their shareholders" has no conceptual referent in the first sentence. Use "thus" or "therefore" to express this cause-and-effect relationship.

B. Correct. "Consumer" names a category for ISM. You understand that "as the consumer," ISM will be liable for the tax.

1.7 Placing Modifiers and Contrasting Terms

1.7.1   Placing "However"

Reasonable people disagree about the placement of "however." Some stylists advise lawyers not to reverse logical direction with this adverb at the beginning of a sentence. They suggest using "however" in that position only when it serves as an adverb and means "in whatever way" or "to whatever extent":

1.   *However low the stock value dropped, the Plimpton board resisted BayCo's hostile takeover bid.*

2.   *However his attorney advised, Mr. Rosewood continued to dump hazardous waste behind the Poughkeepsie warehouse.*

These stylists suggest placing "however" in other positions when it changes the direction of the argument. Your choice will depend on your intended emphasis. The negative stress of "however" falls on the term that precedes it. For example, "however" can follow an introductory phrase for emphasis:

> 3.   On November 15, <u>however</u>, Ms. Cole purchased 12,130 of the 17,546 outstanding shares of common stock of BCG.

Stressing "November 15," the adverb might contrast with the earlier date of a previous fact.

You also can insert "however" after the subject:

> 4.   O.R.C. § 5739.01(E)(2) and § 5741.02(C)(2), <u>however</u>, prohibit the tax assessments.

Here "however" emphasizes the two sections, perhaps contrasting with other sections that permit the use-tax assessments.

"However" can appear after the verb:

> 5.   The Tax Commissioner held, <u>however</u>, that Greene must pay tax on 20 percent of the materials.

The previous sentence might have discussed the commissioner's reasoning that seemed to contradict the holding.

Moreover, you can place "however" after the object:

> 6.   The judge denied the exemption, <u>however</u>, because the structure is not a permanent improvement to the property.

In this sentence, "however" modifies "exemption," which might contrast with a zoning application that the judge approved.

Finally, "however" can end the sentence:

> 7.   Indiana courts have rejected this argument, <u>however</u>.

In this position, "however" modifies not only the entire sentence, but also the preceding term. "This argument" could be juxtaposed with other arguments discussed.

But these rules about the placement of "however" are changing. If you begin a sentence with this conjunctive adverb, it signals that the entire sentence, not just one part of it, changes the direction of the argument. Many lawyers like the directness of this placement. If you insert "however" between major grammatical elements, the conjunctive adverb interrupts the sentence's flow. The separation is short, and proponents of this view like the precision of targeting the term that receives negative emphasis. They suggest using "but" or "yet" at a sentence's beginning to avoid the awkward sound of the multisyllabic "however."

As you place "however," determine where you want to change the direction of the argument. Note the intended emphasis and the effect of interrupting grammatical elements.

Exercise

Determine possible positions for "however" in this sentence, explain the modification, and, where appropriate, name a potential contrasting word or phrase.

Last year Italico Shoe Company maintained two warehouses in Georgia.

Answers

1. At the beginning of the sentence: "however" modifies the entire statement.

2. After "last year": "however" stresses the adverbial phrase. Might contrast with two years ago.

3. After "Company": "however" stresses the subject. Might contrast with another shoe company.

4. After "Georgia": "however" stresses the object of the preposition or the entire statement. Might contrast with South Carolina.

1.7.2 Placing "Only" and Other Adverbs

Place "only" just before the modified word or phrase. This adverb is like a flashlight shining "soleness" on one particular term. Without thinking, many speakers insert "only" before the verb. But in the wrong position, this adverb can change the meaning of a sentence. As you revise, check the position of "only." Move this adverb, if necessary, to make your writing more precise and persuasive.

CHAPTER ONE

In a memo concerning patent law, a lawyer used "only" before the adjective "apparent":

>   1(a)   *The segmented quality of the tire tread is <u>only</u> apparent when the tire is evaluated in one direction.*

This attorney meant that the tire tread's quality is apparent under only one set of conditions: when the tire is evaluated in one direction. Yet "only" in this sentence precedes and modifies the adjective "apparent." "Only" establishes the "apparentness," not the conditions. For clarity, insert "only" before "when":

>   1(b)   *The segmented quality of the tire tread is apparent <u>only</u> when the tire is evaluated in one direction.*

In sentence 2(a), "only" modifies the verb "receive":

>   2(a)   *The nephew will <u>only</u> receive the gift if one or both of the daughters fail to survive their mother.*

The lawyer wanted to state that the nephew will receive the gift under only one condition: if one or both of the daughters fail to survive their mother. "Only" should precede the "if" clause:

>   2(b)   *The nephew will receive the gift <u>only</u> if one or both of the daughters fail to survive their mother.*

The placement of "only" in sentence 3 is ambiguous:

>   3.   *In* Lafayette, *the court concluded that the Parker doctrine <u>only</u> exempted anticompetitive conduct when the government was acting as a sovereign.*

According to this writer, the court concluded that the Parker doctrine "only exempted" particular conduct under certain conditions. To correct this sentence, you need to know the writer's intention. Does this lawyer mean that the doctrine exempted "only anticompetitive conduct" under the conditions described? Or that anticompetitive conduct was exempted "only when the government was acting as a sovereign"?

Be careful when you place other modifiers as well. Consider the two meanings of sentence 4(a):

>   4(a)   *Most couples who consider the matter <u>seriously</u> decide to use trusts in their estate planning.*

Does "seriously" modify "consider" or "decide"? Does this lawyer say that most couples "seriously decide" to use trusts after considering the matter? Or that most couples who "seriously consider" the matter decide to use trusts? The second meaning is more likely. For clarity, insert "seriously" before "consider":

>   4(b)   *Most couples who <u>seriously</u> consider the matter decide to use trusts in their estate planning.*

Exercise

A. Identify two possible terms modified by "frequently" in the sentence below. Revise the sentence to eliminate ambiguity. Punctuate as needed.

Applying this definition frequently courts have ruled that a stamp collection does not fit into the category of "personal effects."

B. Note five meanings that depend on the placement of "only" in this sentence.

Bob Gorham only plays tennis on Saturdays.

Answers

A. 1. "Frequently" modifies "applying."

Revision: Frequently applying this definition, courts have ruled that a stamp collection does not fit into the category of "personal effects."

2. "Frequently" modifies "have ruled."

Revision: Applying this definition, courts frequently have ruled that a stamp collection does not fit into the category of "personal effects."

B. 1. <u>Only</u> Bob Gorham plays tennis on Saturdays. (Only Bob Gorham plays; no one else does.)

2. Bob Gorham <u>only</u> plays tennis on Saturdays. (He only plays tennis; he refuses to watch it on television.)

3. Bob Gorham plays <u>only</u> tennis on Saturdays. (He plays tennis only; he refuses to play other sports.)

4. Bob Gorham plays tennis <u>only</u> on Saturdays. (He won't play tennis on any other day of the week.)

5. Bob Gorham plays tennis on Saturdays <u>only</u>. (This sentence has the same meaning as B[4].)

1.7.3   Antithesis: Placing Contrasting Phrases

To achieve a strong contrast, place contrasting elements next to each other. When you juxtapose two parallel phrases, you emphasize the contrast:

> 1.   *Unlike <u>members of Congress</u>, <u>state officials</u> do not conduct foreign policy.*

Do not separate parallel phrases with intervening words. These interrupters weaken the contrast and can create confusion:

> 2(a)   *<u>Grim Company</u> should wear the label "forum shopper" in this action, not <u>Marsh, Inc.</u>*

The writer argues that the label "forum shopper" has been applied to the wrong party. Although the first contrasting element serves as subject of the sentence, the parallel phrase appears at the end of the independent clause. Place "not Marsh, Inc." after "Grim Company" for a stronger contrast:

> 2(b)   *<u>Grim Company</u>, not <u>Marsh, Inc.</u>, should wear the label "forum shopper" in this action.*

This change clarifies that "Marsh, Inc." is parallel to "Grim Company," not to "action."

Intervening words also separate antithetical phrases in sentence 3(a):

> 3(a)   *<u>The facts in existence when a suit is filed</u> determine a court's jurisdiction, not <u>later events</u>.*

To create a more powerful contrast, juxtapose the underlined noun phrases:

> 3(b)   *<u>The facts in existence when a suit is filed</u>, not <u>later events</u>, determine a court's jurisdiction.*

Exercise

Place contrasting phrases correctly in these sentences.

A. Common law will likely govern in this case, not the U.C.C.

B. Nasco must demonstrate clear and convincing evidence to establish all facts giving rise to the trust, not a mere preponderance of evidence.

C. The act of conversion gives rise to a claim, not the intention to convert.

D. The seller bears the burden of determining whether to register, not the purchaser or its agent.

Answers

A. Common law, not the U.C.C., will likely govern in this case.

B. Choose between two revisions, depending on the placement of the "to" phrase:

Revision: Nasco must demonstrate clear and convincing evidence, not a mere preponderance of evidence, to establish all facts giving rise to the trust.

Revision: To establish all facts giving rise to the trust, Nasco must demonstrate clear and convincing evidence, not a mere preponderance of evidence.

C. The act of conversion, not the intention to convert, gives rise to a claim.

D. The seller, not the purchaser or its agent, bears the burden of determining whether to register.

1.7.4   Misplaced Modifiers

Place modifiers close to the term they explain. Separating a clause or phrase from the modified word creates awkwardness and ambiguity. For example, a lawyer misplaced the final phrase in sentence 1(a):

1(a)   The court held that expenses will be charged to principal, <u>including expenses of Mr. Morton's counsel</u>.

The final phrase "including expenses of Mr. Morton's counsel" modifies "principal," the preceding noun. But the writer obviously intended for this phrase to explain "expenses." By inserting the phrase "including expenses of Mr. Morton's counsel" after "expenses," you eliminate the awkwardness and ambiguity:

1(b)   The court held that expenses, <u>including expenses of Mr. Morton's</u> <u>counsel</u>, will be charged to principal.

But repetition of "expenses" is awkward. Use the pronoun "those" after "including":

1(c)   The court held that expenses, including those of Mr. Morton's counsel, will be charged to principal.

Exercise

Place modifiers correctly in these sentences.

A. The database also will group important firm documents for historical purposes and for future use, such as legal opinions and research memoranda.

B. The options for disposing of irradiated reactor fuel were explained by Ms. Brown, e.g., reprocessing, permanent disposal, off-site facility storage, and on-site storage.

Answers

A. The database also will group important firm documents, such as legal opinions and research memoranda, for historical purposes and for future use.

- Put the phrase "such as legal opinions and research memoranda" after "documents," the modified noun.

B. Ms. Brown explained the options for disposing of irradiated reactor fuel, e.g., reprocessing, permanent disposal, off-site facility storage, and on-site storage.

- The "e.g., . . . storage" phrase modifies "options." Because "options for disposing of irradiated reactor fuel" is one unit, add the "e.g." phrase after "fuel." Then convert the sentence from passive to active.

1.7.5   Placing Prepositional Phrases

Do not separate major grammatical elements with long prepositional phrases. Instead, move the intervening structure to another position. Note the long prepositional phrase between a noun and its modifier in sentence 1(a):

1(a)   The trustee shall be the judge, <u>in the trustee's reasonable discretion</u>, of a person's competence, suitability, and availability to give any consent or consultation.

A prepositional phrase, "in the trustee's reasonable discretion," separates a noun, "judge," from its modifier, "of a person's competence, suitability, and availability." An adverbial phrase, "in the trustee's reasonable discretion," properly explains "shall be." But the position of that phrase implies that it modifies "judge." To correct this problem, move the intervening prepositional phrase to the beginning:

> 1(b) *In the trustee's reasonable discretion, the trustee shall be the judge of a person's competence, suitability, and availability to give consent or consultation.*

This change links the noun "judge" with its modifying prepositional phrase, "of a person's competence, suitability, and availability." But repeating "trustee" is awkward. Change the introductory phrase to eliminate this repetition:

> 1(c) *Using reasonable discretion, the trustee shall be the judge of a person's competence, suitability, and availability to give consent or consultation.*

A prepositional phrase separates the subject and verb in sentence 2(a):

> 2(a) *If a widow remarries, her second husband, absent a valid prenuptial agreement, is entitled under state law to receive up to one-half of his wife's estate.*

The phrase "absent a valid prenuptial agreement" modifies "is entitled" and explains the conditions under which a second husband may receive part of his wife's estate. This phrase separates the sentence's major elements, the subject and the verb. To revise this sentence, move the intervening phrase. The inheritance depends on the conditions expressed in two structures: "if a widow remarries" and "absent a valid prenuptial agreement." First, combine these ideas:

> 2(b) *If a widow remarries, absent a valid prenuptial agreement, her second husband is entitled under state law to receive up to one-half of his wife's estate.*

Then eliminate the awkward preposition "absent":

> 2(c) *If a widow remarries <u>without a valid prenuptial agreement</u>, her second husband is entitled under state law to receive up to one-half of his wife's estate.*

1.8 Transitions

1.8.1 The Importance of Transitions

Use transitions to show the relationships among ideas. Serving as signals to the reader, transitions bridge the gap between parts of a sentence, between sentences, between paragraphs, or between sections of a longer work. The etymology of transition relates to this function. "Transition" derives from the Latin term "trans-," which means over or across, and the verb "ire," to go. Thus, a transition literally "goes across" between elements of meaning.

Weak transitions make sentence 1(a) hard to understand:

> 1(a) *A deposit will not be available for setoff if the facts show fraud or collusion between LIM and BLH; or if BLH holds the funds not on open account, but for a special purpose known to BLH; if the deposit was not made or accepted in the ordinary course of business; or if the deposit was made or accepted for the purpose of obtaining or granting to BLH a right of setoff.*

The writer crammed a statement and four conditions into a long and confusing sentence. It lacks signals to guide the reader through five clauses. Inconsistent placement of "or" and of punctuation (colon, semicolon) contributes to the ambiguity.

To revise this sentence, assume that all four conditions are separate and that any one will preclude setoff. First, add "under any one of the following conditions" after "setoff" in line 1:

> 1(b) *A deposit will not be available for setoff <u>under any one of the following conditions</u>:*

The noun "conditions" establishes a category for the tabulated items. Introduce the four conditions with "if," tabulate them, separate them with semicolons, and insert "or" after the third:

> *1(c)   A deposit will not be available for setoff under any one of the following conditions:*
>
> > *i.   If the facts show fraud or collusion between LIM and BLH;*
> >
> > *ii.   If BLH holds the funds not on open account, but for a special purpose known to BLH;*
> >
> > *iii. If the deposit was not made or accepted in the ordinary course of business; or*
> >
> > *iv.   If the deposit was made or accepted for the purpose of obtaining or granting to BLH a right of setoff.*

1.8.2   Coordinating Conjunctions

Use coordinating conjunctions to join words, phrases, and clauses. These conjunctions are "and," "but," "or," "nor," "for," "so," and "yet." Although "yet" and "nor" can be used correctly at the beginning of sentences, experts disagree about starting sentences with "and," "but," "or," "for," and "so." Some stylists believe that this structure creates a fragment. Others argue that sentences beginning with "and," "but," and "or" can be effective in persuasive writing, especially when a conversational tone is appropriate.

1.8.3   "And": Our Weakest Connective

1.8.3.1   At the Beginning of a Sentence

Consider context, tone, and audience carefully before you start a sentence with "and." Many lawyers and judges were taught that this structure is an incomplete sentence, i.e., a fragment. Even if that rule has changed, "and" creates a flabby, indirect beginning for a sentence.

As you revise, look for sentences starting with "and." Analyze the meaning you intended to express with the conjunction. Then substitute another word or phrase that communicates the logical relationship clearly and gracefully.

CHAPTER ONE

In example 1(a), a lawyer began the last sentence with "and":

> 1(a) *You can obtain private nuclear liability insurance from two nuclear liability insurance pools: American Atomic Insurance and Mutual Nuclear Energy Liability Underwriters. Together, they will write coverage of up to $160 million. Accordingly, the Commission has required primary insurance coverage of that amount for licensees required to have the maximum amount of financial protection. Since seventy-three commercial reactors are now licensed to operate under C.F.R. Part 50, the secondary insurance pool provided by the reactor licensees is $365 million. <u>And</u> the total amount of privately available insurance, both primary and secondary, is $525 million.*

The writer used "and" to signal the conclusion to the paragraph. In this formal context, however, the sentence seems flabby and weak.

To revise this structure, first analyze the logical development of the paragraph. After identifying two sources of private nuclear liability insurance, the lawyer explains the amounts of their coverage. "And" introduces a summary sentence about the total private insurance available. Substitute "thus" for "and" to express this cause-and-effect relationship:

> 1(b) <u>*Thus*</u>*, the total amount of privately available insurance, both primary and secondary, is $525 million.*

Do not use "and" to communicate a precise meaning that is not clear to the reader. For example, in passage 2(a), "and" appears to mean only "in addition." But the logical relationship between the final two sentences is more complex:

> 2. *In holding that Rhode Island and Commissioner Sullivan lacked standing, the court below adopted an extraordinarily pinched view of the law of standing. As the lower court reasoned, apparently the only proper plaintiffs to put in issue the validity of the SEC's purported preemption of Rhode Island's takeover statute are "the tender offerors whose activities are subject to regulation." [Citation] <u>And</u> the only available "remedy" for Rhode Island and Commissioner Sullivan is to await the commencement of a tender offer and then attempt to enforce the Rhode Island statute: [Quotation from lower court's ruling].*

By beginning the last sentence with "and," the writer weakens the force of the statement and creates ambiguity. "And" is the blandest connective we have; it simply indicates that two elements belong together. Unlike other coordinating conjunctions, "and" does not show a more specific relationship between two elements. In the final sentence of the passage, the writer started with "and" to reinforce the phrase "as the lower court would have it," which introduces the previous sentence. He added "and" to establish that the rest of the sentence states the court's analysis.

That meaning is not clear, however, especially after a long intervening sentence and citation. "And" does not imply that the final sentence states the court's view. In fact, the sentence begins as if it were the writer's own assertion. Only the final quotation clarifies that these ideas are the court's.

If you delete "and," you have not solved the problem, because the sentence requires more information, not less, to explain the source of the ideas. Repetition of "as the lower court would have it" would be monotonous. Instead, emphasize the extension of the court's ideas with a different introductory phrase. "According to the lower court" will provide both variety and precision.

1.8.3.2   In a Series

Place "and" just before the last element of a series. To avoid flabby prose, do not insert this conjunction between other elements. An extra "and" weakens the series in sentence 1(a):

> 1(a)   *Functions such as assessment collection _and_ benefits distribution _and_ negotiation of health plans do not involve the trustees' exercising broad discretion.*

This series needs only one conjunction; commas between elements also will clarify the structure. Delete "and" after "collection":

> 1(b)   *Functions such as assessment collection, benefits distribution, _and_ negotiation of health plans do not involve the trustees' exercising broad discretion.*

With these revisions, the series is concise and clear.

1.8.3.3 Between Clauses

Overuse of "and" to link clauses creates flabby prose. This conjunction joins two elements that belong together, but it does not show a more specific relationship between them. When possible, use subordination, a more sophisticated linking technique. Subordination establishes a hierarchy between clauses. The main clause receives more emphasis than the dependent, subordinate clause.

Subordination will improve sentence 2(a):

2(a) *Mr. Lukov protested against the current regime, <u>and</u> then he was threatened, beaten, and arrested without charges.*

To revise this sentence, first analyze the logical relationship between the two clauses. Then choose an adverb to express it. "After" states the time relationship in this sentence. Insert "after" before the first clause; then delete "and":

2(b) <u>*After*</u> *Mr. Lukov protested against the current regime, then he was threatened, beaten, and arrested without charges.*

Next, cut "then" from the independent clause:

2(c) <u>*After*</u> *Mr. Lukov protested against the current regime, he was threatened, beaten, and arrested without charges.*

Even short independent clauses joined by "and" can create a flabby sentence. Instead, use a more precise connective or subordination. "And" links two independent clauses in 3(a):

3(a) *The request was denied, and the hearing proceeded.*

This structure might be effective in a short story, but not in legal writing. By using subordination, you create a clearer relationship between the clauses:

3(b) <u>*When*</u> *the request was denied, the hearing proceeded.*

Exercise

A. Suggest an alternative to "and" at the beginning of the last sentence below.

The "financial protection" required of licensees must be insurance that provides protection against public liability. The term "public liability" is broadly defined to include any legal liability, without regard to whom or by whom owed, arising out of a "nuclear incident." And the insurance protects not only the licensee, but also any other person who may incur liability as a result of a nuclear incident.

B. Tighten flabby prose in this sentence.

The police arrested and imprisoned Mr. Cherdin without charges and Ms. Ellis warned that he was on a dissident list and would not be released.

Answers

A. To express the cause-and-effect relationship between the last two sentences, replace "and" with "thus," "consequently," or "therefore."

B. After the police arrested and imprisoned Mr. Cherdin without charges, Ms. Ellis warned that he would not be released because his name was on a dissident list.

• Use subordination:
  i. Add "after" at the sentence's beginning;
  ii. Drop the second "and";
  iii. Add a comma after "charges";
  iv. Move "his name was on a dissident list" to the end of the sentence; and
  v. Insert "because" before "his."

1.8.4 "But" and "Yet"

"Yet" is a more versatile conjunction than "but." You can use "yet" at the beginning of sentences and clauses. Although "but" is correct at the beginning of a dependent clause, stylists disagree about using this conjunction to start a sentence. Some believe that an independent clause introduced by "but" is a fragment, or incomplete sentence:

1. *But neither DR 7-1-4 (A)(1) nor Model Rule 4.2 prohibits ex parte communications with former employees.*

Of course, "but" is correct when it introduces the second clause in a compound sentence:

2.   *Trexco proposed a 5 percent increase in wages, but the union rejected the offer.*

The rule against beginning a sentence with "but" appears to be changing. In some contexts, this technique can be effective. For example, "but" should introduce only a short sentence:

3.   *But Plaintiffs still have access to and from their homes via the Elm Street easement.*

Moreover, use this structure only in writing with an informal tone. Otherwise, "but" creates a weak beginning:

4.   *But Friedman is not precluded from advocating that it is entitled to an EAJA award because the Ninth Circuit Court of Appeals has not addressed the issue of EAJA applicability in the context of grand jury-related motions and because the Second and Third Circuits have applied different reasoning to circumstances distinct from those presented here.*

"Yet" is more formal than "but" and is strong enough to begin a sentence:

5.   *The class members possess a leasehold interest in individual units. Yet the property description specifies only the tracts of real estate.*

Like "but," "yet" is also effective in a compound sentence:

6.   *There were several other adults in the house, yet the child was left unattended by the father.*

Alternatives to these coordinating conjunctions include conjunctive adverbs and prepositional phrases. To begin a sentence, you can use adverbs like "nevertheless" and "however," which have a formal tone.

7.   *Nevertheless, our clients stopped filing reports with the secretary.*

8.   *However, most jurisdictions grant mercantile rating agencies a qualified privilege against liability.*

You also can use "on the contrary" before a short main clause:

9.   *On the contrary, Ms. Little paid off the line of credit on June 30.*

Exercise

Suggest alternatives to "but" in these sentences.

A. The father read the drain cleaner's warning label. But he allowed his child to touch the product.

B. Oakton's motor was a standard "off-the-shelf" motor that Lasar selected for inclusion in the meat grinder. But Oakton did not participate in the design of the meat grinder.

Answers

A. You have three choices:

   1. Retain two separate sentences. Begin the second with "yet," "however," or "nevertheless." Add a comma after all of these transitions except "yet."

   2. Create a compound sentence. Add a comma between the clauses, and use "but" or "yet."

   3. Insert a semicolon between the sentences. Use "however" or "nevertheless," and follow the transition with a comma.

B. Follow the first option above. The sentences are too long for the second and third options.

1.8.5   "Nor" and "Or"

Like all coordinating conjunctions, "nor" and "or" introduce the second independent clause in a compound sentence. Yet these conjunctions differ in their function at the beginning of a sentence.

"Nor" has three appropriate functions. First, you can use "nor" at the beginning of the second independent clause:

1.   *Mr. Moore did not see the report, <u>nor</u> did he discuss it with the committee.*

You also can add "nor" at the beginning of a sentence when the previous sentence contains a negative:

> 2. *Glase Company does not supply maintenance products for industrial, commercial, or institutional applications. <u>Nor</u> does Glase Company manufacture firefighting accessories such as nozzles, valves, portable tanker units, specialized tools, and protective clothing.*

"Nor" stresses the negative in both sentences and links them. The negative aspect receives far more emphasis with "nor" than it would with "in addition . . . not." Of course, "nor" is also part of the expression "neither . . . nor":

> 3. *The court <u>neither</u> analyzed medical monitoring under state law <u>nor</u> certified the question to the Supreme Court of Pennsylvania.*

Not all grammarians agree about "or" at the beginning of a sentence. This conjunction correctly links two independent clauses in a compound sentence:

> 4. *Plaintiffs may seek to amend their complaint to cure the pleading defect, <u>or</u> they may refile, opening a new lawsuit.*

In persuasive writing with a conversational tone, a short sentence that starts with "or" can be effective. Yet in formal writing, a sentence that begins with "or" may be read as a fragment:

> 5(a) *Antagonism and dissension between partners may be sufficient grounds for dissolution. <u>Or</u> serious misconduct by one partner may serve as sufficient grounds for dissolution.*

Both sentences in 5(a) have the same predicate. To eliminate the fragment, combine both subjects with one predicate:

> 5(b) *Antagonism and dissension between partners <u>or</u> serious misconduct by one partner may serve as grounds for dissolution.*

Combining two predicates will also improve the "or" structure in 6(a):

> 6(a) *To satisfy the debt, Pama Steel could borrow $500,000 from Colco National Bank. <u>Or</u> the company could liquidate its investments in Lion Corporation.*

6(b)   To satisfy the debt, Pama Steel could borrow $500,000 from Colco
        National Bank _or_ liquidate its investments in Lion Corporation.

1.8.6   "For" and "So"

Use "for" and "so" to link two independent clauses in a compound
sentence. These conjunctions designate specific relationships between
the two clauses. Do not insert "for" or "so" at the beginning of a sentence
in formal writing.

"For" signals that a causal relationship exists between two sentences.
The second clause explains the reason for the action or state of being in
the first. Many lawyers avoid this usage because of its awkward, formal
tone:

1.   In Green, amendment was not an option, _for_ it could not have cured
        the defect.

When you add "for" as a causal connective at the beginning of a sentence,
you create a fragment:

2.   _For_ amendment could not have cured the defect.

The conjunction "so" designates a cause-and-effect relationship between the clauses. Use "so" at the beginning of the second independent
clause in a compound sentence. The second clause explains a conse-
quence that follows from the first:

3.   Mr. Clemmer's allegations are not factually supported, _so_ he lacks
        standing to maintain this suit.

Most grammarians agree that a clause introduced with "so" is a fragment:

4(a)   _So_ the board of directors canceled the quarterly dividend.

You have several options for converting the fragment to a complete sentence. First, add an independent clause at the beginning:

4(b)   Foreign competition limited Plimpton's profit margin, _so_ the board of
        directors canceled the quarterly dividend.

With this change, the cause-and-effect relationship is clear. You also can substitute a conjunctive adverb for "so":

> 4(c) Foreign competition limited Plimpton's profit margin. _Thus_, the board of directors canceled the quarterly dividend.

> 4(d) Foreign competition limited Plimpton's profit margin. _Therefore_, the board of directors canceled the quarterly dividend.

> 4(e) Foreign competition limited Plimpton's profit margin. _Consequently_, the board of directors canceled the quarterly dividend.

All these revisions express the relationship between the two clauses and satisfy the constraints of sentence structure.

Exercise

Identify coordinating conjunctions in these sentences. Revise structural problems as needed.

A. "Kill switches" to stop boat motors were available last year. But the plaintiff purchased her boat two years ago.

B. Carriers may obtain Section 214 authorization to construct a transmission facility. Or they may submit semiannual reports regarding any new circuits.

C. The alternative safety devices were technologically possible. Yet they were not practical due to inordinate economic costs.

Answers

A. Conjunction: "but." The sentence is correct but may be converted to a compound sentence.

   Revision: "Kill switches" to stop boat motors were available last year, but the plaintiff purchased her boat two years ago.

B. Conjunction: "or." Convert to a compound sentence with a comma before the conjunction.

   Revision: Carriers may obtain Section 214 authorization to construct a transmission facility, or they may submit semiannual reports regarding any new circuits.

C. Conjunction: "yet." The sentence is correct but may be converted to a compound sentence.

   Revision: The alternative safety devices were technologically possible, yet they were not practical due to inordinate economic costs.

1.8.7 Causal Connectives: "Because," "As," and "Since"

Choose carefully between connectives to express cause and effect. "Because," "as," and "since" express causal relationships, but "as" and "since" can also denote time. For clarity, use "because" in any potentially ambiguous sentence.

Do not use "as" in contexts involving time. This adverb can mean either "because" or "at the same time that." In sentence 1(a), the relationship between the two clauses is confusing:

1(a)   *These cases are irrelevant <u>as</u> the court did not award injunctive relief.*

Are the cases irrelevant because the court did not award injunctive relief or while the court did not award injunctive relief? The causal meaning is more likely, but the reader must stop briefly to interpret the meaning. Use "because" to avoid ambiguity:

1(b)   *These cases do not apply <u>because</u> the court did not award injunctive relief.*

If you use "as" in the causal sense, place the adverb clause at the sentence's beginning. Use "as" only in contexts with no confusion about time or cause:

2.   *<u>As</u> the Public Utilities Act supercedes the Franchise Ordinance, it is impossible to perform.*

The adverb "since" also creates ambiguity in contexts related to time:

3(a)   *The judge granted the motion for change of venue <u>since</u> the psychiatric reports were released on July 1.*

The judge may have granted the motion for change of venue because the reports were released on July 1 or after their release. Substitute "because" or "after" for "since":

3(b)   *The judge granted the motion for change of venue <u>because</u> the psychiatric reports were released on July 1.*

3(c)   The judge granted the motion for change of venue <u>after</u> the psychiatric reports were released on July 1.

You can use "since" correctly as a causal connective in contexts with no reference to time:

4.   The "obsolete doctrine" does not apply to the Franchise Ordinance <u>since</u> it is a contract, not a statute.

"Because" is the safest causal connective. Use "since" or "as" for variety in sentences with no ambiguity about time or cause.

Exercise

Identify ambiguous causal connectives in these sentences. Revise as needed.

A. The current legislative proposals do not apply to Buxton's claim as they rely on the Plat Act.

B. Many DOJ lawsuits have alleged violations of the Act since ECOA broadly prohibits discrimination in credit transactions.

C. Mr. Monroe's psychiatric report is significant as he is free on bail.

D. The Franchise Ordinance does not grant Axton a license to use the streets since the city's Municipal Code governs this relationship.

Answers

A. Ambiguous connective: "as"

   <u>Revision</u>: The current legislative proposals do not apply to Buxton's claim because they rely on the Plat Act.

• Substitute "because" for "as."

B. "Since" is not ambiguous in this context unrelated to time.

C. Ambiguous connective: "as"

   <u>Revision</u>: Mr. Monroe's psychiatric report is significant because he is free on bail.

• Substitute "because" for "as."

D. "Since" is not ambiguous in this context unrelated to time.

1.8.8   Introducing a Series: The "Category Noun"

To introduce a series, use a "category noun" and a colon. The noun should name a category for the elements and provide a context for the reader. Place the category noun as close to the colon as possible.

Some lawyers bury the category noun in the middle of a long lead-in:

1(a)   *The Sixth Circuit uses a <u>three-step analysis</u> to determine whether a tying arranging will cause anticompetitive effect and thus violate the Sherman Antitrust Act:*

[Three Steps]

Seventeen words separate the category noun from the series. Some readers will not identify "three-step analysis" as the category noun because it does not occupy the expected slot just before the colon. At the very least, the intervening words obscure the category noun.

Revise this lead-in to meet your readers' expectations. First, move the intervening words to the beginning of the sentence. With this revision, the category noun appears just before the colon and leads directly into the series:

1(b)   *To determine whether a tying arranging will cause anticompetitive effect and thus violate the Sherman Antitrust Act, the Sixth Circuit uses a <u>three-step analysis</u>:*

[Three Steps]

In sentence 2(a), a lawyer inserted information about attachments between the category noun and a series:

2(a)   *The following <u>unexpired patents</u>, copies of which are attached as Exhibit A, were located by Ms. Jackson:*

[List of ten patents and inventors]

The writer began with the category noun, explained its relationship to attachment A, and continued with a passive verb. Instead, convert the main clause to the active voice:

> 2(b) *Ms. Jackson located the following <u>unexpired patents</u>, copies of which are attached as Exhibit A:*
>
> *[List of ten patents and inventors]*

To place the category noun just before the colon, change the relative clause about attachment A to a sentence, and move it after the series:

> 2(c) *Ms. Jackson located the following <u>unexpired patents</u>:*
>
> *[List of ten patents and inventors]*
>
> *Copies of these patents are attached as Exhibit A.*

Exercise

Place the category noun correctly in this lead-in.

> The following four-pronged test will be applied by the court to determine whether ModBank's prepayment policy violated Oregon law:

Answer

> To determine whether ModBank's prepayment policy violated Oregon law, the court will apply the following four-pronged test:

- First, move the "to" phrase to the beginning of the sentence. Then convert the main clause to the active voice, and place the category noun, "four-pronged test," just before the colon.

1.8.9 Awkward Transitions

Do not clutter your writing with transitions that are wordy, awkward, and repetitious. These transitions repeat previous material, provide a preview of ideas to come, or make an appeal to the reader, such as "let us now turn to. . . ."

In a legal memorandum, an attorney ended a section by "previewing":

1.   *We may now discuss the provisions found in the Federal Alcoholic Beverage Labeling Act and California's Proposition 65 that raise the preemption issue.*

Immediately below, the same material appeared in a heading:

> *The Warnings Required Under the Alcohol Labeling Act and California Proposition 65.*

The transition is unnecessary because the heading announces the topic.

Some superfluous transitions summarize previous material and state a general principle that is developed more specifically in a heading. For example, the transition below concluded a section in a memo:

2.   *Now that the two warning requirements have been stated, it is necessary to analyze whether federal law will preempt the state law.*

The next section began with this heading:

> *Application of the Doctrine of Preemption to the Conflict Between the Requirements of the Alcohol Labeling Act and California Proposition 65.*

To avoid repetition, delete the transition and explain the applicable federal and state law after the heading.

In the concluding sentences below, attorneys introduce the topic of the next paragraph. Instead, omit the superfluous preview and begin the next paragraph as shown in brackets:

3.   *To find the answer, we must explore the Congressional intent behind the Act.*

     [Discuss Congressional intent.]

4. *A thorough analysis of Congressional intent behind the legislation can be had only by reviewing Congressional debates that occurred while the Act was still being considered for passage.*

    [Review Congressional debates.]

5. *An overview of the legal, as well as practical, ramifications of using designated funds may illustrate the pros and cons of such use.*

    [Summarize ramifications.]

Conclude every paragraph by "hammering home" its main point, not by justifying the material that follows.

Exercise

Revise this transition sentence.

> Having determined that in many cases the investment of other charities' funds will be considered a legitimate role for community foundations, what follows is an examination of four alternative investment structures.

Answer

> Community foundations have four alternative structures for investing other charities' funds.

- A long introductory phrase repeats previous material and is a dangling modifier. Begin the next paragraph with the idea in the main sentence.

CHAPTER TWO

~ *Persuasion* ~

Before you write to persuade, analyze your goals. Of course, you want to convince the reader to think in a certain way. At times you also want to persuade the reader to act in a certain way. Plan how to achieve those goals. Consider diction, tone, sentence structure, logical development, and organization. All these factors will affect the persuasiveness of your writing.

Not only litigators write to persuade. Lawyers in other practices must write persuasive letters, faxes, and e-mails. The principles of persuasion are consistent in all practice areas. The tone of written communication, however, may differ. The most aggressive corporate letters may be less strident than some briefs.

Topics such as diction, tone, and sentence structure, which were discussed generally in chapter 1, will focus on persuasive techniques in this chapter.

2.1 Diction and Tone

In persuasive writing, pay careful attention to diction. Your word choice will affect tone, an important factor in persuasion. As a general rule, choose simple words over complicated ones. If a short word expresses the same meaning as a long one, use the shorter form. Essential legal terms often create a formal tone. To offset this awkward quality, use short, simple words when appropriate in context. Dense prose is not persuasive.

As you draft, choose diction for grammatical slots in each sentence. Consider your options for each verb, noun, adjective, and adverb. Base your decision on context, goal, and intended tone. Analyze the relative strengths of potential choices. If necessary, use a thesaurus, but always check the definition of unfamiliar synonyms. Consider your options for each verb, noun, adjective, and adverb.

2.1.1   Verbs

The verb is the heart of a sentence. Verbs express action (e.g., "steal") or a state of being (e.g., "was"). All other structures, such as subject, object, complement, and their modifiers, depend on the verb. When you write to persuade, choose the verb for each sentence first. Analyze the most effective action or state of being. By carefully selecting the verb, you begin to control each sentence's persuasive power.

A litigator used two types of verbs successfully in a brief arguing against the claims of Mr. Little, a cartoonist. Twenty years after signing an agreement with Atlantic News Syndicate, Little challenged the validity of the agreement. At that point, Atlantic had invested heavily in promotions for Little. In sentence 1, the litigator chose short verbs:

1.   *Now that Atlantic News Syndicate has <u>sowed</u> for cartoonist Little, Little believes that he alone should <u>reap</u>.*

Like other words derived from Anglo-Saxon, these verbs represent actions related to life's basic needs, e.g., "agriculture." In this context, the verbs, which echo Biblical language, stand figuratively for investing and profiting. These simple, direct action words help persuade the reader that Little is wrong.

Later in the same brief, the litigator used a different type of verb:

2.   *Little cannot wait twenty years and then <u>abscond</u> with the fruits of that effort.*

"Abscond," a formal, somewhat stilted verb, derives from Latin. Because it rarely appears in legal writing, "abscond" attracts the reader's attention. Its negative connotation, i.e., running away to escape the law, also contributes to the verb's strength. Its Anglo-Saxon object, "fruits," offsets the formality of the verb.

Exercise

Analyze the strength or weakness of the verb phrase in this sentence, depending on the writer's goal.

> Defendant Carla Lang <u>seems to be claiming</u> that these interrogatories are burdensome and therefore need not be fully answered.

Answer

If the writer represents the defendant, the underlined hedging verb is weak. If the writer represents the plaintiff, the verb phrase strengthens an attack on Ms. Lang. The hedging verb implies that her claims are weak and thus she is unable to communicate them clearly.

2.1.2   Nouns

After you choose a verb for each sentence, focus on noun slots. A noun is a part of speech that names a person, place, or thing. Noun slots include the subject, complement, direct object, indirect object, and object of a preposition.

While drafting a brief, a litigator inserted different nouns in the complement slot. First, she used a gently persuasive phrase:

> *1(a)   Plantex's Motion to Recover Excess Costs is a <u>meritless effort</u>.*

To make the tone more accusatory, she substituted "sham" for "meritless effort":

> *1(b)   Plantex's Motion to Recover Excess Costs is a <u>sham</u>.*

With this contrast, she could analyze the overall tone of the sentence in context and select the more persuasive noun.

Sets of underlined nouns below illustrate similar differences in tone:

> *2(a)   This case constitutes a bold <u>challenge</u> to national labor law policy.*

> *2(b)   This case constitutes a bold <u>attack</u> on national labor law policy.*

3(a)   *Axco's attempted <u>changes</u> regarding the discovery schedule were obvious to Defendants.*

3(b)   *Axco's attempted <u>sleight of hand</u> regarding the discovery schedule was obvious to Defendants.*

2.1.3   Adjectives

Choose adjectives carefully. Adjectives, which modify nouns or pronouns, can be descriptive ("long brief"), limiting ("both motions"), or proper ("Texas law").

In a brief arguing against the expense and delays of proxy contests, a litigator used a strong adjective to emphasize the relatively small administrative costs:

1(a)   *The administrative expense is <u>trifling</u> when compared to the costs of the transactions.*

"Trifling," a forceful adjective rarely used in legal writing, attracts the reader's attention. The lawyer could have chosen one of the modifiers below:

1(b)   *The administrative expense is <u>small</u> . . . ;*

1(c)   *The administrative expense is <u>minimal</u> . . . ; or*

1(d)   *The administrative expense is <u>slight</u>. . . .*

These adjectives are weaker than "trifling" but appear frequently in briefs. Overused adjectives with general meanings are as bland in legal writing as the word "nice" has become in speech.

2.1.4   Adverbs

Before you add adverbs to your draft, consider their effect on the style and tone of your document. Adverbs, which modify verbs, adjectives, and other adverbs, explain how, why, where, or in what manner. Compare the two columns below:

1. broad categories—*absurdly* broad categories

2. ignores—*studiously* ignores

The adverbs make both phrases more descriptive and more accusatory. Use adverbs sparingly, however. When overused, they weaken persuasive writing.

2.1.4.1 "Clearly" and "Totally"

Do not try to strengthen an argument by inserting "clearly" or "totally" before a verb. Avoid these overused adverbs. "Clearly" will not bolster a weak statement. Choose more precise words to explain why something is clear.

Writers use "totally" so frequently that it is no longer persuasive. How many times have you read "totally fails"? What impact does the phrase have for you? Instead, choose stronger verbs, nouns, adjectives, and adverbs.

2.1.4.2 "Importantly" and "Significantly"

Avoid using adverbs like "importantly" and "significantly" for emphasis at the beginning of a sentence. Although these modifiers appear to add persuasive power, their impact is limited:

1. *Significantly, Defendant Greene did not serve Axco with his motion to vacate until August 1.*

2. *More importantly, Ms. Lear failed to appear in court on her young client's behalf.*

These adverbs merely tell readers that the statement is important. They must then infer why, but may not understand your meaning. To use these adverbs persuasively, you should explain the reasons for the statement's importance. Show the reader why you began the sentence with "importantly" or "significantly." For example, after sentence 1, the lawyer could explain that because August 1 is more than thirty days after the motion period, the motion should be denied.

2.1.5 Legalese

Do not use unnecessary legal terms in persuasive writing. Archaic words distract the reader and contrast with the persuasive tone of a brief or letter. You often can delete terms such as "said," "such," "infra," "supra," "arguendo," "inter alia," "hereto," "herein," and "foregoing." Distinguish between essential legal language and superfluous terms of art.

Incorrect use of "such," for example, can weaken an argument:

1(a)   Petitioners' conclusory _allegations set forth in paragraphs 25 and 26_ _fulfill neither of the requirements. Petitioners fail to set forth who made_ such _allegations, when_ such _allegations were made, how petitioners relied upon_ such _allegations, and how petitioners were allegedly damaged by reliance._

The first "such" refers to specific allegations, those "set forth in paragraphs 25 and 26." You can make the sentence more persuasive by replacing "such" with "these." Substitute "the" for "such" in the other two examples:

1(b)   Petitioners' conclusory _allegations set forth in paragraphs 25 and 26_ _fulfill neither of the requirements. Petitioners fail to set forth who made_ these _allegations, when_ the _allegations were made, how petitioners relied upon_ the _allegations, and how petitioners were allegedly damaged by reliance._

In persuasive writing, use "such" only to mean "of that type."

2.1.6   "Hidden" Verbs

When you write to persuade, convert long nouns to their verb forms. Many long nouns are based on a verb form, e.g., "limitation—limit." The verb is more direct, and therefore more persuasive, than the noun. Some of these nouns also require extra prepositions, such as "of." Review each sentence to identify nouns that contain hidden verbs. If possible, substitute more concise verb forms.

Hidden verbs limit the persuasive power of sentence 1(a):

1(a)   In the event of the occurrence of a default by Payco that brings about the termination of the agreement, there will be no obligation for Smith to repurchase the San Francisco accounts.

Note the four nouns that contain hidden verbs:

1(b)   In the event of the _occurrence_ of a _default_ by Payco that brings about the _termination_ of the agreements, there will be no _obligation_ for Smith to purchase the San Francisco accounts.

You can convert "default," "termination," and "obligation" to their verb forms:

1. default—*defaults*

2. termination—*terminates*

3. obligation—*obligates*

Delete "occurrence," which requires no substitution. These changes also eliminate the verb phrase "brings about"; the impersonal expression "there . . . be"; the articles "a" and "the"; and the prepositions "of," "for," and "by." Finally, replace the wordy phrase "in the event of" with "if" and add "thus":

> *1(c)*   *If Payco <u>defaults</u> and thus <u>terminates</u> the agreement, Smith will not <u>be obligated</u> to purchase the San Francisco accounts.*

With a 60 percent reduction in words, the revised version is more persuasive than its original form.

2.1.7   Gauging Tone

You do not have to shout to be persuasive. Do not instinctively choose the most aggressive diction available. Of course, use strong words if their tone is appropriate for your audience, goal, and context. Yet logic also persuades, and a reasoned approach can influence readers without offending them.

Note the contrast in tone in the litigation writing below:

<u>Forceful</u>

1. Titanic struggles

2. an atmosphere free of economic coercion

3. did not deploy any exotic defense

4. attempted sleight of hand

Calm

1. Defendant's request constitutes wishful thinking, not reasoned argument.

2. It would be illogical to provide a means for recovery.

3. Plaintiff's theory is inconsistent with derivative actions.

4. In sum, the evidence showed no conflict between the board and the shareholders.

In the first four phrases, litigators chose words carefully to create strong arguments. "Titanic," "coercion," "exotic," and "sleight" communicate powerful meanings. Yet the writers of the "gentler" statements seem to have examined the legal context and then made reasoned judgments. Logic and observation inevitably lead to these conclusions.

2.1.8   Aggressive Language

Strong language is not always persuasive. Overblown rhetoric and frequent attacks on opposing counsel can alienate even the most impartial reader. Too much aggressive language weakens the force of each phrase.

Counsel for plaintiff Zip Stores misjudged the tone of a brief in opposition to defendant Shoe City's motion to recover excess costs. Shoemaker had sold the infringing shoe product to Shoe City, and Shoemaker's counsel had represented Shoe City in previous litigation. Excerpts from the ten-page brief appear below:

1. *The most recent Motion filed by counsel for Shoe City Stores, Inc. ("Shoe City") is but the latest in a series of shabby efforts by counsel to divert the court's attention from the merits of this case and, specifically, the merits of Zip Stores' ("Zip") recent Motion for Summary Judgment. The length to which counsel for Shoe City will go to avoid the salient issues in the Motion for Summary Judgment is appalling.*

2. *This is a fallacious and illusory argument without any supporting legal basis.*

3. *Rather than taking simple procedural steps so as to be in a position to argue that the consent judgments can have no effect on it, Shoemaker and its counsel use and adopt the consent judgments! Likewise, they raise the spurious requirement that Shoemaker actually controls settlement negotiations in order to be bound by consent judgments. That is fluff without substance.*

4.   *The Motion to Recover Excess Costs is by any standard only a transparent effort by Shoemaker and Shoe City's counsel to cover up their horrendous tactical errors in permitting consent judgments to be entered without seeking intervention or in any other manner objecting to their entry. Shoemaker and Shoe City's counsel now find themselves in the professionally embarrassing position of having squandered whatever chance Shoemaker had to succeed in its case in Chicago, or on its customers' Counterclaims filed here and elsewhere.*

5.   *It is regrettable that counsel for Shoemaker feel pushed to this extreme and mortifying position by their own mistakes.*

6.   *Shoe City's Motion to Recover Excess Costs is a sham, entirely frivolous, and no more than a dejected and obvious effort to detract the court's attention for the merits of Zip's Motion for Summary Judgment. Shoe City's Motion serves to exemplify the errors of Shoemaker and Shoe City's own counsel, and seeks to cover up those errors from the court and from the clients as well.*

The litigator's strong language numbs the reader. After the first few examples, each word has little impact. Some readers find the cumulative effect humorous. If your overblown rhetoric amuses readers, you cannot persuade them.

Two other techniques in passage 3 weaken this argument:

1. At the end of a fifty-five-word sentence describing legal dynamics, the exclamation point has no effect.

2. The last phrase, "That's fluff without substance," is redundant. What other type of fluff is there?

2.2 Sentence Structure

2.2.1   Short Sentences

Use short sentences with clear structures in persuasive writing. In long sentences, readers must trace the meaning through each clause and phrase. An argument that forces readers to work so hard will not be persuasive. Divide long sentences if possible. When you must draft a long sentence, use parallelism, tabulation, and accurate punctuation to clarify structural relationships.

Remember two basic sentence structures: subject-verb-object and subject-verb-complement. Both can be effective, even for topic sentences. For example, after discussing two effects of plaintiffs' delay in bringing a damage claim in *Fifth Third Bank v. West*, a litigator began a paragraph this way:

1.   *Atlantic News Syndicate suffered both types of prejudice.*

In this subject-verb-object structure, "types" is the direct object, a noun that receives the action of the verb. The sentence serves as a transition from a discussion of *Fifth Third Bank* to two types of prejudice against the client. Each word in the "bare bones" sentence has a strong impact.

The subject-verb-complement structure can also be persuasive. In this context, the complement is a noun or adjective that completes the subject. The short topic sentence below followed a discussion of the court's reasoning in *Osborne*:

2.   *This case is far stronger.*

With five words, the litigator powerfully characterizes her argument. In addition, the topic sentence links the application of *Osborne* to the client's situation.

2.2.2   Awkward Sentences

When you edit, analyze the structure of each long sentence to determine if logical connections are clear. Note your experience as you read sentence 1(a):

1(a)   *The committee's suggestion that the debtor-in-possession orders violate* United Savings Ass'n of Texas v. Timbers of Inwood Forest Assoc., *484 U.S. 365 (1988), in which the Supreme Court held that an undersecured creditor may not receive interest on its collateral, and* Shapiro v. Saybrook Mfg. Co. (In re Saybrook Mfg. Co.), *963 F. 2d 1490 (11th Cir. 1992), in which the Eleventh Circuit concluded that post-petition liens may not be granted to secure pre-petition debt, warrants little consideration.*

CHAPTER TWO

The litigator's goal was to attack a committee that approved debtor-in-possession orders three times but challenged the orders three years later. Yet he will not convince most readers that the committee acted inappropriately. The litigator crammed too much material into one sentence. In addition, the main subject and verb are separated by fifty-five words and two citations. Readers will not be able to link the subject, "suggestion," in line 1 with the verb, "warrants", in the next to last line. Some frustrated readers will skip to the next sentence.

If you want to persuade your audience that the committee was wrong, divide the sentence into four shorter units. First, state the committee's suggestion and add the adverb "erroneously":

1(b)   *The committee erroneously suggests that the debtor-in-possession orders violate* United Savings Ass'n of Texas v. Timbers of Inwood Forest Assoc. *(cite)* and Shapiro v. Saybrook Mfg. Co. (In re Saybrook Mfg. Co.) *(cite)*.

Next, explain the courts' action in the two cases:

1(c)   *In* United Savings Ass'n of Texas, *the Supreme Court held that an undersecured creditor may not receive interest on its collateral. In* Shapiro, *the Eleventh Circuit concluded that post-petition liens may not be granted to secure pre-petition debt.*

Finally, dismiss the suggestion as worthless:

1(d)   *Yet the committee's suggestion warrants little consideration.*

Exercise

Revise the structure of these sentences to make them more persuasive.

A. The Supreme Court, because of Plaintiff's attack on Zinco's discriminatory policy, did not apply, as the *Ajax* court did, the *Green-Burdine* test, but instead applied the policy-presumption test to establish a prima facie case.

B. Of course, Bug-Off Spray was safe if used as directed.

Answers

A. Because of Plaintiff's attack on Zinco's discriminatory policy, the Supreme Court did not apply the *Green-Burdine* test, as the *Ajax* court did. Instead, the Supreme Court applied the policy-presumption test to establish a prima facie case.

• Intervening structures separate the subject, verb, and object in this long sentence. Move the intervening structures and create two sentences.

B. The most direct form of this sentence is "Bug-Off Spray was safe if used as directed." You can add "of course" for emphasis in certain contexts.

2.2.3 Long Sentences

As a California litigator prepared a Verified Petition for Writ of Prohibition and Writ of Mandate, he began with a long sentence. He also did not follow guidelines from a California Continuing Education of the Bar publication. It provides these instructions for the introduction to such a petition: (1) include a short introductory passage that persuasively summarizes the petitioner's equities; and (2) treat your introduction as an important element of a persuasively written petition.

Note the first sentence in the lawyer's introduction:

TO THE HONORABLE COURT OF APPEAL SECOND APPELLATE DISTRICT, AND TO ALL INTERESTED PARTIES AND THEIR COUNSEL OF RECORD:

> *Because the respondent court has exceeded the jurisdiction conferred upon it by C.C.P. § 386 and has permitted the improper interpleading of over $31 million of Petitioners' funds—corporate dividends actually declared in Petitioners' names—Petitioners Andrew and Thomas Olson, defendants and cross-complainants in the action below, respectfully petition this court for a writ of prohibition and a writ of mandate compelling the respondent Superior Court of the State of*

California for the County of Los Angeles (1) to acknowledge that the court lacks subject matter jurisdiction over the instant interpleader action absent the present risk of double or multiple exposure to the interpleading plaintiff; (2) to comply with Code of Civil Procedure § 437c; (3) to vacate that portion of its Order served August 20, which denied summary judgment or judgment on the pleadings on the instant interpleader action; (4) to grant summary judgment or judgment on the pleadings in favor of Petitioners; (5) to vacate its denial of Petitioners' Motion for Preliminary Injunction re Wrongful Withholding of Dividends; and (6) to grant Petitioners' Motion for Preliminary Injunction re Wrongful Withholding of Dividends and compel distribution of the interpleaded funds to Petitioners.

The litigator's introduction begins with a sentence of more than 175 words. He ignored the bar association's guidelines to persuasively summarize petitioners' inequities and to develop the introduction as an important element of a persuasively written petition. Readers cannot easily connect the beginning of the sentence with the end. After several clauses, many readers will skip the rest and move to the next sentence.

To be more persuasive, divide this sentence from the lawyer's introduction, cut extra words, and tabulate points (1)–(6) under the third sentence:

1. *The respondent court has permitted the improper interpleading of over $31 million of Petitioners' funds—corporate dividends actually declared in Petitioners' names.*

2. *Petitioners Andrew and Thomas Olson, defendants and cross-complainants below, therefore respectfully petition this court for a writ of prohibition and a writ of mandate.*

3. *The writ should compel the respondent Superior Court of the State of California for the County of Los Angeles: (1)–(6).*

2.2.4   The Passive Voice

The passive voice is generally not persuasive. Its backward motion contrasts with the directness of the active voice. In a passive sentence, the subject receives the action of a transitive verb:

1(a) *The EPA's rejection of industry data was upheld.*

The actor-agent, if included, appears after the verb:

> *1(b) The EPA's rejection of industry data was upheld by the* Kennecott court.

The passive also requires more words than the active. A passive verb must have at least two forms: a helping verb ("to be") and the past participle of the verb. Most past participles end in "-ed" (e.g., "alleged"), but some verbs have irregular forms (e.g., "hold —held"). With some tenses, four forms are necessary, as in "will have been reviewed." Moreover, you must precede an actor-agent with "by." Thus, every passive sentence is longer than its active counterpart.

When you write to persuade, use the passive voice sparingly in certain contexts.

2.2.4.1 Omitting the Actor-Agent

The passive voice can be effective in persuasive writing when you want to omit the actor-agent. In an active sentence, the actor-agent is the subject and cannot be deleted. If you do not know who committed the action of the verb, use the passive:

> *1. Ms. Bryan's injury occurred when the van's hood latch was not properly fastened.*

Perhaps you know who the actor-agent is, but do not want to say:

> *2. A flammable mixture including kerosene was used as a cleaning solvent for the X-1 machine at Amster Foundry.*

If your client used the solvent, you can concede its use but still protect the client. Use the passive voice also when the actor-agent is unimportant:

> *3. It is possible to incur injury if a product is misused.*

2.2.4.2 Varying Sentence Structure

Employ the passive voice occasionally to vary your sentence structure. The best writers use different structures to avoid monotonous prose. A few passive sentences strategically placed can make your writing more persuasive in a subtle way.

Exercise

A. Determine whether these sentences are passive.

1. Atcam's CEO was determined to increase profits by 15 percent.

2. The deposition will be taken on May 1 in Philadelphia.

3. Ms. Hansel's testimony was very convincing.

B. Your goal is to attack a committee for its late challenge of debtor-in-possession orders. Is the passive voice effective? Revise the sentence as needed.

The committee's challenge of the orders should have been made last year.

C. Revise this sentence to eliminate the awkward "by . . . by" structure:

Those charges can be verified by Medcam by submitting four patient accounts.

Answers

A. 1. Not passive. "To be" is a state-of-being verb, not a transitive verb. "To be" cannot take an object and therefore cannot be passive. "Determined" serves as an adjective, not as the past participle of the verb. Compare the sentence to the passive structure: "It was determined by the committee that. . . ."

2. Passive

3. Not passive. "Convincing" is an adjective after the verb "to be."

B. No, the passive voice is not effective. To attack the committee, use the active voice, eliminate extra words, and convert "challenge" to a verb.

Revision: The committee should have challenged the orders last year.

C. Medcam can verify those charges by submitting four patient accounts.

• Convert the sentence to the active voice.

2.3 Underlining for Emphasis

2.3.1 Choosing a Context for Underlining

If you underscore for emphasis, pick one or two crucial words in your paper. Select significant terms, not just concepts you will discuss. Underlining shows the reader that terms are important but does not tell why. The reader must infer from the context why the writer stressed certain words. For effective emphasis, explain the importance of each underlined term.

When you underscore, analyze your goals. Are you emphasizing the point or merely explaining it? If you are not "pounding your fist on the table," do not underline. Instead, tell the reader why the designated words are significant.

2.3.2 Frequent Underlining

Frequent underscoring distracts the reader and weakens an argument:

> The ALJ erred in resorting indiscriminately to the '764 _specification or disclosure_ when concluding that the '027 patent claims in issue "would be obvious from the subject matter of claim 17 of the '764 patent in light of the _full disclosure_ of the transfer molding process in the '764 patent _specification_." (ID at 152, emphasis added.) See also the ID at 151, where the ALJ considered the _specification_ of the '764 patent. The disclosure of the '764 patent may not be used to evaluate whether the _claims_ of the '027 patent were obvious variations of claim 17 of the '764 patent.

The lawyer wanted the reader to understand certain relationships among the underlined terms: "specification or disclosure," "full disclosure," "specification," and "claims." Yet those relationships are not clear. If the writer had explained the terms' importance, the argument would be stronger.

Frequent underlining creates a "ho-hum" response in the reader, who understands that all the designated terms are not critically important:

> A manufacturer has a _duty to warn_ in _either of these circumstances_:
>
> 1. The product produces a danger that _the user can avoid_ if he is alerted to it and instructed how to avoid it; and

2. *The product creates dangers that <u>cannot be eliminated</u>, but its utility is so great that it may be marketed without subjecting the manufacturer to liability, provided the user is made aware of the danger and has the opportunity to make an <u>informed decision whether to expose himself</u> to it.*

The lawyer underscored five times for emphasis in a short passage. Instead of stressing one significant term, he underscored one or two central concepts in almost every sentence.

2.3.3 Effective Underlining

Underlining can be effective if you emphasize only one critical term. In a twenty-two-page motion for summary judgment, a litigator underlined for emphasis only twice. Moreover, she underscored only one word each time. Because the lawyer did not overuse this technique, the underscoring catches the reader's attention. In the motion, the litigator argued that the judge should dismiss three claims that the plaintiff, Charles Atwood, brought. He claimed that defendant, Greene Company, violated the Age Discrimination in Employment Act, intentionally inflicted emotional distress, and breached an implied covenant of good faith and fair dealing.

The writer first argues that Atwood was dismissed because his performance was inadequate. As sole salesman on the West Coast, plaintiff lost money for the company. To establish that point, the lawyer argued:

> *Greene's monthly West Coast sales for this year were <u>lower</u> than West Coast sales for last year, when Greene did not have a salesman on the West Coast. Plaintiff's own reports demonstrate this fact.*

	Previous Year	Current Year	Decrease
April Sales	$49,830	$32,300	$17,530
May Sales	$49,830	$40,188	$ 9,642
June Sales	$33,975	$30,420	$ 3,555

The attorney's underlining emphasizes an important fact: that Atwood's efforts resulted in fewer West Coast sales than those generated from only East Coast offices in the previous year. This loss will buttress the litigator's argument, and underscoring one adjective, "lower," stresses the contrast.

Later in the motion, the lawyer argued that Greene Company would have to make large investments if it entered the California market. Expenses for increased inventory and an office would be essential. Yet economic circumstances had recently forced Greene to cut costs, an action that precluded expansion on the West Coast. To emphasize plaintiff's poor performance, the litigator wrote:

> *Greene decided to cut its losses and close the California office because Plaintiff failed to increase sales. Greene also questioned Plaintiff's performance and whether he would <u>ever</u> generate the sales necessary to maintain the office.*

The underscoring simulates speech, that is, the emphasis you would place on "ever" in oral argument. By underlining "ever," the writer emphasizes the improbability of Atwood's future success.

2.4. Stating the Facts

2.4.1 Anticipating the Argument

As you plan the fact section of a brief, anticipate your argument in subtle ways. Do not simply tell the story in an objective fashion. Instead, select facts and draft a narrative that will prepare the reader for the argument.

In addition, consider your role as master storyteller. Compose a story that will hold the reader's attention. As you draft the facts, follow these guidelines:

1. Organize facts in a step-by-step fashion so that the reader can easily follow the sequence of events;

2. Use short sentences;

3. Cut extra words;

4. Avoid inflated diction and legalese; and

5. Create well-formed paragraphs.

The fact section from the appellate brief in *Chemco v. Robert Martin and Red Laboratory* illustrates these principles. The litigator argues that a judgment against Chemco, manufacturer of Zappo pesticide, should be reversed because Chemco was not at fault. As you read the fact section, note the writer's techniques:

INTRODUCTORY STATEMENT

Robert Martin is a rancher who breeds Santa Gertrudis beef cattle. One of Martin's bulls, identified as "Atlas" ("plaintiff's bull" or "Atlas"), was in the custody of Red Laboratory ("Red Lab"). The owner of Red Lab, Thomas Pax, had used the insecticide Zappo for three years to control flies around the premises, but not to spray animals directly.

On March 15, Pax told his foreman to spray the pens for flies. The foreman in turn instructed two newly hired, illegal aliens, who had never sprayed for flies before, to spray the pens, not the bulls. The foreman then left, and neither the mixing of the Zappo nor the spraying was supervised.

A veterinarian was summoned shortly afterward. He found two bulls down and one going down, smelled an insecticide, suspected an overdose, found the Zappo can, and as directed on the label, administered an antidote. Two bulls recovered, but Mason's did not. When the foreman returned, the two employees told him they had sprayed the bulls directly, and the employees immediately disappeared.

The Zappo label contains prominent and detailed warnings, cautions, and instructions for use of the product. (See appendix A.) Pax read the label before he first used the product three years earlier. On the occasion in question, however, there is no evidence that the label instructions were followed as to dilution, method, or rate of application, or in any other respect. The foreman did not read English, and neither of the newly hired employees who did the spraying spoke or read English.

This fact section is successful for two reasons. First, the facts lend themselves to the creation of a good story. The clear narrative involves animals, objects, and actions familiar to most readers. In addition, the litigator applied the principles of effective storytelling. She presents the narrative in an immediate step-by-step manner, as if the reader were standing in a barn watching the dramatic events unfold. Diction is simple, e.g., "rancher," "spray," "flies," and "left." Complicated words are limited to essential legal terms, such as "custody"; scientific terms, such as "antidote"; and words for which no synonym exists, such as "veterinarian." The litigator uses short, direct sentences and logical paragraph structure.

Moreover, the fact section anticipates the argument that Chemco is not at fault. The writer has interwoven the argument's strands with the story's events. Without reviewing the brief, the reader can determine main points of the litigator's argument. The reader knows that Pax, the owner of Red Lab, had read the warnings on the Zappo label earlier and had used Zappo regularly for three years. He did not supervise the foreman's instructions to the employees or the spraying. Pax's behavior was especially careless because the foreman did not read English and the two other employees did not speak or read English. No evidence demonstrates that the label instructions were followed. The reader also knows that the employees admitted spraying the bulls directly. Finally, the litigator's characterizing the employees as "newly hired, illegal aliens" makes them and Red Lab seem irresponsible.

These facts effectively "sow the seeds" of the arguments developed in the brief. Note the relationship between the facts and one argument section:

> *The trial court erred in entering judgment against Chemco because there is no evidence, or alternatively in overruling Chemco's motion for new trial because there is insufficient evidence, to support the jury's comparative causation findings that 65 percent of the harm was caused by Chemco's product and 35 percent of the harm was caused by Red Lab's negligence.*

Argument and Authorities

A.   *Red Lab's Independent Negligence Was the Proximate Cause of the Occurrence.*

B.   *Red Lab Is Not Entitled to Indemnity Against Chemco.*

C.   *Claims That Chemco Breached Implied or Express Warranties Are Unsupported in This Case.*

D.   *The Occurrence Was Not Caused by Any Inadequate Warning or Instruction by Chemco.*

The litigator closely correlated the fact section's preview of the argument with points developed in the brief.

2.4.2   Presenting Complicated Facts

Not all fact sections lend themselves to the creation of a good story. Unlike the step-by-step narrative of poisoning the bulls, many fact sections describe complicated corporate transactions occurring over many years. Highly technical facts may not hold readers' attention. Bored readers may skim the passage and miss an argument you weave into the facts.

As you draft complicated facts, follow the suggestions on page 106 and the guidelines below:

1. Group facts in short paragraphs;

2. Draft strong topic sentences and concluding sentences to frame the information in each paragraph; and

3. Avoid unnecessary technical terms.

A litigator successfully used these techniques in the facts of an appellate brief regarding break-up fees. The writer argues that Glimmer's costs connected with unsuccessful white knight transactions are deductible. GobbleCo attempts to take over Glimmer, the target company. Note the litigator's techniques in an excerpt from the middle of the fact section:

> On March 15, the search for a white knight bore fruit when the Glimmer Board received a merger proposal from Friends & Company, Inc. ("Friends"). Friends proposed $73.80 per share for approximately 80 percent of the Glimmer shares, with stock in the new company to be exchanged for the remaining shares. The Friends' proposal also demanded the inclusion in the merger agreement of a provision for break-up fees if the merger did not occur for various reasons. After the March 15 board meeting, the board authorized negotiation of a merger agreement with Friends, which included the provision for break-up fees.

> On March 16, the Glimmer board reconvened. It learned that the negotiators from Glimmer and Friends had worked out a proposed Agreement and Plan of Merger (the "Friends Merger Agreement"), under which Friends would pay $74.50 per share for about 80 percent of Glimmer shares and exchange stock in the new company for the balance. The board was advised that synergies would be realized from merging these two successful retailing companies. Consequently, a combined Friends/Glimmer entity could provide much higher long-term values to shareholders. The board resolved to reject the latest GobbleCo proposal and approved the proposed merger with Friends. After

the Friends Merger Agreement was executed on March 17, the struggle appeared to be over.

GobbleCo, however, reacted with a sharp counterthrust, changing its previous proposal to a coercive front-end loaded tender offer. . . .

The litigator skillfully guides the reader through complicated material. The writer analyzed the overall story and divided it into clear conceptual units. Most sentences are short. In addition, strong topic sentences and concluding sentences provide an organizational framework for the details of complex corporate transactions:

1. *On March 15, the search for a white knight bore fruit when the Glimmer Board received a merger proposal from Friends & Company, Inc.*

2. *On March 16, the Glimmer Board reconvened.*

3. *After the Friends Merger Agreement was executed on March 17, the struggle appeared to be over.*

4. *GobbleCo, however, reacted with a sharp counterthrust, changing its previous proposal to a coercive front-end loaded tender offer.*

Moreover, the writer selected diction carefully. Most words in the fact section are short and uncomplicated. No unnecessary legal or business terms clutter the narrative. Moreover, he used contrasting diction in some overview sentences. Words unrelated to law or business anchor the reader. For example, the topic sentence of the first paragraph contains the metaphor "bore fruit." This agricultural phrase communicates succinctly and directly. After discussing the Friends merger agreement, the writer concludes the second paragraph with "the struggle appeared to be over." These simple words stress the human side of the business transactions. Then the litigator signals a change in tone in the third paragraph with diction related to fighting. Strong language like "coercive" and "sharp counterthrust" describes GobbleCo's action that disturbs Glimmer's relief after the Friends Merger Agreement was executed.

2.5 Tightening an Argument

As you draft an argument, plan the function of every sentence. First, determine how each one fits into the logical development of the brief. Then compose a sentence that fulfills each role. After you write the argument, scrutinize it and delete sentences that do not fit. With this technique, you can create a strong logical framework.

An argument's relative tightness is very important, especially in long and technical briefs. Unnecessary sentences break up the argument's flow. Even a short interruption weakens thought development.

As he wrote an appellate brief, a lawyer planned the purpose of each sentence. The writer argues that costs connected with unsuccessful white knight transactions are deductible. The target company is Glimmer; GobbleCo makes the takeover attempt. Note the argument's tight structure in the excerpt below:

A.   *The Bankruptcy Court Properly Concluded That the White Knight Trans-*
     actions Were Abandoned and That the Costs Incurred in Connection
     with Them Are Deductible Abandonment Losses.

> *Appellees entered into binding contractual commitments to merge*
> *with their white knights: Nichols with Malls and Glimmer with Friends.*
> *In both instances, these proposed merger transactions were aban-*
> *doned. The expenses incurred by Appellees in connection with the*
> *abandoned mergers therefore are losses deductible under § 165. The*
> *statutory language and the case law, as well as an administrative*
> *determination by the IRS itself, on facts virtually identical to those pre-*
> *sented here (see § A.1, infra), all make clear that costs associated with*
> *abandoned business mergers are fully deductible in the year in which*
> *the mergers are abandoned.*

> *The losses associated with abandoned white knight transactions*
> *manifestly are within the plain language of § 165. The statute permits*
> *the deduction of "any loss sustained during the taxable year and not*
> *compensated for by insurance or otherwise." Appellees were contrac-*
> *tually committed to pay the fees and expenses at issue as part of the*
> *abandoned white knight transactions, and did pay them during the ap-*
> *plicable tax year. These payments thus constitute a "loss" for which no-*
> *body has ever suggested that Appellees have been compensated.*

This writer carefully structured the argument's paragraphs. Each sentence has a clear function in logical development. No extraneous statements distract the reader from the argument. Strong conclusions reinforce the writer's main points. Moreover, you can identify the role of each sentence:

LEGAL WRITING

Paragraph I

Facts: *Appellees entered into binding contractual commitments to merge with their white knights: Nichols with Malls and Glimmer with Friends. In both instances, these proposed merger transactions were abandoned.*

Conclusion: *The expenses incurred by Appellees in connection with the abandoned mergers therefore are losses deductible under § 165.*

Rules: *The statutory language and the case law, as well as an administrative determination by the IRS itself, on facts virtually identical to those presented here (see § A.1, infra), all make clear that costs associated with abandoned business mergers are fully deductible in the year in which the mergers are abandoned.*

Paragraph II

Application: *The losses associated with abandoned white knight transactions manifestly are within the plain language of § 165.*

Rule: *The statute permits the deduction of "any loss sustained during the taxable year and not compensated for by insurance or otherwise."*

Fact: *Appellees were contractually committed to pay the fees and expenses at issue as part of the abandoned white knight transactions, and did pay them during the applicable tax year.*

Conclusion: *These payments thus constitute a "loss" for which nobody has ever suggested that Appellees have been compensated.*

The concise style of this argument complements the tight paragraph structure. Given the context, word choice is simple and direct; the litigator does not use legalese or inflated diction. Most sentences are short. Concluding statements, however, would be more effective if they were shorter and less complicated.

CHAPTER TWO

Exercise

Identify persuasive techniques in this conclusion to an appellate brief:

This case constitutes a bold attack on the national labor law policy expressed in § 9(a) of the National Labor Relations Act, 29 U.S.C. § 159(a), which makes a bargaining agent, once certified, the "exclusive representative" of employees for the purpose of negotiating terms and conditions of employment. If plaintiffs prevail, virtually every provision of every labor agreement may become the subject of a federal court action filed by some disgruntled union member, dissatisfied with his individual lot, heedless of the interests of other members, and acting as a self-appointed bargaining agent. It was this very possibility that the Supreme Court sought to foreclose in *Ford Motor Co. v. Huffman*, when it held that federal courts are not free to interfere with a bargaining agent's judgment concerning seniority provisions such as those at issue here:

> Inevitable differences arise in the manner and degree to which the terms of any negotiated agreement affect individual employees and classes of employees. The mere existence of such differences does not make them invalid. The complete satisfaction of all who are represented is hardly to be expected. A wide range of reasonableness must be allowed a statutory bargaining representative in serving the unit it represents, subject always to complete good faith and honesty of purpose in the exercise of its discretion.

345 U.S. at 338.

The judgment of the court below should be affirmed.

Answers

A. Strong language: "bold attack," "virtually every . . . every," "disgruntled," "dissatisfied," "heedless," "self-appointed," and "this very possibility"

B. Parallelism in four phrases that begin with adjectives: "disgruntled union member, dissatisfied with his individual lot, heedless of the interests of other members, and acting as a self-appointed bargaining agent"

C. Emphatic syntax: "It was this very possibility that the Supreme Court sought to foreclose. . . ."

D. Paragraph structure: This tight paragraph begins with a strong topic sentence. Every sentence plays an important function. A concluding sentence after the long quotation would strengthen the paragraph.

E. Sentence structure: Sentences are long, but strong language and varied syntax make them easy to read.

F. Use of quotation: The persuasive quotation fits the context.

G. Conclusion: The short, direct final sentence contains no unnecessary modifiers or complicated words.

2.6 A Corporate Letter

A corporate lawyer planned to use an aggressive, yet courteous tone in a letter for a client, Transbank, to send to the opposing party. Transbank wanted to persuade the opposing party to act in a certain way. As you read the excerpt, note the tone of the underlined persuasive language:

Dear Mr. Marlowe:

Your previous written and oral criticism of MidSouth's investment in Transbank has left me well advised of your opinion concerning it. _I am particularly concerned_ about the characterization that you have given the MidSouth transaction in your July 7th letter and the manner in which you have disseminated your views.

Your allegations that the transaction is unlawful _are both completely unfounded and potentially harmful_ to Transbank. _I fear that you have created the incorrect impression_ that MidSouth's investment in Transbank will be invalidated and that therefore _you could be causing injury_ to Transbank's shareholders and its banking business.

[Discussion of positive reactions of regulatory agencies to MidSouth's investment.]

Finally, _I am dismayed_ with your request to participate in the management functions of Transbank. _Your request_ to negotiate a revision of the agreement _is wholly inconsistent_ with your shareholder rights under the corporation law of Georgia and under Transbank's Bylaws. Furthermore, _your actions are an attempt to influence_ the management and policies of Transbank. _I question if this interference is not_ the type of action that would lead the Federal Reserve Bank of Atlanta to change the view stated in its letter of May 18 with respect to your group's control over Transbank.

After you have reflected on these matters, _I sincerely hope_ that _you will be dissuaded_ from interfering to any further extent in Transbank's relations with its governmental regulatory agencies (Emphasis added).

The corporate lawyer blends aggressive and calm language to persuade the opposing party to stop interfering in Transbank's activities. Using gentle persuasion, the writer begins with "I am particularly concerned." In the next paragraph, the tone becomes accusatory: "Your allegations . . . are both wholly unfounded and potentially harmful." The lawyer then takes a more moderate approach. The clause "I fear that you have created the incorrect impression" is indirect and cautious. To maintain that tone, he uses a conditional verb in "you could be causing injury."

The last two paragraphs also contain a mixture of strong and gentle language. The beginning, "I am dismayed," establishes a restrained tone, but the writer soon becomes more aggressive. He characterizes the opposing party's behavior in two ways: "your request is wholly inconsistent" and "your actions are an attempt to influence the management and policies of Transbank."

Finally, the corporate lawyer uses two indirect persuasive structures. In the last sentence of the third paragraph, he begins: "I question if this interference is not the type of action that would lead the Federal Reserve Bank of Atlanta to change its view." The circuitous lead-in, "I question if this interference is not," creates a convoluted sentence. Contrast this beginning with a more concise, aggressive statement: "This type of action would lead the Federal Reserve Bank of Atlanta to change its view."

The writer concludes with a gently persuasive request: "I sincerely hope that you will be dissuaded from interfering to any further extent. . . ." The beginning, "I sincerely hope," seems courteous but may contain a veiled threat. With the formal verb "dissuaded," the lawyer communicates a serious, yet impersonal tone. To be more direct, he could have ended with "I hope that you will not interfere . . ." or the more combative "Stop interfering in Transbank's relations. . . ." He chose to maintain a gentle tone despite the extra words.

Throughout this excerpt, the corporate attorney used both aggressive and calm language to persuade the opposing party. Strong diction contrasts with gentler words. By mixing these two tones, the writer created a defensive, yet restrained letter.

CHAPTER THREE

~ *Writing with Flair* ~

If you want to add flair to persuasive writing, first analyze audience, context, and tone. Then consider the most effective technique. Metaphor, strong language, wordplay, literary and historical references, and repetition can make legal writing distinctive. But use these techniques sparingly. Too much flair can weaken the power of each example. Experiment in early drafts to develop a keen judgment on these techniques.

3.1 Metaphorical Language

3.1.1 Metaphors

An effective image strengthens an argument by creating a vivid picture in the reader's mind. When you choose a figure of speech, select a fresh, original metaphor, not a cliché. Use metaphors that add persuasive power to your argument.

Because they appear so frequently in legal writing, the underlined examples below have lost their impact:

1.   *Movants apparently are quite unaware that the wheels of justice grind slowly when form is allowed to take precedence over substance.*

2.   *The fatal flaw in Kelly's brief is that it contains factual assertions not found in the pleadings before the court.*

Avoid metaphors that appear frequently in general usage as well. Certain figures of speech weaken a legal argument:

3.   *The present cases are part of plaintiff's attempt to avoid having to reap the consequences of its own sharp practices.*

4.　　*How ironic it is that <u>the needles of justice</u> can <u>be buried in so huge a haystack</u>.*

Fresh and original figurative language will attract readers' attention:

5.　　*Florida has a well-developed body of voluntary payment law. Mr. Young and Ms. Astor, however, apparently cannot find a Florida case to support their argument; they rely instead on a Michigan case. Even that Michigan case predates the twentieth century; it comes from an era <u>when trolleys, not television, traveled on cables</u>.*

6.　　*The fear of losing cable service cannot constitute legal "compulsion" or "coercion." With all due respect to both client and country, it is inconceivable—even in America today—that threatening to cut off cable television service constitutes duress. MTV and ESPN are not inalienable rights. Losing Nickelodeon and the Cartoon Network is not <u>like losing electricity in the winter</u>. Being condemned to watch broadcast television (or to listen to a radio, or to read a book) is not the same <u>as being condemned to the abyss</u>.*

7.　　*Hattori and its American subsidiaries do maintain some independence —<u>about as much as the egg and vegetables in a western omelette</u>. Just as from a culinary point of view we focus on the ultimate omelette and not its ingredients, from a jurisdictional standpoint the effect of the integrated international operation of Hattori activities in New York is our primary concern.*

Exercise

Identify clichés in these sentences.

A. Six potential problems mine the trail for our client.

B. Palmer's rising profits were spawned by the fact that Power Words, Inc. conducted the advertising campaign.

C. Although an eye was kept on the law in other jurisdictions, nothing appeared on forced conversions. Perhaps a second look in Ohio and other jurisdictions for provisions of that nature would be helpful.

D. Bankco should pull in the reins on Automax's short-term credit line.

Answers

A. "Mine the trail" is an overworked war image. Use literal language.

Revision: Our client faces six potential problems.

B. The phrase "is spawned" is a cliché originating in the reproductive patterns of fish. The writer has applied the metaphor awkwardly to an increase in sales. Use literal language and the active voice.

Revision: Power Words, Inc.'s advertising campaign led to Palmer's rising profits.

C. Ocular imagery, "an eye was kept on the law" and "a second look," represents legal research. Convert these clichés to literal language.

Revision: Although I reviewed the law in other jurisdictions, I found nothing on forced conversions. Perhaps a careful search in Ohio and other jurisdictions for provisions of that nature would be helpful.

D. The cliché "pull in the reins" depicts Bankco officials as riders and Automax as a horse. The diction is not appropriate for a formal context.

Revision: Bankco should tighten Automax's short-term credit line.

The verb "tighten," with "credit line" as object, is a metaphor. This expression is an accepted financial term, not a cliché. To avoid a metaphor, use "limit."

3.1.2   Choosing between Two Drafts

Reasonable persons often disagree about the effectiveness of a specific metaphor in a brief. "Writing by committee" can lead to heated debates about whether to include figures of speech. At times, committee members must choose between two drafts: one with dramatic imagery and one with literal language.

LEGAL WRITING

A committee of attorneys drafted two paragraphs for the introduction in a memorandum in support of application for a preliminary injunction. At first, the lawyers could not agree on a final version. Contrast the two paragraphs below:

1(a)   *Accordingly, when Trax-Co and Ace Oil are viewed in the context of their industry with its unique composition and characteristics, the cases cited and the facts illustrated above point inexorably in the direction of illegality and the need for a preliminary injunction. The court could properly base a finding of illegality on those cases and facts alone. Yet. . . .*

1(b)   *Accordingly, when the economists have stopped expounding theories, the lawyers have quit making distinctions, and the courtroom is still, the cases cited and the facts illustrated above will continue to point inexorably in the direction of illegality and a preliminary injunction. This court could appropriately and correctly go no further. Yet. . . .*

As you review the paragraphs again, consider these questions:

1.   Which version is stronger?

2.   What techniques make each draft persuasive?

3.   Would you employ the same techniques in your writing?

4.   Which version do you believe the committee chose?

While the tone of paragraph 1(a) is logical, paragraph 1(b) is more dramatic and emotional. The initial contrast occurs in the "when" clauses:

1(a)   *Accordingly, when Trax-Co and Ace Oil are viewed in the context of their industry with its unique composition and characteristics. . . .*

1(b)   *Accordingly, when the economists have stopped expounding theories, the lawyers have quit making distinctions, and the courtroom is still. . . .*

In version 1(a), the writer describes a corporate context that will serve as a backdrop for the desired outcome. The second draft, however, opens with a dramatic image: a courtroom quiet after the intellectual efforts of economists and lawyers are over. The writer makes the economists and attorneys sound dispensable, because the law and facts point to only one result. The longer verb phrase, "will continue to point inexorably," extends the image's power.

The drafts differ also in the second sentence's content and tone. The first paragraph continues the earlier intellectual argument. The writer points out the logically predetermined outcome: "The court could properly base a finding of illegality on those cases and facts alone." Yet in the second, more concise version, the writer makes a strong value judgment: "This court could appropriately and correctly go no further." The adverbs "appropriately" and "correctly" reinforce the earlier courtroom image, and establish that the evidence and law show only one possible outcome.

The committee members chose paragraph 1(a) for the final version of the memorandum. Do you agree with their decision?

3.1.3   Mixed Metaphors

Do not mix metaphors. Within each sentence, use consistent figurative language, i.e., metaphors that sustain the same image. Otherwise, their juxtaposition may be jarring or even ludicrous.

Note the mixed metaphors in sentence 1:

1.   *Although this argument may go too far, it has some weight for debtors who are going under.*

The writer begins with an implied comparison of the statement to a measure of distance in the phrase "may go too far." Next, the figurative phrase "has some weight" suggests the image of Justice with her scales. Finally, the lawyer compares the debtors to drowning persons who are "going under."

Together these metaphors create an impossible image. To revise the sentence, first convert the figures of speech to literal language:

Metaphor	Literal Language
go too far	be extreme
has some weight	is relevant
going under	unable to pay

If you retain only one figure of speech, you can maintain the intended tone without mixing metaphors.

Exercise

Identify the mixed metaphors in this sentence. Convert each figure of speech to literal language.

Today's newspapers are jammed with articles and editorials screaming for a halt to the growing mushroom of government regulation on business.

Answer

Mixed metaphors: "are jammed with," "screaming for," "a halt," and "growing mushroom"

Metaphor	Literal Language
are jammed with	are filled with
screaming for	that call for
a halt	an end
growing mushroom	rapid growth

Retain only one figure of speech to avoid mixed metaphors.

3.1.4 Tone

Overblown rhetoric creates a shrill tone. Histrionic prose will not persuade readers and may make them chuckle. Note the underlined figures of speech as you read the passage below from a memorandum of points and authorities to dismiss a motion for summary judgment. While attacking the plaintiff's bank, the writer sprinkles metaphors throughout the argument:

> "You may think that we are diamond dealers," _trumpets_ the advertising for London Discount Bank, co-parent, with Peterson's Bank International, of Plaintiff Peterson's Discount Bank.
>
> In the motions before the court, however, plaintiff _presents another and very different face_. _Wrapping itself in the hoary respectability_ of the 1855 British Bills of Exchange Act, plaintiff here _passes itself off as an uninvolved holder_ in due course of commercial paper, _put upon by frivolous deadbeats and liars_ resisting payment of their just debts in bad faith. Plaintiff _assumes the air of a respectable institution_ being _ripped off by defendants_ who have the temerity to insist on their day in court.

> *A closer look at such pretensions, however, discloses that Peterson's has <u>feet of clay</u>. An avid participant in the <u>high-flying diamond market</u>, Peterson's extended credit against phony trust receipts to evade British banking law, and when the market <u>turned sour</u>, tried to <u>cover its excesses</u> by <u>framing</u> Rochester and calling in the <u>fictitious diamonds</u>. The present cases are part of Plaintiff's attempt to avoid having <u>to reap the consequences</u> of its own sharp practices.*

> *For a <u>host</u> of reasons, the motions for summary judgment as to Defendants Johnson and Holmes must be denied. (Emphasis added.)*

In this argument, the sheer number of metaphors limits the impact of any one. The cumulative effect is too dramatic. Moreover, the attorney used clichés, including "ripped off," "feet of clay," "turned sour," and "to reap the consequences." Instead, develop one effective metaphor to create a more persuasive argument.

Exercise

How would you rewrite the attack on Peterson's if you were limited to one metaphor?

3.1.5 Extended Metaphors

A litigator developed a musical theme as an extended metaphor in a brief submitted to the International Trade Commission. Most of the commission's members are not lawyers. According to the litigator, the musical theme emphasized "that the ALJ's decision was out of 'harmony' with the law."

Throughout a sixteen-page section of the brief, the attorney used metaphors and similes to stress the parallel between the erroneous ruling and discordant music. He began with a simile:

1. *<u>Like a cacophony of clashing cymbals</u>, the ALJ's erroneous findings and conclusions on double patenting show a complete and utter disregard of (1) the proper statutory construction of the restriction/double patenting statute, (2) the law of double patenting, and (3) proper claim interpretation and Patent Office procedure.*

Additional figures of speech appear throughout the argument. For example, the attorney asserts:

> 2. *Reference to transfer molding in claim 17 of the '764 patent cannot invalidate the '027 patent, <u>any more than the first four notes of Beethoven's Fifth Symphony play the entire piece</u>.*

A paraphrase of Thoreau extends the musical image in a subsequent simile:

> 3. *<u>Like the person marching to the beat of a different drum</u>, the ALJ erred in resorting indiscriminately to the '764 specification or disclosure in her conclusion.*

The lawyer then compares the ruling to a musical instrument:

> 4. *Thus, the ALJ's double patenting ruling is <u>like a screeching violin in the symphony of law</u>.*

The litigator's attack on the ALJ continues with another simile:

> 5. *<u>Like an out-of-tune honky-tonk piano</u>, the ALJ erroneously concluded that the public must be free to use the invention of an expired patent.*

In the conclusion, the lawyer returns to his original parallel:

> 6. *The ALJ's double patenting findings and conclusions are clearly erroneous and should be reversed <u>to bring the discordant decision in harmony with the facts and law</u>.*

As you review these examples, consider these questions:

1. <u>How disparate should the "poles" of your comparison be?</u>

    By definition, a metaphor compares two unlike things by creating a common connection between them. This paradox draws readers' attention to the figure of speech. Are the connections between music and patent law strong enough for effective comparisons?

2. <u>How broad should the field of comparison be?</u>

    Is music too general a field for an extended metaphor? Should all the examples refer to classical music? Is the leap from Beethoven's Fifth Symphony to a honky-tonk piano too broad?

3. <u>How appropriate is each image?</u>

    In example 4, is the comparison of a ruling to "a screeching violin" effective? Too harsh? What about the reference to "the symphony of law"? Do the musical terms "discordant" and "in harmony" blend smoothly with the language of law in sentence 6?

For many readers, the extended metaphors seem forced. Some are successful; others are contrived. Would fewer, more consistent metaphors be more persuasive?

Look for opportunities to use extended metaphor in persuasive writing. Experiment with comparisons to strengthen your argument. As you draft, consider the most effective number of metaphors and field of comparison.

3.2 Analogy

If you use an analogy in persuasive writing, choose an effective parallel. Correlate it carefully with your own argument. Then develop the analogy step by step. Describe it in short sentences and, where possible, simple words.

In an appellate brief, a lawyer used an analogy to argue that cable television subscribers' voluntary payment of late fees bars a claim for their recovery:

> *The voluntary payment doctrine serves two purposes. First, a free market cannot lightly recognize a cause of action for buyer's remorse. Perhaps the Porsche was a bit expensive, but absent some justification—such as fraud, duress, or the like—one cannot voluntarily buy the car and then sue to get the extra money back.*

The lawyer compares plaintiffs to a consumer who purchases a Porsche and then sues to recover part of its cost. With this ridiculous parallel, the writer asserts that plaintiffs' claims are barred.

Another litigator included a persuasive analogy in a memorandum in opposition to a motion to dismiss counterclaims. A former employee had sued her client, a greeting card company, for copyright infringement. The defendant counterclaimed on the same theory. Plaintiff then moved to dismiss the counterclaims on various grounds. She argued that defendant's counterclaims denied plaintiff access to the courts and violated her constitutional right to petition for redress of grievances. To ridicule this theory, the litigator used an analogy in the brief:

> *If Plaintiff were to purchase a "Mickey Mouse" T-shirt and then change its coloration, make several photocopies of it, register it with the U.S. Copyright Office, and file a complaint for copyright infringement against Walt Disney, attaching a photocopy of the T-shirt to her complaint, it would be absurd to think that a counterclaim by Walt Disney for copyright infringement based on Plaintiff's unauthorized use and unauthorized copying of Walt Disney's copyrighted design should be dismissed on a theory that it might "chill" Plaintiff's First Amendment rights. Such an absurd result is precisely what Plaintiff's Motion to Dismiss seeks in this case.*

The judge commented that this analogy persuaded him to dismiss the motion. Like the judge, most readers will recognize the character Mickey Mouse. Moreover, they instinctively object to anyone's tampering with such an endearing and all-American figure. The step-by-step process in the analogy demonstrates the ridiculousness of plaintiff's claim. Readers understand that changing the colors on Mickey Mouse's picture does not create an original design.

The analogy's sole weakness lies in the litigator's writing style. The parallel is drawn in an eighty-six-word sentence. Shorter sentences would make this analogy even more effective.

3.3 Repetition for Effect

3.3.1 Persuasive Repetition

You can use repetition for emphasis at the beginning of clauses or sentences in persuasive writing. This technique is especially useful when you want to place responsibility on one party.

In a products liability case, a lawyer sought to blame the father for the injury to his one-year-old daughter, who had been burned by a drain cleaner. To discredit the father as a reliable parent, the writer used repetition in the appellate brief. With this technique, she portrayed the father as an unreliable person and thus minimized the role of the drain cleaner's manufacturer. First, she describes the father's lack of awareness at the earlier trial:

> For example, *he was unable to remember* when he had moved into the house where the accident occurred, where he had been on the day of the accident, when he left home that day, why he had returned, or whether he had eaten.
>
> . . . .
>
> *He was unable to remember* who was with the child when he picked her up, why he had left the child unattended in the hall, or even the shape of the bathroom.

The repeated words, plus the simple questions that follow, depict a father out of touch with the basic events of his life and with his daughter's movements.

Later in the brief, the attorney used repetition to emphasize the father's irresponsible behavior at the time of the accident:

> Thus, the father was clearly aware that the product he was about to use had certain dangers attendant to its use. *He knew* it could cause severe burns. *He knew* the label said to keep the product away from children. Yet in the face of that knowledge, *he* did the following:
>
> (1) *He* carried the child upstairs with him, the container in one hand, the child in the other.

(2) *He put the child down in the hall, outside the bathroom where he was going to use the product; the child was completely unattended and able to crawl.*

(3) *He opened the container, used part of the contents, and then set the container down on the ledge of the sink without bothering to replace the cap.*

(4) *After the container remained on the ledge for a period of time, he knocked it to the floor.*

(5) *He permitted the child to enter the bathroom at some point, and he maintained at trial that he was not even aware of the fact that the child had entered the small bathroom.*

(6) *Then after the accident, he totally failed to follow the procedures set forth on the container.*

Initial repetition of "he knew" and "he" stresses both the father's responsibility and his careless behavior. The litigator portrays the father as the sole actor and depicts his movements step by step. With repetition, the attorney emphasizes that the father's negligence caused the injury to his daughter.

3.3.2 Monotonous Repetition

Some repetition creates monotonous prose. For example, an attorney overused a favorite phrase for emphasis in a brief. He repeated "the very (noun)" to stress the inconsistent behavior of the plaintiff and his lawyers. The litigator began his argument with sentence 1:

1. *Johnson's Amended Complaint challenges a transaction that he, as Chairman of the Board of Directors and President of the TAP Companies, negotiated with the help of the very law firm that filed the Amended Complaint.*

In this attack, the litigator depicts plaintiff's dual role in straightforward, unemotional language. He writes more forcefully when he characterizes opposing counsel as "the very law firm that filed the Amended Complaint." After introducing the phrase, "the very law firm," the lawyer planned to repeat it and vary it for emphasis.

Several pages later, the litigator used the same phrase to focus his attack:

> 2.   *Finally, as a condition precedent to the execution of the Settlement Agreement, the TAP Companies were required to deliver an opinion of their counsel that the Settlement Agreement and each of the Closing Documents that were executed in conjunction with the Settlement Agreement were valid and enforceable. Ross and Myers, <u>the very law firm</u> that now claims that the Amended Lease was the result of "extortion" and "coercion," provided a legal opinion stating "that each of the closing documents is valid and enforceable according to its terms."*

When stressing Johnson's role, the litigator changed the phrase slightly:

> 3.   *Johnson must be disqualified as a plaintiff because he not only acquiesced, but actively participated, in negotiating and procuring shareholder and board approval of the Settlement Agreement and the Amended Lease, <u>the very act</u> that he now is attacking in his derivative claim.*

With a plural noun, this variation appears two more times within five pages:

> 4.   *Therefore, Johnson is estopped from asserting the claims against Lease Co. because he participated in <u>the very acts</u> that now form the basis of his complaint.*

> 5.   *Johnson actively participated in the negotiation and approval of the terms of the Amended Lease, <u>the very acts</u> that now form the basis of his complaint.*

Repeating this structure at a brief's beginning and end weakens the argument. To attract the reader's attention, vary the phrase slightly. For example, you can change "the very law firm [or acts]," to "the same law firm [or acts]." Moreover, a different structure would emphasize the inconsistent behavior of Johnson and his counsel. Juxtapose earlier and current actions in this pattern: "After <u>providing</u> . . . , Ross and Myers now <u>claims</u>":

Original

> *Ross and Myers, <u>the very law firm</u> that now claims that the Amended Lease was the result of "extortion" and "coercion," provided a legal opinion stating "that each of the closing documents is valid and enforceable according to its terms."*

Revision

> *After providing* a legal opinion stating "that each of the closing documents is valid and enforceable according to its terms," *Ross and Myers now claims* that the Amended Lease was the result of "extortion" and "coercion."

Exercise

Analyze the effect of repetition in this passage.

> [After a government investigation, a criminal indictment was brought against a former United States senator. In his brief, the lawyer argued that the senator had been a victim of illegal government entrapment.]
>
> It was the Government that suggested that Senator Little must have an interest and that his interest should be concealed. It was the Government that held out the lure of vast financial assistance, first of $13 million, then of $100 million, and eventually of $170 million. It was the Government that suggested "government contracts." It was the Government that produced a supposed prince. It was the Government that suggested the incorporation of the mining venture, in order to have something tangible to transfer to Senator Little. It was the Government that then found additional mine owners and proposed the sale of stock. Finally, it was the Government that staged the asylum scene of January 15 in a desperate effort to make a provable cause, since we now know that it was the Government's conclusion that it did not have a case before that time. The January 15 session resulted in a disappointment for the Government, despite its actions in cutting off Senator Little's explanation to the prince.

Answer

Repetition of "it was the Government that" (1) establishes and reinforces the government's active role in "trapping" Senator Little, and (2) minimizes Little's guilt.

3.4 Literary and Historical References

Choose literary and historical references carefully. Select an allusion that parallels your argument and will be familiar to your readers. An esoteric reference will not be persuasive. The decision to include references from literature or history depends on these factors as well as audience, context, and style.

3.4.1 Ambiguity

Before writing a brief, a litigator planned how to attract the attention of the judge. The judge, a voracious reader of English literature, liked abstractions. In the attack on the plaintiff's brief, the writer used a reference to Coleridge:

> *Mr. Ackerman's self-serving affidavit is incomplete, presenting a misleading picture of the material facts at issue here. As Coleridge wrote, "Veracity does not consist in saying, but in the intention of communicating truth." Several examples demonstrate that Mr. Ackerman's affidavit is just as revealing for what it does not say as for what it does.*

Although at first this quotation appears to complement the argument, note the ambiguities between Coleridge's words and the context. Coleridge states that a person's intention to tell the truth is more important than the spoken or written words. Does the litigator imply that if Mr. Ackerman intended to be truthful but was not, he was being honest? This interpretation weakens the writer's argument. Or do Coleridge's words emphasize the attorney's point? Do they convince you that even if Ackerman's sentences were literally true, they were misleading?

Out of context, you can read the quotation both ways. When you select a literary reference, consider both the quotation's content and potential ambiguities in interpretation.

3.4.2   Context and Accuracy

In a brief in opposition to a motion in limine, a litigator characterized opposing counsel's previous allusion and suggested a more appropriate one. The writer, who represents defendant Summit Motors, argues against the exclusion of expert testimony and evidence of profitability. Central Summit Dealership is the plaintiff. Two literary references appear below:

> *In attempting to make its point, Plaintiff derisively compares Summit Motors' "new defense" (to be presented through Mr. Johnson's testimony) to "the fictional stories of Robinhood" (sic). (See P's Mem. at 1, 2, 4.). While in this vein, Plaintiff should also have considered another legendary character from fiction, Don Quixote. For Central is tilting at windmills.*

> *Whatever the merit of Central's assault on the relevance of Johnson's testimony to the question of violation of § 818.9(a)(3), Plaintiff's real enemy (like Don Quixote's) lies elsewhere—in § 818.20. That section provides as follows:*

> *[Paraphrase: The right to bring a civil action is limited to those franchises who are "so injured in business or property by a violation of a provision of this act." . . . Central cannot prove actual injury.]*

The litigator first debunks the plaintiff's comparison of Mr. Johnson's expert testimony to "the fictional stories of Robinhood." But she wrote "Robin Hood" incorrectly, i.e., with one word, not two. She also ignored his legendary role as folk hero. Although Robin Hood stole from the rich, he gave his bounty to the poor and did not seek personal gain.

Defendant's attorney then introduces a more effective literary reference. Comparing plaintiff to Cervantes' hero, Don Quixote, the litigator describes both men as "tilting at windmills." He refers to Don Quixote's attacking windmills because he believed they were giants.

This reference is familiar and appropriate in context. Don Quixote's assault on windmills was misplaced. Similarly, the litigator asserts, plaintiff errs as he argues against the testimony's relevance. Like Don Quixote's attack on windmills, plaintiff's argument is ludicrous. Plaintiff focuses on the wrong section of law, not on the "real enemy," a different section establishing a standard that plaintiff cannot meet.

Exercise

A Texas supreme court judge alluded to a Greek legend in *City of Houston v. Sam P. Wallace and Co.* In that case, one of two plaintiffs secretly had settled with the defendant and agreed not to argue negligence against it. Is the Trojan Horse reference effective?

> At the commencement of the trial, both City of Houston and Little had actions against Wallace Company as their common adversary. The trial court properly and fairly cast them as plaintiffs after the consolidation of the two cases. . . . The fairness of the alignment turned into unfairness when, unknown to City of Houston, its ally and confederate became its adversary. City of Houston, under an adversary proceeding, had the burden to develop and present its own case, but it did not have the additional burden to defeat the Trojan Horse that had secretly invaded City's camp. Counsel for Little switched sides and then undermined his co-plaintiffs and his own case as alleged.

Answer

The reference to the Trojan Horse expresses an effective thematic parallel with *City of Houston.* In the Greek legend, two enemies, the Trojans and the Greeks, were at war. The Greeks built a large wooden horse, and Greek soldiers hid inside. After the rest of the Greeks pretended to sail away, the curious Trojans pulled the horse inside the city walls. At night, the Greek soldiers crept out of the horse and opened the city gates to the other Greek forces, who defeated the Trojans. As in *City of Houston,* one side achieved victory by disguising itself and deceiving its enemy. The *City of Houston* co-plaintiff secretly settled with the defendant and invaded Houston's "camp," causing Houston to lose.

3.4.3 Extended Literary References

As he drafted a reply brief, a litigator saw a parallel between the opposing counsel's argument and the actions of a Shakespearean character. To express this connection, he began with a simile comparing plaintiffs' argument to Lady Macbeth. He developed this metaphor in the introduction and set the tone for the rest of the brief.

Throughout the introduction, the writer echoes Shakespeare's language and the themes of *Macbeth*. The litigator refers to Lady Macbeth's behavior after she attempts to disguise her husband's murder of Duncan by rubbing bloody daggers on the pillows of sleeping attendants. The lawyer also alludes to her famous sleepwalking scene, in which she utters "Out, damned spot!" as she tries to wash the murdered king's blood from her hands.

Extending these themes, the lawyer crafted the figures of speech underlined below:

> *Like Lady Macbeth vigorously scrubbing the spot that she could not remove from her hand, SMIB's Opposing Memorandum energetically but fruitlessly sweeps over the facts that will not disappear. No amount of massaging in SMIB's Memorandum can dissipate the facts established in Potter's motion papers and confirmed in SMIB's own affidavits. Thus, while SMIB asserts factual conclusions in its Memorandum that are not supported by SMIB's affidavits, the affidavits themselves, taken alongside the evidence presented by the Potter and Smith defendants, establish the facts that show that personal jurisdiction is lacking. These spots cannot be rubbed out.*

> *Not one word in SMIB's Memorandum is devoted to the* Jones Dairy Farm *decision, the leading case in this district regarding the appropriateness of a transfer under 28 U.S.C. § 1404. Yet the facts here are closer to those found to control that decision than in any case cited by SMIB. The* Jones Dairy Farm *case is yet another spot that cannot be rubbed out.*

> *SMIB is simply left with making the purely cosmetic argument that because it is a state agency spending state money and being represented by a state attorney, it should be able to force foreigners into its home forum* ipso facto. *This argument serves only as make-up, unsupported as it is by any case law authority. It cannot hide the ineradicable spots.*

> *This reply brief will demonstrate that the facts that SMIB has not disputed with admissible evidence require a finding that personal jurisdiction is absent in this court. In any event, the*

case must be transferred to the situs of the claims in suit, the Southern District of Florida, since SMIB's arguments opposing transfer reveal nothing more than SMIB's tactical desire to maintain this case in a forum where only SMIB will have the capability of putting on its evidence live.

As you review this passage, consider these questions:

1. <u>How appropriate and familiar is the literary reference?</u>

   Will all readers know the story of Macbeth?

2. <u>Is the image effective when it is first presented?</u>

   Is the comparison between writers who try to ignore facts and Lady Macbeth fresh and original? Is the first sentence convincing?

3. <u>How successful are the extended comparisons?</u>

   The litigator later refers to "massaging," "spot that cannot be rubbed out," "purely cosmetic argument," "make-up," and "in-eradicable spots." Do these references reinforce the original simile? Do some of them seem contrived? Would one example of figurative language be more powerful than an extended meta-phor? How far should a writer extend a figure of speech?

To most readers, the later comparisons to Lady Macbeth seem awk-ward. The original metaphor would be more effective without extended comparisons.

3.4.4 Poetry

While crafting a figure of speech, a litigator recalled a favorite poem and considered whether to use it in a brief. He hoped the poem would complement his metaphor about the role of corporate officers. He figura-tively describes the officers' behavior in the last sentence below:

Apart from all of the above, however, it seems clear, since the individual defendants are all alleged to be officers and employees of Wiltex, Inc., that an allegation that they conspired with themselves as directors of Computone would not be sufficient in law. The image of them with their Wiltex hats on making a conspiratorial proposal to themselves as Computone directors

that, while the sound waves were still reverberating in the room,
they accepted after changing quickly to their Computone hats, is
too ludicrous to warrant further comment.[1]

After developing the image of the directors' "changing hats" as representatives of two corporations, the writer remembered a poem by Edwin
Arlington Robinson. The litigator saw a connection between the metaphor in his argument and the behavior of the poem's central figure. The
writer added the poem in a footnote, which ended with an application of
case law to the poem's main character.

The litigator used the poem to debunk plaintiffs' argument that Wiltex
directors "changed hats" and conspired with themselves. In the poem,
Eben Flood plays the role of his own drinking companion. He calls himself
by name and offers himself a drink from the jug. Next Eben changes roles
and graciously accepts the invitation. Drawing parallels between Eben
Flood and the Wiltex directors, the writer dismisses plaintiffs' assertion.

Reasonable persons disagree about the relative success of including
"Eben Flood" in the brief. Some readers find this long footnote pretentious
and distracting. Other lawyers think that the connection between Wiltex
directors and Eben Flood is clever.

---

1.   *The first two stanzas of Edwin Arlington Robinson's delightful poem, "Mr. Flood's Party,"*
come to mind:

> *Old Eben Flood, climbing alone one night*
> *over the hill between the town below*
> *and the forsaken upland hermitage*
> *that held as much as he should ever know*
> *on earth again of home, paused warily.*
> *The road was his with no native near;*
> *and Eben, having leisure, said aloud,*
> *for no man else in Tilbury Town to hear:*

> *"Well, Mr. Flood, we have the harvest moon*
> *again, and we may not have many more;*
> *the bird is on the wing, as the poet says*
> *and you and I have said it here before.*
> *Drink to the bird." He raised up to the light*
> *the jug that he had gone so far to fill, and*
> *answered huskily: "Well, Mr. Flood, since*
> *you propose it, I believe I will."*

Under the theory that plaintiff would be forced to advocate, if Eben Flood were an employee of
one corporation and a director of another, both he and the two corporations (if this were authorized
business entertainment) could be found guilty of conspiring to violate applicable prohibition laws.
Such a holding would rest solely on poetic license, for the law is otherwise. Windsor Theatre Co. v.
Wallbrook Amusement Co., *(D. Md. 1950) 94 F. Supp. 388 at 396, affirmed (4th Cir. 1951) 189*
F. 2d 797; Goldlawr, Inc. V. Shubert, *(3rd Cir. 1960) 276 F. 2d 614 at 617. Compare* Rogers v.
American Can Co., *(D. N.J. 1960) 187 F. Supp. 532 at 540, where the stockholder (Can Co.) was*
alleged to have conspired with directors of the corporation in which it held stock, only some of
whom were (and some of whom therefore were not) connected with Can Co.

If you wrote the brief, would you have used the poem? When does poetry strengthen an argument? When is a poem distracting? Which readers will like this technique? Which ones will be put off? Consider these questions when your writing reminds you of a favorite poem.

3.5 Historical References

A litigator chose an unusual historical reference for his argument against an award of attorneys' fees. Smith Taylor, a law firm that did not serve as class counsel in the case, had demanded $300,000 in fees. After describing Smith Taylor's limited role, the writer quotes Joseph Welch, who challenged Senator Joseph McCarthy in congressional hearings in 1954. The litigator implies that Smith Taylor's behavior, like McCarthy's, is reprehensible:

> *Finally, with all due respect, even the lodestar amount claimed by Smith Taylor is incredible. Elton & Bammel, Class Counsel, have worked on this case for the last seven months. They have been in constant communication with Plexco's counsel, have monitored work being done on the settlement, and have made innumerable telephone calls to class members. Yet they testify that they have spent only 400 hours working on this case.*

> *By contrast, Smith Taylor has done little, and accomplished less. It prepared a settlement proposal that was copied from Sears. It filed a complaint that was modeled on the Sears complaint. Smith Taylor attended one meeting—that lasted for less than half of one day—with Plexco's counsel, and had some telephone calls. Yet Smith Taylor claims to have spent more than 300 hours—a full six weeks of lawyer time—working for the benefit of the class. In the words of Joseph Welch, the one man willing to stand up to Senator Joseph McCarthy: "Have you no sense of decency?"*

> *Smith Taylor is entitled to neither a multiple of its lodestar nor even the lodestar itself.*

The lawyer chose this historical reference to express outrage at Smith Taylor's request. Since the case took place in federal court in Massachusetts, Welch's home state, readers would undoubtedly recognize the allusion. In a less dramatic context, this quotation might be too strong and therefore ineffective. Because the lawyer developed a reasoned argument throughout the brief, this reference provides a persuasive conclusion.

3.6 Justices' Flair

3.6.1 Inflated Diction

In *Crummer Co. v. du Pont*, the judge's inflated diction and awkward sentence structure weaken his opinion. The district judge dismissed the plaintiff's complaint alleging an antitrust conspiracy by various defendants. But the court agreed that plaintiffs had stated no course of action as to other defendants. Using flowery language in his opinion, the judge emphasized that facts, not conjecture, are required:

> *The Complaint does not charge, or even suggest that the State Board of Administration, in bringing the suit, was a party to any unlawful combination or conspiracy, and no facts are alleged which show or indicate that Gall or Crummer Sons Cypress Company was knowingly or consciously a part of a conspiracy in violation of the federal Antitrust Laws. Charges as to such conspiracies must be based on substantial and affirmative allegations, and no mere gossamer web of conclusion or inference, as here, trifles light as air, to the suspicious strong as proofs from Holy Writ, will suffice, and we are in no doubt that the court did not err in dismissing Gall and Crummer Sons from the suit.*

Note the pretentious quality of the judge's writing. Both sentences in the passage are long and convoluted. In the first sentence, two phrases separate major grammatical elements. A complicated structure and Latinate diction in the second sentence confuse even the most perceptive reader. The writer develops metaphors in the second independent clause's long subject: "no mere gossamer web of conclusion or inference, as here, trifles light as air, to the suspicious strong as proofs from Holy Writ." With three phrases between the main subject and the verb, these metaphors are hard to understand. Is "trifles" a noun or a verb? How does "to the suspicious strong as proofs from Holy Writ" fit in? What is the subject of "will suffice"?

Moreover, the judge's word choice creates an awkward tone in this short passage. Latinate diction includes "conspiracies," "substantial," "affirmative," "allegations," "gossamer," "conclusion," "inference," "suspicious," "suffice," and "dismissing." Using complicated words and sentence structure, the judge has gone too far in his attempts at flair.

3.6.2 Wordplay

Judges sometimes write playfully to attract the reader's attention. At times they also wish to make an argument amusing or to have fun with language. Creative efforts surprise us because they do not match our expectations. In most legal contexts, readers expect to see traditional forms.

A judge who loved sports used football terms to write about a case involving the trademark of a college team. As you read excerpts from his opinion, note his creative techniques:

University of Georgia Athletic Association v. Laite et al.

> In the fall . . . , when the fancy of Georgia sports fans turned to thoughts of college football, Bill Laite Distributing Co. ("Laite"), a Macon, Georgia wholesaler of novelty beers, began marketing "Battlin' Bulldog Beer." The beer was sold in red and black cans bearing the portrayal of an English bulldog wearing a red sweater emblazoned with a black "G." The bulldog had bloodshot eyes, a football tucked under its right "arm," and a frothy beer stein in its left "hand."

> Laite hoped that the "Battlin' Bulldog" would pile up yardage and score big points in the always-competitive alcoholic beverage market. Unfortunately, however, the pug-faced pooch was thrown for a loss by the University of Georgia Athletic Association, Inc. ("UGAA"), which obtained preliminary and permanent injunctive relief in federal district court based on the "likelihood of confusion" between the "Battlin' Bulldog" and the "University of Georgia Bulldog." Laite now cries "foul," arguing that (l) the "University of Georgia Bulldog" is not a valid trade or servicemark worthy of protection, (2) the district court used the wrong factors in comparing the "Battlin' Bulldog" with the "University of Georgia Bulldog," and (3) the court's conclusion that the sale of "Battlin' Bulldog Beer" created a "likelihood of confusion" is clearly erroneous. After viewing a "replay" of the proceedings below, we conclude that no error was committed and affirm the judgment of the district court in all respects.

> . . . .

> We kick off our discussion by noting that the district court, in granting preliminary injunctive relief to UGAA, discussed only the Lanham Act claim and did not mention the claims arising under Georgia law.

CHAPTER THREE

. . . .

While the "clearly erroneous" standard of review is less stringent than the well-known sports rule, "The referee is always right," it nevertheless presents a formidable challenge to appellants who, like Laite, seek to overturn the factual finds of a district court.

. . . .

The "Battlin' Bulldog's" football career thus comes to an abrupt end. Laite devised a clever entrepreneurial "game plan," but failed to take into account the strength of UGAA'S mark and the tenacity with which UGAA was willing to defend that mark. Like the University of Georgia's famed "Junkyard Dog" defense, UGAA was able to hold its opponent to little or no gain. Because we find that the district court did not err, in fact or in law, when it granted permanent injunctive relief to UGAA, we hereby AFFIRM.

The judge in *Arthur Murray Dance Studios of Cleveland, Inc. v. Witter* also used wordplay in his opinion. He chose terms from the case's subject matter to establish a light tone in the first paragraph:

> *When the defendant, Clifford Witter, a dance instructor, waltzed out of the employment of the plaintiff, the Arthur Murray Dance Studios of Cleveland, Inc., into the employment of the Fred Astaire Dancing Studios, the plaintiff waltzed Witter into court. For brevity, the two studios are called "Arthur Murray" and "Fred Astaire." At the time Witter took his contentious step, Arthur Murray had a string attached to him—a certain contract prohibiting Witter, after working for Arthur Murray no more, from working for a competitor. That Arthur Murray and Fred Astaire are rivals in dispensing Terpsichorean erudition is not disputed. Now Arthur Murray wants the court to pull that string and yank Witter out of Fred Astaire's pedagogical pavilion.*

These judges have fun superimposing the football or dance language on the details of the case. In addition, they implicitly ask us to enjoy wordplay that distinguishes these opinions from more conventional ones.

3.6.3   Parallel Arguments

Judges often use parallel arguments for emphasis in persuasive writing. Each parallel leads the reader to the central argument's intended conclusion. In addition to wordplay, the judge in *Arthur Murray Dance Studios of Cleveland, Inc. v. Witter* employed parallel arguments. The case involves a dance instructor, Clifford Witter, who left Arthur Murray's studios to teach at Fred Astaire's school. Murray's contract with Witter prohibited him from working for a competitor. The parallel arguments concern "customer contact," i.e., whether customers will follow Witter to Fred Astaire's studio.

The judge added flair to his argument with humor, Cleveland names, references to the legal profession, and rhetorical questions. For example, in discussing whether customers will follow an elevator operator to another building, the judge refers to three Cleveland office buildings:

> *Yet whoever heard of a tenant moving from the Union Commerce Building to the Terminal Tower or Caxton Building because an elevator operator did?*

These allusions make the argument more engaging to readers who recognize these buildings. Eight more rhetorical questions follow:

> *Because he likes the elevator operator, will he break his lease and incur damages? Will he endure the trouble of packing, moving, reestablishing? And the expense? Will he sacrifice the advantage of customers being accustomed to doing business with him at his present stand? Will he leave an advantageous location he likes to follow to a disadvantageous one he dislikes? How far will he follow? Two buildings away? Two miles away?*

The judge then draws other parallels to the inconvenience of customers' following a departing receptionist, apartment manager, college professor, milkman, and even a law school administrator:

> *If the deans of the Harvard and Yale law schools exchanged chairs, it might be very unflattering to see how few, if any, of their students would try to follow them.*

CHAPTER THREE

The judge extends the parallel to the college context:

> As every school knows, there is such a thing as an "institutional hold" that may be greater than the hold of one teacher, such as the hold it exercises through such things as loyalty, tradition, reputation, the campus, classmates, friends, fraternity brothers, other teachers and the girl who wears one's fraternity pin.

Personal elements in this series increase the sense of "institutional hold" by evoking memories of the reader's own college years.

CHAPTER FOUR

~ *Grammar* ~

Judges, colleagues, and clients expect to see correct grammar in all lawyers' written work. Grammatical errors mar legal writing, even if it is eloquent, clearly reasoned, or brilliant. Mistakes in grammar can change a sentence's meaning, and sloppy usage may confuse the reader. If a writer ignores grammatical rules, readers may wonder whether the substance of a paper is correct.

Use this chapter as a reference to help you identify and fill gaps in your grammar background. You can review the elements of sentence structure, techniques for combining clauses, and lawyers' most common grammatical errors. These include pronoun usage, subject-verb agreement, dangling modifiers, and use of the subjunctive.

4.1 Clauses

A clause is a group of related words that contains both a subject and a predicate. Clauses may be independent or subordinate.

4.1.1 Independent Clauses

A main clause is a grammatically independent unit that can stand alone as a sentence:

1. *On April 30, City Council approved A-1 zoning status for Hollyhock Apartments.*

2. *The Wild and Scenic Rivers Act sets aside certain designated rivers for preservation.*

3. *Tele-Value has installed underground cable, cable television hook-ups, and other related equipment on the property.*

In a compound sentence, two main clauses are linked by a coordinating conjunction such as "and," "but," "or," "nor," "for," "so," and "yet." Add a comma before the conjunction:

> 4. *Richardson resides in Connecticut, and Utah Oil is a Delaware corporation with its principal place of business in Ogden, Utah.*

> 5. *Ms. Belton's videotapes constitute opinion work product, so they are not discoverable.*

Use a semicolon to join main clauses without a coordinating conjunction. The clauses should be short and closely related in meaning:

> 6. *Mr. Hoover withheld facts from the government; he also made an obvious effort to obscure those facts.*

Main clauses also can be linked by a semicolon and a conjunctive adverb, which expresses the relationship between the two clauses:

> 7. *The trial court ruled against the purchaser; however, the court of appeals reversed that decision.*

Exercise

Identify the main clauses in these sentences.

A. No document or consent agreement by American National exists, and no consent was given.

B. The revolving credit terminates automatically in the case of a default.

C. If the joint clients are an insurer and insured, a conflict of interest may arise during the course of the joint representation.

D. Claims of conflict of interest and failure to disclose conflicts usually are not raised until the underlying suit against the insured has been settled or brought to judgment.

Answers

A. Main clauses: "no document or consent agreement by American National exists" and "no consent was given"

B. The entire sentence is an independent clause.

C. Main clause: "a conflict of interest may arise during the course of the joint representation"

D. Main clause: "claims of conflict of interest and failure to disclose conflicts usually are not raised"

4.1.2   Relative Clauses

Relative clauses are dependent on the main clause. These subordinate structures serve as adjectives, i.e., they describe a noun or pronoun. Adjective clauses begin with a relative pronoun, e.g., "who," "whom," "whose," "which," or "that."

When an adjective clause modifies an inanimate noun, use "which" or "that" to introduce the clause. Nonrestrictive clauses begin with "which" and add information in a by-the-way fashion about a precisely identified noun. In sentence 1, the adjective clause is nonrestrictive:

> 1.   *The partner based her argument on Tex. Tax Code Ann. §§ 171.251-171.257, which deal exclusively with the forfeiture of corporate privileges.*

The pronoun serves as subject of the dependent clause, which modifies "Tex. Tax Code Ann. §§ 171.251-171.257," the object of a preposition.

Restrictive clauses identify the modified noun by creating a subcategory. Begin these clauses with "that":

> 2.   *Pharmi-Co manufactured an anti-cholesterol drug <u>that caused harmful side effects</u>.*

The restrictive clause modifies the object of the verb; the relative pronoun "that" functions as subject of the dependent clause.

Use "who," "whose," and "whom" at the beginning of adjective clauses that describe human nouns. If the relative pronoun serves as the subject of the subordinate clause, "who" is the correct form. In sentence 3, "who" is the subject of the verb "purchased":

> 3.   *The class members <u>who purchased individual units in the building</u> sued the seller for breach of contract.*

This adjective clause modifies "the class members," a noun phrase that functions as subject of the independent clause.

When the relative pronoun represents the direct object, indirect object, or object of a preposition in the adjective clause, use "whom":

4. *The witness <u>whom Axco wants to interview</u> was a CEO at Porter when the dispute took place.*

In this dependent clause, "whom" is the object of a verb phrase, "wants to interview." The clause modifies "witness," the subject of the independent clause.

Use "whose," the possessive form of the relative pronoun, to show ownership in an adjective clause. Sentence 5 contains a subordinate clause that modifies the direct object in the main sentence:

5. *The defendant will compensate plaintiffs <u>whose rights have been violated</u>.*

Some adverbs introduce adjective clauses. Examples include "jurisdictions where . . . ," "reasons why . . . ," and "times when. . . ."

Exercise

In these sentences, identify each adjective clause, the relative pronoun, its function in the clause, and the modified noun.

A. Mr. Mead is a shareholder of Pacific Connections, Inc., which was a qualifying S Corporation throughout its last fiscal year.

B. Plaintiff, whom Atco Motors hired as an hourly employee, was fired for falsifying company records.

C. Fager, who is Decedent's legal surviving spouse, will receive 90 percent of his wife's estate.

D. The court limited the total amount of punitive damages that could be imposed upon an individual defendant.

Answers

A. 1. Adjective clause: "which was a qualifying S Corporation throughout its last fiscal year"

   2. Relative pronoun: "which"

   3. Function: subject

   4. Modified noun: "Pacific Connections, Inc."

B. 1. Adjective clause: "whom Atco Motors hired as an hourly employee"

   2. Relative pronoun: "whom"

   3. Function: direct object of "hired"

   4. Modified noun: "Plaintiff"

C. 1. Adjective clause: "who is Decedent's legal surviving spouse"

   2. Relative pronoun: "who"

   3. Function: subject

   4. Modified noun: "Fager"

D. 1. Adjective clause: "that could be imposed upon an individual defendant"

   2. Relative pronoun: "that"

   3. Function: subject

   4. Modified noun: "damages"

4.1.3 Adverbial Clauses

An adverbial clause is a subordinate clause that functions as an adverb. These clauses modify a verb, an adjective, an adverb, or the rest of the sentence. Subordinating conjunctions introduce adverbial clauses. Clauses of this type explain time, location, condition, cause, concession, comparison, purpose, or result.

4.1.3.1 Time

When an adverbial clause indicates time, begin the clause with a conjunction such as "after," "as," "before," "once," "since," "until," "when," "as soon as," "once," "now that," or "while." In each sentence below, the underlined clause modifies the verb and explains when the action expressed by the verb takes place:

1. *<u>Before Lowell Co. purchased 60,000 shares of stock</u>, Mr. Horton's family owned 10 percent of the company.*

2. *<u>After the discovery period expired</u>, Mr. Little's attorneys filed the Motion to Compel.*

3. *<u>When money damages serve as an adequate remedy at law</u>, equity will not intervene.*

4.1.3.2 Condition

Some adverbial clauses explain conditions that govern the action in the main clause. Subordinating conjunctions such as "if," "even if," "unless," and "provided (that)" introduce conditional clauses. Each of the conditional clauses below modifies the verb in the main sentence:

1. *<u>Even if the bill of sale were unenforceable</u>, the sale of Alice Cooper's interest violated her contract with Apex Company.*

2. *According to the agreement, Axco must pay extra charges <u>if Plimpton does not receive payment by February 1</u>.*

4.1.3.3 Concession

Concession adverbial clauses begin with "though," "although," or "even though." These clauses contain an acknowledgment or admission by the writer:

1. *<u>Although Mr. Simon acknowledges that Ms. Reese was entitled to these documents</u>, he did not show her the bill of sale until April 15.*

2. *<u>Even though Dr. Little testified that she exercised her option to purchase stock on June 1</u>, no corporate records reflect the alleged stock transfer.*

Like temporal and conditional clauses, concession clauses modify the main verb.

4.1.3.4 Cause

Begin causal dependent clauses with "because," "since," or "as." Causal clauses explain why the action or state of being expressed in the independent clause occurs:

  1. *The court is familiar with the facts in this dispute <u>because the parties already have filed several motions and supporting briefs</u>.*

4.1.3.5 Comparison

Introduce comparison adverbial clauses with "as if," "as though," "than," or "as far as." These clauses establish a comparison with a verb, adjective, or adverb in the independent clause. For example, the underlined clause in sentence 1 modifies the adjective "more":

  1. *Plaintiff seeks more information <u>than defendant can provide before December 31</u>.*

In sentence 2, the comparison clause modifies the verb and explains how Mr. Miller complained.

  2. *Mr. Miller complains about the blocked easement <u>as if he had suffered irreparable harm</u>.*

4.1.3.6 Purpose

Begin adverbial clauses that explain purpose with "so that" or "in order that." These clauses describe the purpose of an action or state of being in the main sentence:

  1. *Plaintiff's attorneys illegally gained access to the warehouse <u>so that they could read privileged records</u>.*

4.1.3.7 Result

Adverbial clauses also can express the result of action described in the main sentence. Introduce these clauses with "that":

  1. *North's lawyers engaged in such deceptive conduct <u>that they obtained access to privileged files of opposing counsel</u>.*

Exercise

In these sentences, identify adverbial clauses and their function (time, condition, concession, cause, comparison, purpose, or result).

A. The client will receive a refund if he fulfills the terms of the contract.

B. Plaintiff's Motion to Compel should be denied because it was not filed within the time period permitted by Local Rule 225-4(d).

C. Unless Insure-Co can prove that Ms. Fox's claim is invalid, she is entitled to reimbursement.

D. Section 548 avoidance powers are not available to the debtor because that section explicitly grants powers to only the trustee.

E. The court should consider this matter seriously so that the fundamental rights of those who have been victimized will be protected.

F. If the effect of the extrinsic evidence does not contradict or impair any of the deed's terms, the parol evidence will be admissible.

G. Although the plaintiffs may persuade Dr. Seton to substantiate his claims, these affirmations will not ensure a victory.

Answers

A. Clause: "if he fulfills the terms of the contract"
Function: condition

B. Clause: "because it was not filed within the time period permitted by Local Rule 225-4(d)"
Function: cause

C. Clause: "unless Insure-Co can prove that Ms. Fox's claim is invalid"
Function: condition

D. Clause: "because that section explicitly grants powers to only the trustee"
Function: cause

E. Clause: "so that the fundamental rights of those who have been victimized will be protected"
Function: purpose

F. Clause: "if the effect of the extrinsic evidence does not contradict or impair any of the deed's terms"
Function: condition

G. Clause: "although the plaintiffs may persuade Dr. Seton to substantiate his claims"
Function: concession

4.2 Phrases

A phrase is a sequence of grammatically related words without a subject and a predicate. Types include noun, verb, prepositional, participial, gerund, and infinitive phrases.

4.2.1 Noun Phrases

A noun phrase consists of a noun and its modifiers. A noun is a part of speech that names a person, place, or thing. Within each noun phrase, adjectives or articles ("a," "an," or "the") may serve as modifiers.

Noun Phrases

1. a previous action
2. the computer fraud claim
3. an unnecessary delay
4. a collateral estoppel
5. a stipulated final judgment

Noun phrases can occupy any noun slot in the sentence: subject, object, complement, indirect object, possessive, and object of a preposition.

4.2.2 Appositives

An appositive is a noun or noun phrase that stands next to another noun to identify, explain, or supplement its meaning. Appositives can appear in any noun slots. For example, appositives frequently identify the subject:

1. *James Goldberg, General Counsel for the National Alcoholic Beverage Control Association, asserts that no social host or employer should feel free from liability.*

2. *The plaintiff, Sarah Richardson, brought a negligence action for injuries sustained in an automobile accident.*

An appositive also can appear next to a direct object:

3.   *Mr. Thomas failed to prove the first element, <u>irreparable harm if the TRO is not granted</u>.*

Appositives may explain the indirect object, which indicates to whom or for whom something is done:

4.   *The Canadian government granted tax abatements to White Company, <u>a corporation based in Montreal</u>.*

Finally, an appositive can identify the object of a preposition:

5.   *Plaintiffs' allegations stem from Defendant Pharmco's construction of a new store, <u>a drive-through pharmacy at 251 Main Street</u>.*

4.2.3   Verb Phrases

The main verb and any helping verbs make up a verb phrase. Verb phrases denote action, occurrence, or existence.

<u>Verb Phrases</u>

1. will apply
2. may be argued
3. should preclude
4. have asserted
5. had been

Exercise

Identify the noun and verb phrases in these sentences. Explain the role of each noun phrase.

A. LIM stockholders have elected Robert L. Thomson CEO.

B. Under paragraph 5.b, the partnership can unilaterally extinguish all incidents of ownership by canceling the Agreement.

Answers

A. Noun phrase: "LIM stockholders"

Role: subject
Verb phrase: "have elected"
Noun phrase: "Robert L. Thomson"
Role: direct object

B. Noun phrase: "paragraph 5.b"

Role: object of preposition
Noun phrase: "the partnership"
Role: subject
Verb phrase: "can extinguish"
Noun phrase: "all incidents"
Role: direct object
Noun phrase: "the Agreement"
Role: direct object of gerund

4.2.4   Prepositional Phrases

A prepositional phrase contains a preposition and its object. The object is a noun, pronoun, or gerund with optional modifiers. The function of a preposition is to link and relate its object to another word in the sentence. While most prepositions consist of only one word, phrasal prepositions include two or more words.

Prepositions

1. to
2. of
3. against

Phrasal Prepositions

1. according to
2. apart from
3. except for

Prepositional phrases

1. between the two parties
2. by the Apco divisions
3. under New Jersey or Connecticut law
4. of thirty-five jurisdictions
5. in lieu of agency action

Depending on their function, prepositional phrases serve as adjectives or adverbs.

Prepositional phrases that function as adjectives modify nouns or pronouns. These phrases describe or limit the modified words. In the sentence below, the phrase "of public policy" explains the noun "violation":

1.   *The court did not explore the plaintiff's violation of public policy.*

The phrase "for constructive fraud" modifies the noun "claim" in sentence 2:

2.   *Count III's claim for constructive fraud should be dismissed.*

Sentences 3 and 4 also contain prepositional phrases that function as adjectives:

3.   *The discovery requests sought information about National Bank's FSLIC insurance.*

4.   *ABC must have a good faith basis for threatening litigation.*

Adverbial prepositional phrases modify verbs and other forms that function as verbs. These adverbial phrases indicate time, location, or manner. For example, in sentence 5, the phrase "in North America" explains location:

5.   *The recalled vehicles include all Power XL Chargers manufactured in North America last year.*

The prepositional phrase in sentence 6 depicts manner:

6.   *The payments were made <u>without the plaintiff's knowledge and consent</u>.*

Sentences 7 and 8 contain prepositional phrases that indicate time:

7.   <u>*After receiving the goods*</u>, *the retailer refused to pay.*

8.   *Sarah Letterman, the defendant's agent, negotiated the contract <u>on August 15</u>.*

Exercise

Identify each prepositional phrase, its type, and the modified term in these sentences.

A.   The case law does not discuss the composition of indirect cost pools.

B.   Payments made with the full knowledge and consent of the plaintiff do not constitute commercial bribery.

Answers

Phrase	Type	Modified Term
A. of indirect cost pools	adjective	composition
B. with the full knowledge and consent	adverb	made
of the plaintiff	adjective	knowledge, consent

4.2.5   Participial Phrases

A participle is a verb form that serves as part of a verb phrase or as an adjective. To create a present participle, add "-ing" to the verb's present tense, as in "proving," "judging," and "bribing." Regular verbs form their past participle with the present tense plus "-ed" or "-d," e.g., "entered," "alleged," and "adopted." Many verbs have irregular past participles:

1.   blow—*blown*
2.   creep—*crept*
3.   fall—*fallen*
4.   go—*gone*
5.   rise—*risen*
6.   sing—*sung*

7. steal—*stolen*

8. write—*written*

Both the present and past participles can be part of a verb phrase:

1. *LBM maintains that Arthur Company <u>has</u> not <u>discharged</u> its duties.*

2. *While Plaintiffs delayed, Browning <u>has been proceeding</u> with construction.*

Both types of participles also can serve as adjectives, which modify a noun or pronoun:

3. *<u>Acting</u> as an agent, Winter Company arranged for execution of the contract.*

4. *Plaintiff filed an <u>amended</u> complaint against TRICO.*

In sentence 3, a present participle, "acting," modifies the subject, "Winter Company." In sentence 4, "complaint," the direct object of "filed," is explained by a past participle, "amended."

When present participial phrases function as adjectives, they can take objects, complements, or modifiers. Note the phrases with objects below:

5. *Courts often include leave to amend in the order <u>dismissing the complaint</u>.*

6. *Alton and Smith will represent the Chamber of Commerce as an amicus party in litigation <u>involving Lexco</u>.*

Complements also can follow present participles:

7. *<u>Appearing drunk</u>, Plaintiff tested positively for ethanol at work on May 1.*

In addition, some present participial phrases contain modifiers such as adverbs and prepositional phrases:

8. *<u>Arriving late</u> fifteen days last month, Ms. White violated her Last Chance Agreement.*

9. *State and federal courts in Illinois usually apply the same ethical standards to attorneys <u>practicing before them</u>.*

Although past participles cannot take objects or complements, adverbs and prepositional phrases can follow these verbals:

10. *Plaintiff's delay does not demonstrate an "emergency" situation as envisioned by the framers of CR65 (A).*

Exercise

Identify each participial phrase, its structure, and the modified noun in these sentences.

A. State courts allow recovery for future damages related to a present injury.

B. Ms. Cohen filed a complaint proposing a class action lawsuit against Apex Company.

Answers

A. Participial phrase: "related to a present injury"
   Structure: past participle, prepositional phrase
   Modified noun: "damages"

B. Participial phrase: "proposing a class action lawsuit against Apex Company"
   Structure: present participle, modifiers, noun object, prepositional phrase
   Modified noun: "complaint"

4.2.6   Gerund Phrases

Although gerunds and present participles have identical forms (e.g., "arguing"), they serve different grammatical roles. Participles function as adjectives; gerunds serve as nouns. To form a gerund, add "-ing" to the present tense of a verb, as in "testifying," "requiring," and "stating." A gerund can occupy any noun slot in the sentence, i.e., subject, object, indirect object, complement, or object of a preposition.

A gerund phrase consists of a gerund and an object or modifier:

1. phrase with object: "requiring proof"
2. phrase with modifier: "delaying unnecessarily"
3. phrase with complement: "being unduly burdensome"

Like gerunds, gerund phrases can fill any noun slot in a sentence. For example, the phrase can be the subject:

1. *Without a showing of gross negligence, recovering damages from a host driver may be difficult for a nonpaying passenger.*

A gerund phrase can serve as object:

> 2.   *The statute of limitations forecloses <u>refiling the complaint</u>.*

A gerund phrase can also fill the indirect object slot:

> 3.   *Earth-Co has devoted two weeks to <u>repairing the Fifth Avenue easement</u>.*

A gerund phrase can be the complement:

> 4.   *The main rationale for the rule is <u>maintaining the integrity of the attorney-client relationship</u>.*

Finally, a gerund phrase can function as object of a preposition:

> 5.   *Most states restrict a lawyer from <u>inquiring into privileged communi-cations in ex parte communications with former employees</u>.*

Exercise

Identify each gerund phrase, its function, and its structure in these sentences.

A. This state follows other jurisdictions in allowing ex parte contact between opposing attorneys and former employees without approval by the former employer.

B. Filing a class action tolls the statute for all members of the putative class.

Answers

A. Gerund phrase: "in allowing ex parte contact between opposing attorneys and former employees without approval by the former employer"

   Function: object of the preposition "in"

   Structure: gerund ("allowing"), object ("ex parte contact"), and prepositional phrases ("between opposing attorneys and former employees," "without approval," and "by the former employer")

B. Gerund phrase: "filing a class action"

   Function: subject

   Structure: gerund ("filing") and object ("a class action")

4.2.7   Make the Subject Possessive

Use the possessive form for the subject of a gerund phrase. In sentence 1, the possessive form "court's" serves as the gerund's subject:

1.   *Public interest would be served by <u>the court's issuing a temporary restraining order</u>.*

This sentence consists of two central elements. The main sentence is "public interest would be served by (something)." A second independent clause, "the court issued a temporary restraining order," has been converted to a gerund phrase. To create the phrase, express the subject in the possessive case and replace the verb with the new gerund form. Next, insert the new gerund phrase as the object of the preposition in the main sentence.

In sentence 2, possessive nouns serve as subjects of gerunds:

2.   *This suit is premised on <u>the employer's wrongfully terminating the employee</u> and <u>the union's breaching its duty of fair representation of the employee</u>.*

Do not use the possessive before present participles, which look like gerunds but function as adjectives:

4.   *Plaintiffs seek an order <u>creating a medical monitoring fund</u>.*

5.   *The Atco court addressed three issues <u>pertaining to the documents</u>.*

Exercise

Identify the gerund and participial phrases in these sentences. Correct the subject form as needed.

A. In either court, the same rules govern the propriety of Harmon's attorneys contacting the former employee.

B. According to the court, an order dismissing a complaint without prejudice is not a final and appealable order unless. . . .

C. The statute of limitations may prevent the plaintiffs from filing a new lawsuit following dismissal.

D. The fund would cover expenses related to plaintiffs monitoring their health.

Answers

A. Gerund phrase: "attorneys contacting the former employee"

   Correct subject form: "attorneys' "

B. Participial phrase: "dismissing a complaint without prejudice"

C. Gerund phrase: "filing a new lawsuit"

   Participial phrase: "following dismissal"

D. Gerund phrase: "plaintiffs monitoring their health"

   Correct subject form: "plaintiffs' "

4.2.8   Infinitive Phrases

An infinitive is a verb form that functions primarily as a noun. To form the infinitive, insert "to" before the present tense of the verb, as in "to file," "to owe," and "to prove." To create an infinitive phrase, add an object, complement, or modifier.

4.2.8.1   Structure

When an infinitive takes a direct object, that noun receives the action of the verb:

1.   *This change in policy would allow the bank to set off an account.*

The noun phrase, "an account," serves as direct object of the infinitive, "to set off." In sentence 2, "a setoff" is the object of "to effect":

2.   *Despite this conversion, National Central proceeded to effect a setoff.*

CHAPTER FOUR

Modifiers such as adjectives, adverbs, or prepositional phrases can accompany the direct object of an infinitive. For example, a prepositional phrase, "in these accounts," appears after the object, "the funds," in sentence 3:

3.   The bank plans _to set off the funds in these accounts_ if the aggregate balance falls below a specified amount.

The infinitive phrase in sentence 4 contains three types of modifiers:

4.   The right of a bank _to set off a depositor's account against a debt owed to the bank by that depositor_ is well recognized in this state.

The first modifier, "a depositor's," is a possessive noun that modifies "account." Two prepositional phrases, "against a debt" and "by that depositor," follow the object. In addition, "debt" is modified by a past participial phrase, "owed to the bank."

When an infinitive expresses a state of being, you can add a complement and its modifiers. State-of-being verbs include "to be," "to seem," "to appear," and, in certain circumstances, "to remain." A complement is a noun or adjective that completes the meaning of the verb. In sentence 5, the complement is an adjective:

5.   Mr. Butler's chances of winning the appeal appear _to be excellent_.

The modifier "excellent" tells us more about "chances," the subject of the main sentence. A noun also can serve as complement:

6.   Mr. Brown seeks our advice on how _to remain CFO of Alco_ after the merger of Alco and Rose, Inc.

The noun phrase, "CFO of Alco," completes the verb phrase, "to remain."

Exercise

Identify infinitive phrases and their structure in these sentences.

A. Mr. Blanchard wished to obtain certificates of deposit for the plaintiff.

B. Cotter's concentration account appears to be a general deposit.

C. A bank is not permitted to exercise its right of setoff unless mutuality of obligation exists.

D. The bank set off the funds in the contractor's account to satisfy these loans.

Answers

A. Infinitive phrase: "to obtain certificates of deposit for the plaintiff"
   Infinitive: "to obtain"
   Object: "certificates"
   Prepositional phrases: "of deposit," "for the plaintiff"

B. Infinitive phrase: "to be a general deposit"
   Infinitive: "to be"
   Complement: "a general deposit"

C. Infinitive phrase: "to exercise its right of setoff"
   Infinitive: "to exercise"
   Object: "its right"
   Prepositional phrase: "of setoff"

D. Infinitive phrase: "to satisfy these loans"
   Infinitive: "to satisfy"
   Object: "these loans"

4.2.8.2 Split Infinitives

Follow the general rule against split infinitives in most contexts. A split infinitive occurs when an adverb is placed between "to" and the verb form, e.g., "to prejudicially delay." Although many lawyers and judges regard a split infinitive as an error, that rule is changing. At times, a split infinitive may be less awkward than the "correct" form.

When you split an infinitive, first move the adverb outside the infinitive phrase. Then analyze the syntax. If the revision is awkward, you may want to leave the adverb between "to" and the verb form.

In sentence 1(a), a lawyer used "only" to split an infinitive:

1(a)   *The agreement permits Dix Company <u>to only practice</u> the invention that falls within claim 14 of the patent.*

"Only" modifies "the invention" and should appear after "practice":

> 1(b)   *The agreement permits Dix Company <u>to practice only</u> the invention that falls within claim 14 of the patent.*

This revision is smooth and adds precision to the sentence.

Sentences 2(a) and 3(a) also contain split infinitives:

> 2(a)   *On June 1, the Teamsters Local No. 13 voted <u>to immediately object</u> to the hospital's conduct.*

> 3(a)   *The hospital argues that the union had time <u>to directly communicate</u> with the additional employees.*

You can revise sentences 2(a) and 3(a) by moving the adverb after the verb:

> 2(b)   *On June 1, the Teamsters Local No. 13 voted <u>to object immediately</u> to the hospital's conduct.*

> 3(b)   *The hospital argues that the union had time <u>to communicate directly</u> with the additional employees.*

Yet some "unsplit" infinitives create convoluted syntax. In sentence 4(a), the writer placed "specifically" between "to" and "identify":

> 4(a)   *Once again, Plaintiff has failed <u>to specifically identify</u> the essential element of his libel claim.*

If you insert the adverb before "the essential element," the infinitive phrase is intact:

> 4(b)   *Once again, Plaintiff has failed <u>to identify specifically</u> the essential element of his libel claim.*

Because the revision is awkward, the split infinitive may be preferable.

The rule that governs this matter, like so many others relating to style, is breaking down. Purists will never like the divided form. But at times splitting the infinitive creates a smoother phrase than the correct form.

Exercise

Identify and correct split infinitives in these sentences.

A. The bank has informed Mr. Wang of his option to gradually accelerate the loan.

B. The contract contained a clause requiring a premium to promptly be paid for the mortgage loan.

C. The FHLB failed to carefully consider the application.

Answers

A. Split infinitive: "to gradually accelerate"

   <u>Revision</u>: The bank has informed Mr. Wang of his option to accelerate the loan gradually.

• To keep the infinitive phrase intact, move "gradually" to the end of the sentence.

B. Split infinitive: "to promptly be paid"

   <u>Revision</u>: The contract contained a clause requiring a premium to be paid promptly for the mortgage loan.

• Insert "promptly" after "paid."

   <u>Revision</u>: The contract contained a clause requiring prompt payment of a premium for the mortgage loan.

• Convert the passive verb to a noun and change "promptly" to "prompt."

C. Split infinitive: "to carefully consider"

   <u>Revision</u>: The FHLB failed to consider the application carefully.

• Move "carefully" to the sentence's end.

4.2.8.3 Functions

<u>As Noun</u>

Most infinitives that function as nouns are complementary infinitives. This form completes the action of the main verb. According to some grammarians, complementary infinitives are objects of the main verb:

   1.   *If Plaintiff fails <u>to establish irreparable injury as a result of a wrong-ful or illegal act</u>, his applications for a temporary restraining order will be denied.*

   2.   *On February 1, Lapco decided <u>to extend Morris' employment contract</u>.*

   3.   *A party who fails <u>to assert a mandatory counterclaim in one action</u> may not raise it in a separate action.*

An infinitive phrase also can function as subject of a sentence. In this role, the infinitive is the subject of a verb that expresses an action or a state of being:

4.   *To recover future damages will be difficult unless Thermco can show that damages are reasonably certain to follow from the claimed injury.*

In addition, the complement slot can be filled by an infinitive phrase. A complement appears after a state-of-being verb and completes the subject:

5.   *The debtors' goal was to set aside the foreclosure on their property.*

As Adjective

An adjective infinitive phrase modifies a noun. The infinitive describes or further explains the modified term:

1.   *The defendant has the burden to prove the allegations, even though his plea is verified.*

"To prove the allegations" serves as an adjective modifying "burden" and clarifies what the burden is. The infinitive phrase in sentence 2 also serves as an adjective:

2.   *A corporation's failure to issue stock is another factor a court may take into consideration.*

The infinitive phrase, "to issue stock," modifies the noun "failure."

As Adverb

Adverbial infinitive phrases explain the entire sentence and provide a reason for the action expressed in the main clause:

1.   *To support their allegations, Plaintiffs have attached two deeds to their motion.*

2.   *To prevent Dr. Richardson from increasing his business, Defendant made negative statements that stopped potential purchasers from buying the property.*

Exercise

A. Identify the infinitive phrases and their grammatical function in these sentences.

   1. Defendant Cole continues to employ over fifty former members of the union.

   2. Plaintiff's lawyer argues that Defendants conspired to create a monopoly for the Pine Bay Airport.

B. Identify infinitive phrases, their type (adjective or adverb), and the modified term in these sentences.

   1. If the first court has power to adjudicate fully all the matters at issue between the parties, the plea should be granted.

   2. To govern the ethical conduct of lawyers, the Ohio Supreme Court has adopted the Code of Professional Responsibility.

   3. The right to maintain an action in equity for the obstruction of an easement requires a timely objection to the obstruction.

Answers

A. 1. Infinitive phrase: "to employ over fifty former members of the union"
   Function: complementary infinitive

   2. Infinitive phrase: "to create a monopoly for the Pine Bay Airport"
   Function: complementary infinitive

B. 1. Infinitive phrase: "to adjudicate fully all the matters at issue between the parties"
   Type: adjective
   Modified term: "power"

   2. Infinitive phrase: "to govern the ethical conduct of lawyers"
   Type: adverbial
   Modified term: entire sentence

   3. Infinitive phrase: "to maintain an action in equity for the obstruction of an easement"
   Type: adjective
   Modified term: "right"

4.3 Pronouns

4.3.1 Pronoun Reference

Link each pronoun clearly to the noun it represents, i.e., its antecedent. Do not force a puzzled reader to search for the intended referent.

According to the pronoun reference rule, a pronoun refers to the noun that directly precedes it and agrees with it in gender and number (singular or plural). Pronouns cannot "leap" over intervening nouns to an incorrectly placed antecedent.

To correct a pronoun reference problem, substitute a noun for the pronoun. In sentence 1(a), the antecedent for "it" and "its" is ambiguous:

> 1(a) Form BE-605 covers transactions between Motech Systems, as consolidated, and its foreign parent, Chemlo B.V., as well as between *it* and *its* UBO, Chemlo N.V.

The writer wanted "it" and "its" in sentence 1(a) to refer to "Motech Systems." According to the rule, these pronouns refer to "Chemlo B.V." Substitute "Motech" for "it":

> 1(b) Form BE-605 covers transactions between Motech Systems, as consolidated, and its foreign parent, Chemlo B.V., as well as between *Motech* and *its* UBO, Chemlo N.V.

With this change, "its" correctly refers to "Motech."

In sentence 2(a), antecedents for the three underlined pronouns are not clear:

> 2(a) If the seller could have made the second sale in the absence of the original buyer's breach, the resale does not make *him* whole because *he* has lost the profit on a sale *he* otherwise would have been in a position to make.

The lawyer wanted "him" and "he" to refer to "the seller," but the antecedent for these pronouns is "the original buyer." Replace "him" with "the seller":

> 2(b) If the seller could have made the second sale in the absence of the original buyer's breach, the resale does not make *the seller* whole because *he* has lost the profit on a sale *he* otherwise would have been in a position to make.

The other two pronouns then also refer to "the seller."

Exercise

Identify and correct the pronoun reference problems in these sentences.

A. After the exclusive selling agreement expired, Lasco exercised their option and bought the property.

B. The beneficiaries purchased an insurance policy on the taxpayer's life and deposited it in the trust.

Answers

A. "Their," a plural pronoun, has no antecedent. The writer wanted "Lasco" to be the antecedent. Substitute "its" for "their."

   <u>Revision</u>: After the exclusive selling agreement expired, Lasco exercised its option and bought the property.

B. The antecedent for "it" is "the taxpayer's life," but the writer wanted the pronoun to refer to "policy." Substitute "the policy" for "it."

   <u>Revision</u>: The beneficiaries purchased an insurance policy on the taxpayer's life and deposited the policy in the trust.

4.3.1.1 Demonstrative Pronouns

Use clear pronoun reference for demonstrative pronouns, especially at the beginning of a sentence. Demonstrative pronouns include "this," "that," "these," and "those." Each pronoun refers to the preceding noun that matches it in gender and number. When you start a sentence with a demonstrative pronoun, link it precisely to its antecedent.

To clarify the referent of "this," "that," "there," or "those," look for the antecedent in the preceding sentence. If your intended referent is the closest matching noun, no revision is needed. When the pronoun refers to an earlier noun, insert that noun or a synonym after the pronoun. In some sentences, the pronoun stands for a phrase or clause, not just a noun. To correct this problem, choose a noun to express the intended meaning and add that noun after the pronoun.

The antecedent for "this" is ambiguous in passage 1(a). After describing a plan to save inheritance taxes, an attorney explained its advantage:

1(a)   *When his wife dies, the assets will pass to their children free of any tax because her exemption will cover her estate. <u>This</u> is eminently sensible when viewed strictly from a federal tax standpoint.*

According to the pronoun reference rule, "this" stands for "exemption," but the writer wanted "this" to refer to the plan described earlier. Add "plan" after the pronoun:

> 1(b)   *When his wife dies, the assets will pass to their children free of any tax because her exemption will cover her estate. <u>This plan</u> is eminently sensible when viewed strictly from a federal tax standpoint.*

Exercise

Correct the pronoun reference problems in these sentences. Create a context if necessary.

A. The first round of bidding procedures produced no bids. This was remedied by direct negotiations with exhibitors.

B. The Alabama statute is a deliberate and direct regulation of interstate commerce. The Act limits the timing, terms, and manner of entering into interstate contracts and interferes with the movement of motion pictures in commerce from outside the state. This cannot be deemed an act that only "incidentally" affects commerce.

C. The rules that Defendant's attorney cited on June 1 are unclear. Legislative history suggests that this is intentional.

Answers

A. This problem was remedied by direct negotiations with exhibitors.

B. This statute cannot be deemed an act that only "incidentally" affects commerce.

C. Legislative history suggests that this ambiguity is intentional.

4.3.1.2 Collective Nouns

You may use a singular or plural pronoun for a collective noun. Collective nouns, such as "corporation," "management," and "Congress," are grammatically singular, depending on whether the noun refers to one unit or to specific members within the group. Yet by definition, a collective noun designates a group of people. Your choice of pronoun will depend on whether the noun refers to a group or to its specific members. For example, use either a singular or plural pronoun after "committee":

> 1(a)   *The <u>committee</u> presented <u>its</u> arguments before the board of directors.*

In sentence 1(a), the committee acts as a unit. But in sentence 1(b), "committee" is used in the plural sense to designate separate members of the group:

> 1(b)   The _committee_ presented _their_ arguments before the board of directors.

As you choose a pronoun, you may not know whether the members acted as a group or as individuals. Moreover, that distinction may not be important. To express the plural sense, add a plural noun after the collective noun. The plural noun designates individuals who make up the unit described by the collective noun:

> 1(c)   The committee _members_ presented _their_ arguments before the board of directors.

In sentence 2(a), the writer referred to "Whirling Tub Club" with the plural pronoun "they":

> 2(a)   The _Whirling Tub Club_ is advertising that _they_ plan to offer aerobics classes on the roof.

The singular verb "is" shows that "club" is singular here. To correct the reference problem, substitute the singular pronoun "it" for "they":

> 2(b)   The _Whirling Tub Club_ is advertising that _it_ plans to offer aerobics classes on the roof.

Alternatively, you can precede the collective noun with a plural noun phrase, such as "the managers" or "the officers" and a preposition:

> 2(c)   The _managers_ of the Whirling Tub Club _are_ advertising that _they_ plan to offer aerobics classes on the roof.

Exercise

Correct the pronoun reference problems in these sentences. All collective nouns are used in the plural sense.

A. On March 23, Councilman Joseph Morris appeared before the board and urged them to reject the recommendation.

B. The Cut-Co Shears Corporation has determined that they will not be able to repay the outstanding loan.

C. Congress was not able to vote on the proposed legislation before their Christmas recess.

Answers

A. On March 23, Councilman Joseph Morris appeared before the board members and urged them to reject the recommendation.

B. The directors of Cut-Co Shears Corporation have determined that it will not be able to repay the outstanding loan.

• Change "they" to "it" to clarify that the corporation, not the directors, has the obligation to repay.

C. Members of Congress were not able to vote on the proposed legislation before their Christmas recess.

4.3.1.3 "Which"

When you add a relative clause to a sentence, use a clear antecedent for the relative pronoun. A pronoun refers to the preceding noun that matches it in gender and number. If your intended antecedent is not the preceding noun, pronoun reference will be ambiguous:

> 1(a)   Apex's decision is analogous to opening a new <u>plant</u>, <u>which</u> does not create a duty to bargain.

Because a pronoun refers to the preceding noun that agrees with it, "plant" is the antecedent for "which." But the lawyer wanted "which" to refer to the action in the gerund phrase, "opening a new plant."

To correct this problem, add a shorter antecedent just before the pronoun. Choose a noun phrase that expresses the collective idea, "opening a new plant," more concisely:

> 1(b)   Apex's decision is analogous to opening a new plant, an <u>action</u> <u>which</u> does not create a duty to bargain.

"An action" then serves as antecedent for "which." The noun phrase encapsulates the longer intended referent, "opening a new plant." To complete the revision, change "which" to "that," the correct pronoun for a restrictive clause:

> 1(c) *Apex's decision is analogous to opening a new plant, an <u>action</u> <u>that</u> does not create a duty to bargain.*

Exercise

Correct the pronoun reference for "which" in this sentence.

> The Arbitration Decision required Temco to return Mr. Smith to the position of roller, which resulted in bumping Mr. Garfield.

Answer

> The Arbitration Decision required Temco to return Mr. Smith to the position of roller, an action that resulted in bumping Mr. Garfield.

- Add a noun phrase to provide an accurate antecedent for "which." Then change "which" to "that."

4.3.2 Choosing between "Who" and "Whom"

To choose between "who" and "whom," analyze the function of the pronoun. Determine whether the pronoun serves as subject or object.

If the pronoun functions as the subject, use "who" in main clauses:

> 1. <u>*Who*</u> *was fired for falsifying company records at Fastco Motors?*

"Who" is the subject of the verb "was fired."

Use "who" as the subject in subordinate clauses even if the clause serves as object:

> 2. *Defendants' lawyers will not reveal <u>who placed the barricades on the Cherry Street Easement</u>.*

In the dependent clause, "who" serves as the subject of "placed." The relative clause, "who placed the barricades on the Cherry Street Easement," is the object of the verb "will reveal."

When the pronoun functions as object, use "whom":

3.   *Whom did Axco interview?*

"Whom" is the object of the verb phrase "did interview." Choose "whom" also for the object in subordinate clauses, regardless of the grammatical role of the clause:

4.   *Dr. Larson testified about the condition of Ms. Jones, whom he examined on June 30.*

In the subordinate clause, "whom" is the object of "examined." The clause modifies "Ms. Jones," object of the preposition "of."

Exercise

Choose the correct pronoun in these sentences.

A. Ms. Paxton, (*who, whom*) lost two toes, testified about her inability to work.

B. We have been asked to advise Charlotte Evans, (*who, whom*) Plumco Accounting hired in Chicago, regarding her house purchase in Evanston.

C. The partner advised Mr. Little, (*who, whom*) currently lives in New York, about estate tax planning.

Answers

A. Use "who," the subjective form, for the subject of "lost."

B. Use "whom," the objective form, for the direct object of object of "hired."

C. Use "who," the subjective form, for the subject of "lives."

4.3.3 Correct Forms in a Series

4.3.3.1 Subjective Pronouns

To choose the correct form for a pronoun in a series, determine the pronoun's grammatical role. Use the subjective case in the subject and complement positions. Subjective pronouns include "I," "we," "you" (singular and plural), "he," "she," "it," and "they."

When a pronoun functions as subject, it performs the action of an active verb or receives the action of a passive verb. Subjective pronouns appear in the series below:

1.   *Our expert witness, Dr. Simmons, and I will be in New Jersey on December 6 to discuss the exit accumulator tower with Eastland personnel.*

2.   *He and Sarah Richardson are co-chairs of the Business Practice Group in our Denver office.*

To determine the correct pronoun in a series, put parentheses around the first element of the series and the conjunction:

3.   *(Ms. Burton and) I will not compromise the terms of this proposal.*

Then you can see the pronoun alone in the sentence and choose the appropriate form.

4.3.3.2 Objective Pronouns

Use objective pronouns for direct objects, indirect objects, and objects of prepositions in a series. These pronouns include "me," "us," "you" (singular and plural), "him," "her," "it," and "them." Before you choose a pronoun, analyze its grammatical role.

Direct Objects

Use an objective pronoun for a direct object, which receives, or is affected by, the action of a verb:

1.   *If you have any questions about these claims, please call Susan Arnold or me in New York.*

CHAPTER FOUR

Objects of Prepositions

Choose the objective form of a pronoun for the object of a preposition. A preposition is a part of speech that links and relates a noun, pronoun, or gerund to some other word in the sentence. Examples include "at," "by," "of," "from," and "during." To determine the correct pronoun, first identify its role:

> 1. Amy Larson will work with <u>Bob Tanos and me</u> on August 15 to furnish supplemental responses to the interrogatories.

In sentence 1, "me" serves as object of the preposition "with."

Indirect Objects

Use the objective pronoun for an indirect object, which indicates to whom or for whom something is done. A preposition such as "to" or "for" may precede an indirect object:

> 1. Please reply to <u>Mr. Earl or me</u> by September 1.

If you omit the preposition, insert indirect objects after the verb:

> 2. If you fail to provide <u>Ms. More or me</u> with the requested documents by June 30, Thermco will file legal action against you.

Exercise

Identify the role and correct form of the pronouns in these sentences.

1. Thank you for meeting with Sonia Moore and (*I, me*) on Friday.
2. Personal guarantees should be delivered to Stuart Fremont or (*I, me*) by October 15.

Answers

1. Object of preposition: "me"
2. Indirect object: "me"

4.3.4 Correct Forms after "Than"

In a comparison, your choice of pronoun will depend on its grammatical role. First, identify words deleted after "than." Then select the correct form.

If the pronoun functions as subject, use the subjective form:

1(a) Mr. Morton is even more eager than I to avoid litigation with Zipco.

In sentence 1(a), the phrase "am eager" has been deleted after "I." Choosing a pronoun will be easier if you add the omitted words temporarily to your draft:

1(b) Mr. Morton is even more eager than I (am eager) to avoid litigation with Zipco.

When the pronoun serves as object in its clause, use the objective form:

2(a) After breaking her Last Chance Agreement, Ms. Simmons has contacted her supervisor more often than me.

The objective pronoun "me" is correct because it functions as the direct object of the verb "contacted." Sentence 2(a) is a more concise version of sentence 2(b):

2(b) After breaking her Last Chance Agreement, Ms. Simmons has contacted her supervisor more often than (she has contacted) me.

4.3.5 Intensive and Reflexive Pronouns

Attach the suffix "-self" to only two types of pronouns: intensive and reflexive. These pronouns refer to another noun or pronoun that denotes the same person(s) or object(s). Each pronoun should match its referent in gender and number. Singular forms include "myself," "yourself," "himself," "herself," and "itself." Plural forms are "ourselves," "yourselves," and "themselves."

CHAPTER FOUR

Use an intensive pronoun to emphasize its antecedent. Place the pronoun immediately after its referent:

> 1.   *<u>Vincent Company itself</u> has neither authorized nor condoned improper conduct in the employment area.*

Unlike intensive pronouns, reflexive pronouns appear in the predicate and refer to the subject of a sentence. They indicate that the subject acts upon itself. Reflexive pronouns may serve as the object of a verb, the object of a verbal, or the object of a preposition. In sentence 2, the reflexive pronoun is the direct object of the verb:

> 2.   *At all times, my client, Jonathan Berkshire, has attempted to conduct <u>himself</u> in conformity with the law.*

To be reflexive, a pronoun must refer to a noun in the sentence. Writers often use these pronouns incorrectly at the end of a letter:

> 3(a)   *If you have any questions regarding this matter, please call John or <u>myself</u>.*

In this example, "myself" has no referent. Use "me," the objective form, as direct object of the verb:

> 3(b)   *If you have any questions regarding this matter, please call John or <u>me</u>.*

Exercise

Identify the pronouns, their type, and their grammatical role in these sentences. Revise incorrect forms.

A. Please fax the information to either Thomas Peters or myself by Friday afternoon.

B. Mr. Hartwell himself will sever his company's relationship with Evergreen before September 30.

C. Ironically, Pal-Mar sees itself as exempt from enforcement of Markham's rights to payment under the Purchase Agreement.

Answers

A. Pronoun: "myself"

   Type: reflexive, but should be objective. "Myself" has no referent in this sentence and therefore cannot function as a reflexive pronoun.

   Role: indirect object

   Correct form: "me"

B. Pronoun: "himself"

   Type: intensive

   Role: emphasizes the subject

C. Pronoun: "itself"

   Type: reflexive

   Role: direct object

4.4 Subject-Verb Agreement

4.4.1 With Intervening Structures

Always match the verb with the subject, not with intervening words. As you revise, check for subject-verb agreement problems:

1(a) *Determination* of ownership of patent rights or shop rights *are a matter of state law.*

In sentence 1(a), the lawyer matched the verb, "are," to "patent rights" and "shop rights," objects of the preposition "of." Because those nouns directly precede the verb, the writer assumed that they were subjects.

To correct this problem, examine the main clause. First, separate the subject and verb from any intervening words and phrases. Set off these modifiers with parentheses:

> 1(b) <u>Determination</u> (of ownership of patent rights or shop rights) <u>are</u> a matter of state law.

Then match the verb to the singular subject, "determination":

> 1(c) <u>Determination</u> (of ownership of patent rights or shop rights) <u>is</u> a matter of state law.

In sentence 2(a), a lawyer used a singular subject with a plural verb:

> 2(a) Federal <u>registration</u> of the trademarks <u>entitle</u> Knowlton, Inc. to a statutory presumption that they are valid.

Under pressure to meet a deadline, the writer saw "trademarks . . . entitle" and did not look back to coordinate the verb with the subject. The verb should match the singular subject, "registration":

> 2(b) Federal <u>registration</u> of the trademarks <u>entitles</u> Knowlton, Inc. to a statutory presumption that they are valid.

Exercise

Correct the subject-verb agreement errors in these sentences.

A. The essential elements of each cause of action is beyond the scope of this memorandum.

B. In *Hedden v. Waldek,* the court held that the transfer of a deed to two attorneys for services rendered in litigation were fraudulent conveyances.

C. The level of benzene methylene and methyl ethyl ketone were measured by Dr. Black.

D. Each claim of the '899 and '194 patents constitute a separate invention.

E. If the price of a product in two areas change correlatively, then the two areas constitute one geographic market.

Answers

A. The plural subject, "the essential elements," requires a plural verb, "are."

B. Use a singular verb, "was," and a singular complement, "a fraudulent conveyance," with the singular subject, "the transfer."

C. If the two chemicals are mixed, the singular subject, "level," requires a singular verb phrase, "was measured." If the chemicals are separated, a plural subject, "levels," will require a plural verb, "were measured."

D. Use "constitutes," a singular verb, with "claim," a singular subject.

E. The singular subject, "price," requires a singular verb, "changes."

4.4.2   With Indefinite Pronoun Subjects

Use a singular verb after indefinite pronoun subjects, such as "each," "either," "neither," "one," "everybody," and "anyone." This subject-verb agreement is obvious when no prepositional phrase intervenes:

> 1(a)   *Each believes that the Paxton warranty will cover the cost of new parts.*

Match the subject with the verb even if a prepositional phrase separates them. For example, if a prepositional phrase, "of the buyers," is added after "each" in sentence 1(a), do not inadvertently match the verb to "buyers":

> 1(b)   *Each of the buyers believe that the Paxton warranty will cover the cost of new parts.*

Put parentheses around the prepositional phrase to clarify that "each" is the subject:

> 1(c)   _Each_ (of the buyers) _believes_ that the Paxton warranty will cover the cost of new parts.

Pronoun subjects such as "all," "any," "some," or "none" may take a singular or plural verb. Base your choice on context. If the noun referent for the pronoun is "countable," i.e., can be counted as separate units, use a plural verb:

> 2.   _All_ of the Pronto computers _were purchased_ from TechQwik.

When the referent for "all" cannot be counted as separate units, use a singular verb:

> 3.   _All_ of the technology in Chemco's Boston office _was upgraded_ last year.

Exercise

Correct errors in subject-verb agreement in these sentences.

A. Neither of the poultry producers have eliminated black pin feathers, which blemish the appearance of dressed chickens.

B. All the Chippendale real estate was sold on February 15.

C. None of the Webster documents was received by June 1.

Answers

A. Use "has," a singular verb, with "neither."

B. Correct

C. Use "were" because "documents" is a countable noun.

4.4.3   With Certain Conjunctions

Singular subjects joined by "or," "either. . . or," or "neither . . . nor" take a singular verb:

> 1.   A _corporation_ or a _partnership_ _qualifies_ for the tax deduction in Section 327(c).

2.   *Either <u>Tom Shannon</u> or <u>his coworker</u>, Alice Murdock, <u>is</u> responsible for the injury he suffered on July 15.*

3.   *Neither the <u>Vermont statute</u> nor the <u>New Hampshire statute</u> <u>applies</u> in this case.*

Use a plural verb with plural subjects linked with "or," "either . . . or," or "neither . . . nor":

4.   *<u>Sales</u> or <u>leases</u> of durable medical equipment to non-profit nursing facilities <u>are</u> exempt from taxation under § 5739.03(3).*

5.   *Either Ms. Smith's HospInsure <u>policies</u> or her MedCo <u>benefits</u> <u>cover</u> the rental cost for her Model 10-Z hospital bed.*

6.   *Neither the <u>Olsons</u> nor the <u>Pattersons</u> <u>have</u> induced former Med-Systems employees to reveal information that the law protects as confidential.*

When one subject is singular and one is plural, match the verb to the closer subject:

7(a)   *Neither the <u>other experts</u> nor <u>Dr. Horton</u> <u>is</u> qualified to testify about the Ridge County groundwater contamination.*

7(b)   *Neither <u>Dr. Horton</u> nor the other <u>experts</u> <u>are</u> qualified to testify about the Ridge County groundwater contamination.*

Exercise

Correct errors in subject-verb agreement in these sentences.

A. Neither Batco nor its subsidiaries plans to file a repletion action.

B. Either the Primary Leases or the Purchase Agreement contain language that will resolve General's claim for damages.

Answers

A. Use "plan" to match the closer subject, "subsidiaries."

B. Use "contains" to match the closer subject, "Purchase Agreement."

4.5 Dangling Modifiers

A dangling modifier is a verbal phrase or an adverbial clause that does not refer to its intended subject. A verbal is a verb form used as a noun, an adjective, or an adverb. Infinitives ("to show"), participles ("showing," "shown"), and gerunds ("showing") are verbals. To correct a "dangler," make its subject clear to the reader.

When no subject appears in an introductory verbal phrase, the phrase "links itself" to the subject of the main sentence:

> 1. After _installing_ asbestos for thirty years, _the plaintiff_ developed asbestosis.

"The plaintiff," subject of the independent clause, serves also as the subject of the introductory phrase.

Always note the relationship between the introductory phrase and its intended subject. In sentence 2(a), the introductory phrase is a dangling modifier:

> 2(a) In _determining_ whether Telcon breached the agreement, _the New Jersey standard_ was adopted by the court.

According to grammatical rules, the introductory phrase links itself to "the New Jersey standard," which serves as the subject of "determining." Yet the writer intended "the court" to be the subject of "determining." If you convert the independent clause to the active voice, "the court" will serve as the subject of both structures:

> 2(b) In _determining_ whether Telcon breached the agreement, _the court_ adopted the New Jersey standard.

You also can revise dangling modifiers by adding a subject to the verbal phrase. In sentence 3(a), "applying" links itself to "rash," which is not the intended subject:

> 3(a) _Applying_ Weed-O Pesticide, a _rash_ appeared on the plaintiff's skin.

To clarify the subject of "applying," insert "while the plaintiff was" in the introductory phrase:

> 3(b)   *While <u>the plaintiff was applying</u> Weed-O Pesticide, a rash appeared on her skin.*

Finally, substitute a noun for a gerund to correct some dangling modifiers. In sentence 4(a), the introductory phrase lacks an appropriate subject:

> 4(a)   *Without <u>proving</u> that a causal nexus exists between the pesticides and Ms. Fox's injury, <u>this evidence</u> is inadmissible.*

For clarity, substitute "proof" for "proving":

> 4(b)   *Without <u>proof</u> that a causal nexus exists between the pesticides and Ms. Fox's injury, this evidence is inadmissible.*

Unlike "proving," the noun "proof" does not require a subject.

Exercise

Eliminate the dangling modifier in this sentence.

> Showing "good faith and reasonable investigation," the burden of proof was met by Maxco.

Answer

> Showing "good faith and reasonable investigation," Maxco met the burden of proof.

4.5.1   Dangling Participles

Link each participial phrase clearly to its intended subject. A participial phrase consists of a participle followed by an object, a complement, or other modifiers. A participle is a verb form that functions as part of a verb phrase or as an adjective. To form the present participle, add "-ing" to the present tense of a verb, as in "judge—judging." For regular verbs, past participles consist of the present tense followed by "-ed," e.g., "recalled," "attached," and "measured." Irregular verbs use a different root word for the past participle, as in "catch—caught," "lead—led."

4.5.1.1 Introductory Phrases

Many dangling participles introduce a phrase that precedes a main clause. When no subject is present in the introductory phrase, the participle links itself to the subject of the main sentence. If that noun is not the intended subject, the participle is a dangling modifier:

> 1(a)　*Reassessing its earlier position, the regulation was changed by the FTC.*

The lawyer intended the introductory phrase, "reassessing its earlier position," to modify "the FTC." Yet according to grammatical rules, the initial phrase links itself to "the regulation," the subject of the independent clause.

To correct this problem, move the participial phrase next to the term it modifies. If you convert the main clause in sentence 1(a) to the active voice, "the FTC" will move to the subject position. The introductory phrase in sentence 1(b) then links itself to the correct subject:

> 1(b)　*Reassessing its earlier position, the FTC changed the regulation.*

The past participle in sentence 2(a) is a dangling modifier:

> 2(a)　*Blocked by barriers on the Oak Street easement, irreparable harm was suffered by Plaintiffs.*

The introductory phrase "blocked by barriers on the Oak Street easement" links itself to the subject of main sentence, "irreparable harm." Yet the intended subject is "Plaintiffs." To clarify the subject of "blocked," convert the independent clause to the active voice:

> 2(b)　*Blocked by barriers on the Oak Street easement, Plaintiffs suffered irreparable harm.*

You also can change the introductory phrase to a causal clause and place it at the end of the sentence:

> 2(c)　*Plaintiffs suffered irreparable harm because they were blocked by barriers on the Oak Street easement.*

Exercise

Correct the dangling participles in these sentences.

A. Informed of the deficit, a post-petition loan was requested by the company's president.

B. Applying the *Gibbons* reasonableness standard, it was held by the court that Home-Co did not unreasonably interfere with Mr. Johnson's rights.

C. Maintained under seal by Judge Epstein, Genex's attorneys reviewed the privileged documents on June 1.

D. Being a binding, bilateral contract, Defendant cannot cancel the Spantel Agreement.

Answers

A. Informed of the deficit, the company's president requested a post-petition loan.

B. Applying the *Gibbons* reasonableness standard, the court held that Home-Co did not unreasonably interfere with Mr. Johnson's rights.

C. 1. Maintained under seal by Judge Epstein, the privileged documents were reviewed by Genex's attorneys on June 1.

2. On June 1, Genex's attorneys reviewed the privileged documents, which Judge Epstein had maintained under seal.

D. Defendant cannot cancel the Spantel Agreement because it is a binding, bilateral contract.

4.5.1.2 Participles in Other Positions

Clarify the subject of participles in or after the main clause. These participles link themselves to the preceding noun if they are not preceded by a comma. When participles follow a comma, they link themselves to the subject of the main clause.

In sentence 1(a), the subject of "seeking" is not clear:

> 1(a) *Western Company filed suit in the district court <u>seeking</u> an injunction to stay the state court action.*

"Western Company" is the intended subject of "seeking," but because of its placement, "seeking" links itself to "district court." To clarify the subject, you can insert the participial phrase either at the sentence's beginning or just after the modified term:

> 1(b) *<u>Seeking</u> an injunction to stay the state court action, <u>Western Company</u> filed suit in the district court.*

1(c)   *Western Company, seeking* an injunction to stay the state court action, filed suit in the district court.

Sentence 2(a) contains a misplaced participle:

2(a)   *The Commission distinguished two cases from the PXO circumstances citing genuine issues of material fact with regard to PXO's rate design.*

The participle "citing" modifies "circumstances," but its intended subject is "the Commission." If you insert a comma before "citing," the participle will correctly link itself to "the Commission":

2(b)   *The Commission distinguished two cases from the PXO circumstances, citing genuine issues of material fact with regard to PXO's rate design.*

Divide long sentences that contain misplaced participles:

3(a)   *Stepco's annual report disclosed the initiation of a shareholder derivative action in California Supreme Court for the County of Los Angeles stemming from the company's investment in the hotel joint venture.*

In this sentence, two prepositional phrases separate the participle "stemming" and its subject, "action." To clarify the subject of the participle, divide the sentence before "stemming." Then change the participle to the past tense and add "this action" as subject:

3(b)   *Stepco's annual report disclosed the initiation of a shareholder derivative action in California Supreme Court for the County of Los Angeles. This action stemmed from the company's investment in the hotel joint venture.*

Exercise

Revise this sentence to clarify the subject of the participle.

BallCards, Inc. sued the National Players Association asserting six state law claims.

Answer

The correct subject of "asserting" is "BallCards, Inc.," not "National Players Association."

Revision: BallCards, Inc. sued the National Players Association, asserting six state law claims.

Revision: Asserting six state law claims, BallCards, Inc. sued the National Players Association.

4.5.2   Dangling Gerund Phrases

Avoid dangling gerund phrases. A gerund is a verb form that ends in "-ing" and functions as a noun. In sentence l(a), the gerund "testing" is a "dangler":

1(a)   After _testing_ positively for cocaine, _Teleco_ fired Ms. Turner.

According to grammatical rules, if no subject for a gerund phrase appears in the sentence, the gerund links itself to the subject of the main sentence, "Teleco."

You can correct a dangling gerund phrase in two ways. First, add a subject for the verb in the introductory phrase and change the gerund to the past tense of the verb:

1(b)   After _Ms. Turner tested_ positively for cocaine, _Teleco_ fired her.

You also can convert the main sentence in 1(a) to the passive voice. Then the intended subject for the gerund serves as subject of the main sentence:

1(c)   After _testing_ positively for cocaine, _Ms. Turner_ was fired by Teleco.

Exercise

Correct the dangling gerund phrases in these sentences.

A. In determining whether a servient estate owner interferes with the dominant owner's easement, a reasonableness standard has been adopted by New York courts.

B. After arriving at the hospital, an insurance number was assigned to Ms. Johnson.

Answers

A. In determining whether a servient estate owner interferes with the dominant owner's easement, New York courts have adopted a reasonableness standard.

B. 1. After arriving at the hospital, Ms. Johnson was assigned an insurance number.

   2. After Ms. Johnson arrived at the hospital, she was assigned an insurance number.

4.5.3   Dangling Infinitive Phrases

Clarify the subject of dangling infinitive phrases. These "danglers" result when an introductory infinitive phrase does not refer clearly to its intended subject. For example, the "to" phrase in sentence 1(a) is a dangling modifier:

> 1(a)   <u>To be certified</u> as a class pursuant to Rule 23, <u>all prerequisites</u> must be met by the Denfield Plaintiffs.

Because no subject appears in the infinitive phrase, it links itself to "prerequisites," the subject of the independent clause.

To correct this problem, move the intended subject of the infinitive phrase. In sentence 1(a), "the Denfield Plaintiffs" is the subject of "to be certified." Move that noun phrase into the subject position of the independent clause:

> 1(b)   <u>To be certified</u> as a class pursuant to Rule 23, <u>the Denfield Plaintiffs</u> must meet all prerequisites.

Then try a second technique, adding a subject before the infinitive phrase:

>   *1(c)   For the Denfield Plaintiffs to be certified as a class pursuant to Rule 23, all prerequisites must be met.*

Because this sentence is awkward, use the revision in sentence 1(b).

Exercise

Correct the dangling infinitive phrases in these sentences:

A. To transfer shares, the prior written consent of the other shareholders must be obtained by a party.

B. To be held liable as aiders and abetters, Section 14(e) must have been violated by Ms. Vail and Mr. Eaton

Answers

A. To transfer shares, a party must obtain the prior written consent of the other shareholders.

B. To be held liable as aiders and abettors, Ms. Vail and Mr. Eaton must have violated Section 14(e).

4.5.4   Dangling Adverbial Clauses

Avoid dangling adverbial clauses. In these clauses, the subject is implied, not stated. An adverbial clause that does not refer to its intended subject is a dangling modifier.

If no subject appears in an introductory clause, it links itself to the subject of the main sentence:

>   *1(a)   When offered a Last Chance Agreement, a drug test was refused by Mr. Powell.*

The subject of the main sentence, "a drug test," serves as subject of "offered." The verb's intended subject is, of course, "Mr. Powell."

To correct this problem, use the two solutions discussed earlier for dangling modifiers. You can convert the main sentence to the active voice:

> 1(b)   When _offered_ a Last Chance Agreement, _Mr. Powell_ refused a drug test.

The introductory clause then links itself to "Mr. Powell," the subject of the main clause.

Alternatively, add a subject to the adverbial clause. Move "Mr. Powell" into the introductory clause, add "was," and use a pronoun as subject for the main sentence:

> 1(c)   When _Mr. Powell was offered_ a Last Chance Agreement, _he refused a drug test._

Exercise
Correct the dangling modifier in this sentence.
While crossing the Park Street easement, Tarco Paving prevented Plaintiff from turning onto Oak Street.
Answer
While Plaintiff was crossing the Park Street easement, Tarco Paving prevented her from turning onto Oak Street.

4.6 The Subjunctive Mood

Writers may choose among three moods: indicative, imperative, and subjunctive. Moods require different verb forms and reflect the function of an assertion. Statements and questions are expressed in the indicative. The imperative mood is used in command forms. Lawyers employ the subjunctive mostly in two contexts: in contrary-to-fact clauses and after "urge-demand" verbs.

4.6.1   Forms

The subjunctive mood differs from the indicative in only three forms:

Verb "to be"

Present, singular or plural: "be"
Past, singular or plural: "were"

Other Verbs, with third-person singular subjects

Present, singular only: "see"

To create the third-person singular of all verbs except "to be," drop the "-s" ending from the indicative form, e.g., "sees—see."

4.6.2   In Contrary-to-Fact Clauses

Your choice between the indicative and subjunctive depends on whether a clause is contrary to fact. Use the subjunctive in an "if" clause to express a condition that is not true. Choose an indicative verb if the condition may or may not be true.

In the sentences below, subjunctive verbs convey contrary-to-fact conditions:

1.   *If the property <u>were</u> zoned for commercial use, the commission would have approved Ms. Conlon's building permit.*

2.   *If the court <u>were</u> to grant Plaintiff's motion, Alco would suffer severe and irreparable harm.*

Yet not every "if" clause is contrary to fact. Many clauses that begin with "if" express a condition that may or may not be true. For example, in sentence 3 the indicative verb is correct:

3.   *Courts will not uphold a damage award if it <u>is</u> "grossly excessive," clearly not supported by evidence, or based on speculation only.*

4.6.3   After "Urge-Demand" Verbs

Use the subjunctive in "that" clauses after verbs of urging or demanding:

1.   *BriCorp <u>insisted</u> that Mr. Byron <u>relocate</u> to its Los Angeles office despite an implied contract that he would work in Houston.*

2.   *After submitting the plan for approval, the partner <u>urged</u> that the site <u>be zoned</u> "commercial—fourth height and area."*

Verbs in this category include "demand," "recommend," "urge," "insist," "request," "move," "propose," and "suggest."

Many nouns formed on the basis of these verbs also are followed by the subjunctive in a "that" clause:

3.   *Scholl's <u>demand</u> that Layco <u>pay</u> damages is unreasonable.*

When a verb outside the "demand-urge" category is followed by a "that" clause, use the indicative:

4.   *Ms. Williams erroneously <u>claims</u> that Ridgwood Company <u>is</u> responsible for the line breakage.*

Exercise

A. Correct the mood of the underlined verbs as needed.

1. Mr. Little asserts that if he <u>was</u> female, he would not have been fired.

2. Plaintiff's lawyers erroneously claim that the Mother Hubbard clause <u>covers</u> this indebtedness.

3. The court held that the Jackson Purchase Agreement <u>is</u> enforceable.

4. In-house counsel recommends that Dentex <u>claims</u> damages based on the market price of goods under Section 2713.

B. Identify the mood of the underlined verbs. Create a context that makes each choice correct.

1. If Mr. Williams <u>was</u> in charge of the PetroChem fuel tank excavation, he failed to carry out his duties.

2. If the Compatibility Standard <u>were</u> applicable, Wood's apartment project would have been prohibited.

Answers

A. 1. Use "were," the subjunctive, in a contrary-to-fact clause.

2. Correct

3. Correct

4. Use "claim," the subjunctive, after "recommends."

B. 1. Mood: indicative

   Context: uncertainty

   Mr. Williams may or may not have been in charge.

2. Mood: subjunctive

   Context: contrary-to-fact

   Because the project was not prohibited, the standard was not applicable.

CHAPTER FIVE

~ *Punctuation* ~

Punctuation clarifies logical relationships between sentences and between parts of sentences. Readers rely on punctuation to guide them. To punctuate correctly, analyze the grammatical structure of each sentence and apply the rules discussed in this chapter.

5.1 Commas

5.1.1 Commas in Compound Sentences

Use a comma before the conjunction in a compound sentence. A compound sentence contains two independent clauses joined by a coordinating conjunction. These "glue words" include "and," "but," "or," "nor," "for," "so," and "yet." Each clause must contain a subject and a verb, and be able to stand alone as a complete sentence. Before you place a comma before a coordinating conjunction, try a simple test. Analyze the structure of each clause. Does it have both a subject and a verb? Could it stand alone as a sentence? If so, add a comma before the conjunction. Note the correct punctuation in the compound sentences below:

1. *Johnson's title was "Midwest Consultant," and his responsibilities included assisting in the development of ABC's national consulting practice.*

2. *An employer's legitimate decisions may offend an employee's subjective preference, but they do not violate the reasonable person test.*

3. *Dr. Collins did not cite Jones Dairy Farm, nor did she discuss the appropriateness of a transfer under 29 U.S.C. § 1404.*

Omit the comma if the sentence contains a compound predicate (one subject and two verbs):

4. *The conduct fell within the NLRA's exclusive jurisdiction and did not violate a general law.*

5. *Baxco denied Mr. Plimpton's request to transfer and did not investigate his complaints.*

In sentence 4, "the conduct" serves as the subject of "fell" and "did not violate." No subject appears before the second verb phrase. In sentence 5, the writer also used a compound predicate. Because "Baxco" is the subject of "denied" and "did not investigate," no comma precedes "and."

Omit the comma in a compound sentence with short clauses:

6. *Jackson did not respond and counsel provided no answers to the discovery.*

But add the comma if the series near the conjunction could create confusion:

7. *The carriers' denial forced Phonco to sue them and their affiliates, and to pursue its claims through extensive discovery and trial preparation.*

The comma guides the reader through three series joined by "and."

Exercise

Add commas as needed in these sentences.

A. The parties did not resolve the dispute by June 30 so the Plan Assumption documents became the Product Plan for the next year.

B. BankTwo and its agents conspired to mismanage the Oakwood Trust Tree Farm and attempted to conceal their actions from the client.

C. Ertex submitted claims for the environmental cleanup costs to its comprehensive general liability carriers but all the claims were denied.

Answers

A. Add a comma before "so" in this compound sentence.

B. No comma. The second verb phrase has no subject.

C. Add a comma before "but" in this compound sentence.

5.1.2   Correcting Comma Splices

Do not link independent clauses with only a comma. A comma is not strong enough to join independent clauses without a conjunction. Note the comma splice in sentence 1(a):

1(a)   *Central wanted to change the zoning to M-2 Heavy Manufacturing, City Council did not approve the request.*

As you revise, look for comma splices. Analyze the context and logical relationship between the two sentences. Then use one of four techniques to correct the error.

Revision 1:   Add a coordinating conjunction, such as "and," "but," "or," "nor," "for," "so," or "yet" after the comma:

1(b)   *Central wanted to change the zoning to M-2 Heavy Manufacturing, but City Council did not approve the request.*

This correction makes the sentence smoother and less abrupt.

Revision 2:   Insert a semicolon between the main clauses:

1(c)   *Central wanted to change the zoning to M-2 Heavy Manufacturing; City Council did not approve the request.*

This revision pushes the independent clauses together to emphasize their close conceptual relationship.

Revision 3:   Separate the main clauses with a semicolon and a conjunctive adverb. These adverbs include "thus," "furthermore," "hence," "however," "indeed," "instead," "moreover," "nevertheless," "nonetheless," "therefore," and similar terms. The adverb adds a specific relationship between the two clauses:

1(d)   *Central wanted to change the zoning to M-2 Heavy Manufacturing; however, City Council did not approve the request.*

If you prefer, place the adverb after the subject:

> 1(e) *Central wanted to change the zoning to M-2 Heavy Manufacturing;*
> *City Council, however, did not approve the request.*

Revision 4:   Create two separate sentences:

> 1(f) *Central wanted to change the zoning to M-2 Heavy Manufacturing.*
> *But City Council did not approve the request.*

With this revision, each sentence receives equal and separate emphasis.

Exercise

Revise this comma splice.

> Ms. Roth cannot state a claim for the administrative fee's recovery, Count I should be dismissed.

Answers

Correct this comma splice with any of the four methods. You can add coordinating conjunctions and conjunctive adverbs to clarify the relationships between the two clauses:

1. Ms. Roth cannot state a claim for the administrative fee's recovery, so Count I should be dismissed.

2. Ms. Roth cannot state a claim for the administrative fee's recovery; Count I should be dismissed.

3. Ms. Roth cannot state a claim for the administrative fee's recovery; thus, Count I should be dismissed.

4. Ms. Roth cannot state a claim for the for the administrative fee's recovery. Thus, Count I should be dismissed.

5.1.3   Commas after Introductory Structures

Use a comma after adverbial clauses, long phrases, and transitions at the beginning of a sentence. The comma signals a break in thought between the introductory element and the main clause.

Introductory adverbial clauses, which contain a subject and a verb, function as adverbs. These clauses indicate time, place, cause, condition, concession, comparison, purpose, or result. Set off introductory clauses with a comma:

1. *Because Mr. Lily's back injury does not substantially limit a major life activity*, he does not have a disability.

2. *Although the two courts disagree about when a cause of action accrues, the* Kilgore *decision gives more weight to the state court's prior opinion.*

3. *If the court dismisses the complaint*, Bushnell can move to reopen the judgment under Rule 59(e).

Add a comma after long introductory phrases. A phrase is a sequence of grammatically related words without a subject and a predicate. Introductory phrases begin with prepositions or participles. In the following sentences, commas set off phrases that precede the main clause:

4. *During each contract negotiation*, ABC Steel proposed expanded rights to use supervisors to perform bargaining unit work.

5. *In Rutland v. Swift Chemical Co., 351 So. 2d 324 (1977), the plaintiff brought an action for damages relating to poor performance of fertilizer manufactured by the defendant.*

6. *After installing asbestos insulation for forty years*, Mr. Winslow developed asbestosis.

Use a comma after conjunctive adverbs and other transitions at the beginning of a sentence:

7. *Moreover*, Plastica owes no special duty to Ms. Ames.

8. *Thus*, the statute would bar all Plaintiff's warranty claims.

9. *Finally*, Hirsch lacks standing to challenge the behavior of Zephyr's Alaska affiliates.

To prevent misreading, insert a comma after some short introductory elements:

10(a) *During processing chemicals sometimes escape into the atmosphere and are carried beyond the plant grounds.*

Add a comma to mark the end of the introductory phrase:

> *10(b) <u>During processing</u>, chemicals sometimes escape into the atmosphere and are carried beyond the plant grounds.*

Exercise

Add commas after introductory elements in these sentences.

A. To succeed Morton must establish that his working conditions were so intolerable that a reasonable person would have felt compelled to quit.

B. Since the fertilizer did not include a promise of future performance the case did not fit into the statute's narrow exception.

C. As table 14 shows our client, Hobbs, plans to acquire 10 percent of Fixco's stock by December 31.

D. Thus the court acknowledged the time of the wrongful act as the time of accrual for the limitation period.

E. With the assistance of Percolator Electric Company Aldersyde installed a mushroom-shaped control button.

F. In intra-enterprise conspiracy corporations that share complete or common ownership allegedly conspire.

G. After the CEO approved the repayment package and the appointment of a conservator Williams prepared a letter to Jean Watkins.

Answers

A. Add a comma after "to succeed," an introductory phrase, to prevent misreading.

B. Insert a comma after the adverbial clause, "since the fertilizer did not include a promise of future performance."

C. Place a comma after "shows" to eliminate ambiguity.

D. Set off "thus," a conjunctive adverb, with a comma.

E. Add a comma after the long phrase, "with the assistance of Percolator Electric Company," to prevent misreading.

F. Insert a comma after the introductory phrase, "in intra-enterprise conspiracy," to prevent misreading.

G. Add a comma after the introductory clause, "after the CEO approved the repayment package and the appointment of a conservator."

5.1.4   Commas before Sentence Modifiers

To prevent misreading, set off sentence modifiers with commas. These adverbial phrases modify or explain the rest of the sentence. In sentence 1, no punctuation separates the independent clause and the sentence modifier:

> 1(a)   *The partner suggested that we base our argument on the ruling in Mitchell given the uncertainty of Dr. Carpenter's testimony.*

Add a comma after "Mitchell" to set off this phrase:

> 1(b)   *The partner suggested that we base our argument on the ruling in Mitchell, given the uncertainty of Dr. Carpenter's testimony.*

Exercise

Add a comma to set off the sentence modifier.

On February 1, Cooper Company will owe Sloan Savings Bank $55,000 as shown in Table 3 of the revised schedule of payments.

Answer

Use a comma before "as shown in Table 3 of the revised schedule of payments," a sentence modifier.

5.1.5   Punctuating Restrictive and Nonrestrictive Structures

5.1.5.1   Relative Clauses

One of the most subtle rules of punctuation applies to restrictive and nonrestrictive clauses. To punctuate a clause, look at its relationship to the modified noun.

5.1.5.2   Nonrestrictive: "Which"

Use a comma and "which" to introduce nonrestrictive relative clauses. These clauses add extra information about the modified noun in a by-the-way fashion. They do not create a subcategory of the noun or limit it to a specific type. To identify a nonrestrictive clause, ask: "Do I need the clause to identify the noun?" If the answer is "no," insert a comma and add "which" at the clause's beginning.

The relative clause in sentence 1 is nonrestrictive:

1.   *The only relevant exception in this case is exception 6(e)(3)(c)(i),* <u>*which allows disclosure "when so directed by a court preliminary to,*</u> <u>*or in connection with, a judicial proceeding."*</u>

The clause modifies "exception," a noun precisely identified by five numbers and letters. The relative clause provides extra information about that noun in a by-the-way fashion.

The nonrestrictive clause in sentence 2 modifies "Section 1.4":

2.   *Section 1.4,* <u>*which states that Barnett Company must pay for*</u> <u>*materials*</u>, *also gives Carlton-Tex authority over the plans.*

The clause does not distinguish one section from another but provides additional information about the section's contents. The number clearly identifies the section.

In sentences 3 and 4, the relative clauses are nonrestrictive:

3.   *Defendant's brief omits* Jones Dairy Farm, <u>*which is the leading case*</u> <u>*regarding the appropriateness of a transfer under 28 U.S.C. § 1404.*</u>

4.   *The court relied on O.R.C. § 5709.01,* <u>*which states that personal*</u> <u>*property is taxable when "used in business."*</u>

In these sentences, the "which" clause adds extra information about a precisely identified noun.

5.1.5.3 Restrictive: "That"

Do not set off restrictive clauses with commas. These clauses create a subcategory of a general noun. The information in a restrictive clause is essential to the modified noun's meaning. Use "that" to introduce a restrictive clause that modifies an inanimate object.

In sentence 1, a restrictive clause limits the definition of "suits":

1. In constructive trust cases, courts will bar suits *that are not brought "within a reasonable amount of time."*

The restrictive clause identifies the category of suits that courts will bar. They won't bar all suits, but only those not brought within a reasonable amount of time.

The underlined clause in sentence 2 is restrictive:

2. Conscious wrongdoers must surrender any profit *that they obtained from the conversion of the rightful owner's property.*

This relative clause creates a subcategory of the general noun "profit." Although conscious wrongdoers do not have to surrender all profit, they must give up profit obtained from the conversion of the rightful owner's property.

The relative clause in sentence 3 is also restrictive:

3. Directors must not violate any legal or moral duty *that they owe to the corporation or its stockholders.*

The writer uses a "that" clause to identify a specific type of duty. The directors' regulations control only those duties "they owe to the corporation or its stockholders," not all legal or moral duties.

5.1.5.4 Restrictive or Nonrestrictive

Depending on context, the same clause can be restrictive or nonrestrictive:

1. The claim is clearly barred by O.R.C. § 2711.13, *which requires such actions to be filed within three months.*

2. The court applied the O.R.C. section *that requires such actions to be filed within three months.*

The clause in sentence 1 is nonrestrictive because it adds extra information in a by-the-way fashion about a noun precisely identified by its number. Unlike a restrictive clause, the nonrestrictive clause does not create a subcategory of a general noun. Yet in sentence 2, the same clause is restrictive. In this context, many sections of O.R.C. might be relevant. The restrictive clause distinguishes one section from all others. Thus, the identification of "section" depends on information in the clause.

Sentences 3(a) and 3(b) provide a similar contrast. If an office contains only one copy center, which is located on the third floor, the clause in sentence 3(a) is nonrestrictive:

> 3(a)   On July 27, city inspectors discovered dangerous levels of methylene chloride in the copy center, *which is on the third floor*.

Because there is only one copy center in the office, this relative clause provides additional information in a by-the-way fashion.

If the office has two copy centers, one on the third floor and one on the fourth floor, the same clause is restrictive:

> 3(b)   On July 27, city inspectors discovered dangerous levels of methylene chloride in the copy center *that is on the third floor*.

The relative clause in sentence 3(b) identifies the copy center and distinguishes it from the fourth floor center. You can shorten the sentence by dropping "that is":

> 3(c)   On July 27, city inspectors discovered dangerous levels of methylene chloride in the copy center *on the third floor*.

This deletion demonstrates the close relationship between the modified noun and the restrictive clause.

5.1.5.5   "Who," "Whose," and "Whom"

Relative clauses that modify human nouns begin with "who," "whom," or "whose," depending on the noun's role in the clause. To determine the correct punctuation, analyze the clause's relationship to the modified noun.

Nonrestrictive clauses modify human nouns below. The clause in sentence 1 adds extra information about Axco's board chairman:

> 1.   The Axco CFO, *who opposed the move*, suggested a population density requirement.

The modified noun, "the Axco CFO," is precisely identified and does not depend on the clause for clarification. Similarly, in sentence 2, a comma sets off the nonrestrictive clause:

2.   *The City sent tax refunds to all Greenwood residents, <u>who also will receive a credit on next year's return</u>.*

An adjective phrase, "all Greenwood," tells you exactly which residents received the refund. The relative clause provides extra by-the-way information about the modified phrase.

Do not set off restrictive clauses with commas. A restrictive clause identifies "residents" in sentence 3:

3.   *Vinecrest Builders sent a letter about the proposed home for the elderly to all city residents <u>whose property abuts the park</u>.*

The restrictive clause in sentence 4 identifies the City Council members quoted in the *Daily Dispatch*:

4.   *The* Daily Dispatch *quoted three City Council members who voted <u>against the proposal</u>.*

The clause creates a subcategory of "members."

Exercise

A. Determine whether the relative clauses in the sentences below are restrictive or nonrestrictive. Then select the correct relative pronoun and add commas as needed.

1. This section refers to contemptuous acts (*that, which*) also violate federal criminal statutes.

2. The owner paid additional financing costs for the period of delay plus 6 percent interest on the funds (*that, which*) she had invested in the project.

3. The tort is derived from the Restatement Second of Torts, Section 522 (*that, which*) creates a cause of action for information supplied for the guidance of others.

4. When a fraudulent conveyance occurs, the creditor can retrieve the assets (*that, which*) the transferee holds.

5. A debenture is a credit instrument (*that, which*) does not give its holder an equity interest in the issuer.

6. Dr. Walsh did nothing (*that, which*) substantially assisted in his colleague's fraudulent activity.

7. The second statute exempted the Cedar Cemetery Association (*that, which*) objected to the proposed zoning change.

8. Litigation is pending in Michigan against Universal Mail Shopping Service (*that, which*) sells goods by catalog to customers nationwide.

9. Stockholders in a closely held corporation cannot compete for business or clients (*that, which*) in equity or fairness belong to the corporation.

10. The plaintiffs wish to litigate against companies (*that, which*) maintain their principal place of business in New York.

11. Corporate directors have the duty to oppose a takeover offer (*that, which*) would be detrimental to the interests of the corporation and its stockholders.

B. Explain why the clause in this sentence is restrictive.

Plaintiff was not a substantial participant in any fraud that relates to the sale of Apex stock.

C. Explain the difference in meaning between these two sentences. Create a context if necessary.

1. To meet federal regulations, SIPCO will provide a system to inspect interior piping that is not easily accessible.

2. To meet federal regulations, SIPCO will provide a system to inspect interior piping, which is not easily accessible.

D. Determine whether the relative clauses in these sentences are restrictive or nonrestrictive. Correct the punctuation as needed.

1. The union filed Grievance R4252 on behalf of Ronald J. Curtis who complained that Lanco failed to accommodate his religious beliefs and practices.

2. The residents who objected to the new facility comprised only 5 percent of the city's population.

3. Paul L. Shaw, Jr. who has a lien on the Blumenthal property can recover tort damages against parties, who prevent execution of the lien.

Answers

A. 1. Restrictive. Use "that."

2. Restrictive. Use "that."

3. Nonrestrictive. Use "which" and add a comma after "Section 522."

4. Restrictive. Use "that."

5. Restrictive. Use "that."

6. Restrictive. Use "that."

7. Nonrestrictive. Use "which" and add a comma after "Association."

8. Nonrestrictive. Use "which" and add a comma after "Service."

9. Restrictive. Use "that."

10. Restrictive. Use "that."

11. Restrictive. Use "that."

B. The "that" clause is restrictive because it limits the definition of "fraud" to one specific type.

C. 1. The restrictive clause creates a subcategory of the general noun phrase "interior piping." In this context, only some of the interior piping is not easily accessible.

2. This nonrestrictive clause adds extra information about a precisely identified noun phrase, "interior piping." In this context, all interior piping is not easily accessible.

D. 1. Nonrestrictive clause: "who complained that Lanco failed to accommodate his religious beliefs and practices." Add a comma after "Curtis."

2. Restrictive clause: "who objected to the new facility." Punctuation is correct.

3. Nonrestrictive clause: "who has a lien on the Blumenthal property." Add a comma before "who" and after "property."

Restrictive clause: "who prevent execution of the lien." Delete the comma before "who."

5.1.5.6 Adverbial Clauses

Apply the restrictive/nonrestrictive distinction when you punctuate adverbial clauses. These clauses modify verbs, adverbs, or adjectives and explain when, how, or where something is done.

Set off nonrestrictive adverbial clauses with commas. A nonrestrictive adverbial clause adds extra information about a precisely identified modified term. For example, the "when" clause in sentence 1 is nonrestrictive:

1.   *The Whitestone Group submitted items listed on Table A on September 24, <u>when Burton sent its second request for documents</u>.*

"September 24" specifies the day that the Whitestone Group submitted certain items. The clause "when Burton sent its second request for documents" does not define this date or state an essential condition of the submission. Instead, the clause provides additional information in a by-the-way fashion.

The "where" clause in sentence 2 is also nonrestrictive:

2.   *Plaintiff Simon Franklin resides in Evansville, Indiana, <u>where defendant Telecable provides services</u>.*

The city and state names define the location. The "where" clause adds extra information in a by-the-way manner.

Do not set off restrictive adverbial clauses with commas. These clauses establish an essential condition for the action or state of being expressed by the modified term. In sentence 3, a restrictive clause modifies "is enforced" and explains the conditions for enforcing the penalty:

3.   *The penalty is enforced <u>when the owner of the property fails to renew the license</u>.*

The "when" clause limits the scope of enforcement to certain conditions.

In sentence 4, the writer correctly punctuated a restrictive clause:

4.   *Conco's offer is void <u>where it is prohibited by law</u>.*

The clause "where it is prohibited by law" restricts the conditions of the offer. The adverbial clause explains an essential condition for the phrase "is void."

Exercise

Identify restrictive and nonrestrictive adverbial clauses in these sentences. Add commas as needed.

A. The law does not apply when one party fails to pay interest by the end of the fiscal year.

B. Bi-More Company mailed its proof of claim to Mobile, Alabama where the suit was filed.

C. Add sales taxes where they are applicable.

D. Debco must submit a response to the Plan Assumption Documents by June 30 when the board of directors meets in New York.

E. No surcharge applies if payment is received within thirty days.

Answers

A. Restrictive clause: "when one party fails to pay interest by the end of the fiscal year." The clause establishes an essential condition for the law's application. No comma.

B. Nonrestrictive clause: "where the suit was filed." "Mobile, Alabama" is a precisely identified noun. Add a comma after "Alabama."

C. Restrictive clause: "where they are applicable." The clause establishes an essential condition for the addition of sales taxes. No comma.

D. Nonrestrictive clause: "when the board of directors meets in New York." "June 30" is a precisely identified noun. Add a comma after "June 30."

E. Restrictive clause: "if payment is received within 30 days." The clause establishes an essential condition for the application of the surcharge. No comma.

5.1.5.7 Phrases

The principles that govern the punctuation of clauses apply also to restrictive and nonrestrictive phrases. When serving as an adjective, a nonrestrictive phrase adds extra information about a precisely identified noun. Set off nonrestrictive phrases with commas:

1.   Ms. Simmons, *relying on a provision in the defendants' contract*, received $20,000 in damages.

A nonrestrictive phrase, "relying on a provision in defendants' contract," describes a precisely identified noun, "Ms. Simmons," in a by-the-way fashion.

Do not use commas with a restrictive phrase. A restrictive adjective phrase limits the definition of the modified noun by creating a subcategory:

2. *Potter, Inc. must enforce the attendance policy <u>negotiated with the union</u>.*

The phrase "negotiated with the union" establishes a subcategory for the noun phrase "attendance policy."

The same phrase can be nonrestrictive or restrictive, depending on context. For example, the phrase in sentence 3(a) is nonrestrictive:

3(a) *On August 15, the court rejected Claim No. 177, <u>submitted by Exco</u>.*

The nonrestrictive phrase provides extra information in a by-the-way manner about "Claim No. 177," a precisely identified noun. But the same phrase is restrictive in sentence 3(b):

3(b) *On August 15, the court rejected the claim <u>submitted by Exco</u>.*

In this context, claims were also by other parties. The restrictive phrase "submitted by Exco" creates a subcategory of a general noun. No comma precedes the phrase.

Exercise

Identify the restrictive and nonrestrictive phrases in these sentences. Revise the punctuation as needed.

A. Ms. Stockton and Mr. Fox did not discuss any issues, concerning bankruptcy.

B. Mr. Fisher frustrated by Telecable's fees for late payments filed a complaint on March 31.

C. This memorandum will address all issues, raised by Park, Inc.

D. The Uniform Partnership Act enacted on September 17, 1962 established the partners' liability.

Answers

A. A restrictive phrase, "concerning bankruptcy," restricts "issues" to one type. Delete the comma.

B. A nonrestrictive phrase, "frustrated by Telecable's fees for late payments," adds extra information about Mr. Fisher. Set off the phrase with commas.

C. A restrictive phrase, "raised by Park, Inc.," creates a subcategory of "issues." Delete the comma.

D. A nonrestrictive phrase, "enacted on September 17, 1962," adds extra information about the Uniform Partnership Act. Set off the phrase with commas.

5.1.5.8 Appositives

To punctuate appositives, first determine whether they are restrictive or nonrestrictive. An appositive is a noun that stands next to another noun to identify, explain, or supplement its meaning. The appositive plays the same grammatical role as the term that precedes it.

A nonrestrictive appositive adds extra, nonessential information about a precisely identified noun. Set off a nonrestrictive appositive with commas:

> I. *Buy-More Supermarket #834, <u>a class member</u>, failed to file a proof of claim with the clerk of courts.*

Since "Buy-More Supermarket #834" is a precisely identified noun, the appositive, "a class member," provides information in a by-the-way fashion.

In sentence 2, the appositive is also nonrestrictive:

2.   *The Department of Labor refused to grant professional status to Robert M. Jackson, <u>an entrepreneur</u>.*

The name "Robert M. Jackson" is a precisely identified noun. Thus, the appositive, "an entrepreneur," adds extra, by-the-way information about Mr. Jackson.

A restrictive appositive creates a subcategory of a general noun and limits its definition. For example, the phrase "Rickles Dairy" names the class member in sentence 3:

3.   *Class member <u>Rickles Dairy</u> is seeking to overturn the final judgment in an antitrust class action.*

Because it creates a subcategory of the general noun "class member," the appositive is restrictive and is not set off by commas.

A restrictive appositive serves as the object of a preposition in sentence 4:

4.   *The* Trans World Airlines v. Hardison *court focused on the phrase "reasonable accommodation."*

"Reasonable accommodation," the appositive, creates a subcategory of the noun "phrase." Because the appositive is restrictive, no commas are necessary.

Exercises

Identify restrictive and nonrestrictive appositives, describe their grammatical function, and add commas as needed in these sentences.

A. Persons in two professional fields law and medicine can easily attain entry into the United States.

B. Courts define the term "religion" in broad terms.

C. For immigration purposes, the agency reclassified two positions business executives and language translators.

D. Ms. Wilson wishes to establish a trust for her brother Andrew.

E. Satellite Chemical a reprocessor of chemical wastes began operations in Baltimore last year.

F. According to arbitrator Anita Allen, Mr. Curren did not prove he had a bonafide religious belief that conflicted with his work schedule.

G. The government labeled Sharp-O-Darts, a lawn dart game as unsafe.

Answers

A. Nonrestrictive appositive: "law and medicine"

Function: object of preposition. Set off the appositive with commas.

B. Restrictive appositive: "religion"

Function: direct object. Punctuation is correct.

C. Nonrestrictive appositive: "business executives and language translators"

Function: object. Add a comma after "positions."

D. Restrictive or nonrestrictive appositive: "Andrew." If Ms. Wilson has more than one brother, "Andrew" is a restrictive appositive and should not be set off with a comma. If she has only one brother, "Andrew" is a nonrestrictive appositive and should be preceded a comma.

Function: object of preposition.

E. Nonrestrictive appositive: "a reprocessor of chemical wastes"

Function: subject. Set off the appositive with commas.

F. Restrictive appositive: "Anita Allen"

Function: subject. Punctuation is correct.

G. Nonrestrictive appositive: "a lawn dart game"

Function: direct object. Add a comma after "game."

5.2 Semicolons

A semicolon consists of both a period and a comma. This structure reflects the semicolon's functions and relative strength. A semicolon is stronger than a comma, yet weaker than a period.

5.2.1 Linking Independent Clauses with Semicolons

Use a semicolon to join short independent clauses not linked by "and," "but," "or," "nor," "for," "so," or "yet." The clauses should be closely related in meaning:

1. *Ms. White asked for an extension; the committee denied her request.*

Unlike a conjunction or period, a semicolon can link two independent clauses without a pause. A semicolon pushes two clauses together, stressing their juxtaposition and creating a compact, punchy sentence.

You also may use a semicolon to separate two closely related independent clauses joined by a conjunctive adverb or transitional phrase. Conjunctive adverbs include "therefore," "hence," "however," "thus," "moreover," and many others. In addition, phrases such as "for example," "on the contrary," and "in fact" link independent clauses. Semicolons precede the connectives in sentences 2 and 3:

2. *Lanco has requested those documents in written discovery; however, Apson refuses to produce them.*

3. *On March 23, Councilman Robert Avis appeared before the zoning board; in fact, he urged the board members not to grant a temporary Bath Permit.*

Exercise

Add semicolons as needed in these sentences.

A. The prior law likewise established a 6 percent rate in the absence of a specified rate, nevertheless, the law allowed interest upon written contracts after the sum was due and payable.

B. Mr. Lukas signed the Confidential Information Agreement at Ber-Med Labs, but he may have used Ber-Med proprietary information in developing his invention.

C. A patent is property, title to it can pass only by assignment.

Answers

A. Add a semicolon between "rate" and "nevertheless."

B. Correct

C. Add a semicolon between "property" and "title."

5.2.2 Using Semicolons in a Series

To punctuate a series, first look for commas within its elements. If they contain no internal punctuation, use commas to separate them:

> 1. *Plaintiff's duties included measuring roofs for estimates, compiling costs for bids, and analyzing data for clients.*

When elements of a series contain commas, insert semicolons between them. Commas between these elements could confuse the reader:

> 2(a) *To distinguish between an employee and an independent contractor, the court reviewed these factors: payment determined by hours, job, or salary, the provider of the instrumentalities, tools, and place of work, and the degree of supervision.*

The reader must stop and review the sentence to determine the series' structure. For clarity, separate the major elements with semicolons:

> 2(b) *To distinguish between an employee and an independent contractor, the court reviewed these factors: payment determined by hour, job, or salary; the provider of the instrumentalities, tools, and place of work; and degree of supervision.*

The semicolon, a stronger piece of punctuation than the comma, marks divisions between major elements. Within these structures, use commas as needed for clarity.

Exercise

Correct punctuation errors in these series.

A. The interrogatories seek information concerning Whitman's contentions, the basis for his damage claims, and the identity of percipient witnesses.

B. The physicians will work subject to the rules, standards, and regulations set forth by Pacific, with equipment supplied by Pacific, and in a facility provided by Pacific.

C. Paxton, Inc. called three expert witnesses: Dr. Johnson, a microbiologist; Dr. Price, a neurosurgeon; and Dr. Coleman, a geneticist.

D. Inequitable conduct can include actions intended to hinder or harm other creditors; actions that lead to undercapitalization of the borrower; or a breach of fiduciary duty.

Answers

A. Correct

B. The physicians will work subject to the rules, standards, and regulations set forth by Pacific; with equipment supplied by Pacific; and in a facility provided by Pacific.

C. Correct

D. Inequitable conduct can include actions intended to hinder or harm other creditors, actions that lead to undercapitalization of the borrower, or a breach of fiduciary duty.

5.3 Dashes

Use the dash sparingly and only for emphasis. First, analyze the purpose of the dash in your sentence. Do you want to emphasize the point, or are you merely explaining it? If your goal is only to explain, use a comma, semicolon, or colon, depending on context. Add dashes to set off short phrases or clauses in short sentences. If you use dashes to set off a long phrase or clause buried in a long sentence, the isolated material receives little emphasis.

5.3.1 Dashes for Emphasis

The dash emphasizes words by setting them apart conceptually and visually. A litigator used dashes in sentence 1 to stress the time gap between medical services received and the filing of an action:

1. *In March—over one and one-half years after the services at issue were rendered—Dr. Childress filed the instant action against Central Medical.*

216

Dashes in sentence 2 emphasize the value of four metallic elements:

> 2.   *Promoting product life might serve only to place heavier demands on copper, chromium, nickel, and zinc—more valuable and increasingly scarce materials.*

Do not use the dash when you explain information but do not need to emphasize it. In sentence 3(a), a dash and "i.e." introduce a long explanatory phrase:

> 3(a)   *Impax, Inc. cannot utilize this description unless it is appropriately qualified—i.e., by clear and conspicuous disclosure of the fact that certain contents of the product are imported.*

The dash is not necessary here because the writer is not emphasizing the "by" phrase. Replace the dash with a comma:

> 3(b)   *Impax, Inc. cannot utilize this description unless it is appropriately qualified, i.e., by clear and conspicuous disclosure of the fact that certain contents of the product are imported.*

To stress a phrase's importance, use the dash without "i.e."

Finally, do not set appositives off with dashes. Use a comma before short appositives and a colon before long ones. In sentence 4(a), a lawyer added dashes on both sides of a short appositive that identifies producers:

> 4(a)   *Under the agreement, the producers—Milwaukee Diesel and Smith Motor Company—will return 20 percent of the dealer's purchase value.*

Set off these short appositives with commas:

> 4(b)   *Under the agreement, the producers, Milwaukee Diesel and Smith Motor Company, will return 20 percent of the dealer's purchase value.*

Exercise

Analyze the function of dashes in these sentences. Revise as needed.

A. Any attempt to disclaim an implied warranty—which is defined as "an implied warranty arising under state law"—will fail both under the act and under state law.

B. Hospital costs in the year ending in May rose 10 percent over the previous year—twice the rate of inflation of the economy as a whole.

C. Patton asserted that Transbank had made two loans—the pre-petition loan, which was negotiated on January 1, and the post-petition loan, which was offered three months later.

Answers

A. The dash separates a definition from the rest of the sentence. Unless the context requires emphasis on the definition, set off this nonrestrictive clause with commas.

B. This effective dash emphasizes the dramatic increase in hospital costs.

C. This dash sets off a long appositive that contains internal punctuation. Replace the dash with a colon after "loans."

5.3.2 Dashes: Effective Sentence Length

Use the dash to emphasize short groups of words in short sentences. Do not insert a dash before a phrase or clause in a long sentence:

> 1(a) *The Court should avoid the understandable temptation to dismiss everything about this litigation and should instead consider the truly egregious misconduct at issue—misconduct castigated by Federal District Judge Mitchell, found to be "improper" and "not professional" by both Superior Court judges below, and deemed outrageous in the professional opinion of recognized experts in legal ethics.*

This writer used the dash to set off characterizations of the plaintiffs' misconduct. Yet sentence length prevents the reader from focusing on these judgments, which follow a twenty-two-word independent clause. Also, the phrase after the dash contains a long series with three elements. Delete the dash and divide this sentence:

> 1(b) *This court should avoid the understandable temptation to dismiss everything about this litigation and should instead consider the truly egregious misconduct at issue.*

> 1(c)   *This misconduct has been castigated by Federal District Judge Mitchell, found to be "improper" and "not professional" by both Superior Court judges below, and deemed outrageous in the professional opinion of recognized experts in legal ethics.*

Sentence 2 illustrates effective use of the dash. In a short sentence, the litigator employed a dash to set apart only two words:

> 2.   *Petitioners respectfully submit that the facts of record support—indeed compel—disqualification.*

Exercise

Analyze the use of dashes in this sentence. Revise as needed.

A. In *Winston*, the New York judicial system resoundingly put a stop to similar conduct by disqualifying the attorneys—the prominent firm of Smith & Greene—who had misused a deposition and document subpoena to obtain an adversary's files, including privileged files, in the custody of a third party.

B. This memo will analyze five major defenses—unavoidable accident doctrine, error in extremis doctrine, assumption of risk, joint enterprise, and duty to warn.

Answers

This litigator used the dash to stress a law firm's name in a long sentence. Divide it and place the name at the end of the first sentence for emphasis:

A. 1. In *Winston*, the New York judicial system resoundingly put a stop to similar conduct by disqualifying attorneys from the prominent firm of Smith & Greene.

   2. Those attorneys had misused a deposition and document subpoena to obtain an adversary's files, including privileged files, in the custody of a third party.

B. This writer used the dash to explain, not to emphasize. Delete the dash and add a colon after "defenses."

5.4 Quotation Marks

5.4.1 Placing Punctuation with Quotation Marks

Two sets of rules govern the placement of punctuation with quotation marks in the United States. The traditional method reflects eighteenth-century printer practices. Even lawyers outside the U.S. should follow these guidelines when writing for an American audience.

5.4.1.1 Traditional Method

According to these rules, always place the period and the comma within quotation marks:

1. *The pension plan provided for workers' compensation amounts "paid directly or indirectly by an employing company."*

2. *Englewood did not pay most state fund payments "directly or indirectly," as required by the pension plan.*

Insert the period outside the quotation marks, however, if it follows the reference to the source of a direct quotation:

3. *Black's Law Dictionary defines "amicus curiae" as "a person who is not a party to a lawsuit but who petitions the court to file a brief in the action because that person has a strong interest in the subject matter" (p. 32).*

Place two other punctuation marks, the colon and the semicolon, outside quotation marks:

4. *Section 3901.21 defines "unfair and deceptive acts in the business of insurance": [Definition]*

5. *The top line of the label states "KEEP AWAY FROM CHILDREN"; additional instructions for protection from injury include "Danger" and "Call Physician Immediately."*

The placement of the question mark depends on its function. This punctuation mark "floats," depending upon the structure of the sentence.

When a question mark applies to only the quoted words, place it within the quotation marks:

> 6.   *In his deposition, Mr. Whitaker was asked: "What is the total anticipated earnings stream of a seven-year-old child?"*

The question mark appears outside quotation marks if it applies to the entire sentence:

> 7.   *Does Al-Insure's alleged improper conduct fall within the scope of "the business of insurance"?*

If both the entire sentence and the quoted material are questions, use only one question mark and place it inside the quotation marks:

> 8.   *In the June 1 deposition, did Waltex's attorney ask, "What award would be needed to defray the cost of future psychiatric care for a seven-year-old child?"*

Exclamation points, which rarely appear in legal writing, follow the same rules as question marks.

5.4.1.2 New Method

Some writers prefer a new, more consistent method of punctuating with quotation marks:

1. Put all punctuation that is part of quoted material inside the quotation marks.

2. Place punctuation that applies to the overall structure outside the quotation marks.

With these rules, titles of articles, short stories, magazines, songs, compositions, and other phrases do not have extraneous punctuation inside the quotation marks:

> 1.   *Ms. Overton was hired for the position of "Consultant in the Great Lakes Area".*

This method has not yet replaced the earlier conventions, so most writers use the traditional rules.

Exercise

Use the traditional method to punctuate these sentences correctly.

A. When asked to state "work locations desired or geographical preferences", Ms. Kendall wrote "open".

B. Courts have not explained when a religious belief is "bona fide"; however, they equate this expression with the word "sincere."

Answers

A. Incorrect. Put the comma and period inside the quotation marks.

B. Correct

5.4.2 Setting Off Terms with Quotation Marks

When you refer to a word or phrase, set it off with quotation marks. The quotation marks distinguish the term from the object, state, or action represented by that term. For example, quotation marks correctly set off the word "option" in sentence 1:

1. *The court distinguished between two definitions of "option."*

By using quotation marks, the writer refers to the word "option," not to an option itself. Quotation marks also set off "nuclear incident" in the partial definition in sentence 2:

2. *The Act defines "nuclear incident" as a nuclear occurrence inside the United States.*

Because the writer designates the term "nuclear incident," not an actual incident, quotation marks are necessary.

Exercise

Add quotation marks as needed in these sentences.

A. The Steel Industry Compliance Act was popularly known as the steel stretch-out because it permitted companies to delay implementing environmental measures.

B. The State's interests must be designated as either proprietary or quasi-sovereign.

C. The term licensed stationary production facility includes all commercial reactors licensed under Section 7.

Answers

Set off the following terms with quotation marks:

A. "the steel stretch-out"

B. "proprietary," "quasi-sovereign"

C. "licensed stationary production facility"

5.5 Apostrophes

Use apostrophes to show possession, the omission of letters or numbers, and the plural of certain symbols.

5.5.1 Showing Possession with Apostrophes

In a possessive form, the apostrophe signals omission of the word "of." To make singular nouns that do not end in "s" possessive, add an apostrophe and "s," for example, "the unexcused absences of Mr. Moore—Mr. Moore's unexcused absences." Plural nouns that end in "s" form the possessive when an apostrophe is added, e.g., "the termination of the employees—the employees' termination."

Apply different rules for nouns with irregular singular or plural forms. Opinion is divided about singular nouns that end in "s." Writers may add either an apostrophe and "s" or just an apostrophe to show possession. Therefore, either "Mr. Moses's lawyers'" or "Mr. Moses' lawyers" is correct. Many writers prefer using only the apostrophe because the repetition of the "s" sound in the "s's" ending is awkward. To form the possessive of plural nouns that do not end in "s," add an apostrophe and "s." For example, "the rights of children" becomes "children's rights."

Use apostrophes also in the possessive forms of compound nouns and for nouns jointly or individually owned. Compound nouns, such as "the Secretary of State" or "partner-in-charge," become possessive when an apostrophe and "s" are added to the last word, as in "the Secretary of State's speech" and "the partner-in-charge's letter." When individual ownership is indicated, add an apostrophe and "s" to each noun in a series, e.g., "Mr. Patrick's and Ms. Hilton's depositions." For joint ownership, add an apostrophe and "s" to only the last noun in a series or to both nouns, for example, "Ms. King and Mr. Peter's property" or "Ms. King's and Mr. Peter's property." If the couple jointly owns more than one property, the same options for possessive are correct, i.e., "Ms. King and Mr. Peter's properties" or "Ms. King's and Mr. Peter's properties."

Possessive pronouns have possessiveness built into their forms and therefore do not require apostrophes. Personal possessive pronouns include "my," "mine," "your," "yours," "his," "her," "hers," "its," "our," "ours," "their," and "theirs." "Whose" is the relative and interrogative possessive pronoun.

Distinguish carefully between these pronouns and forms that are similar but have different meanings. For example, writers often use "it's" for a possessive form, but this word is actually a contraction of "it is" or "it has." "Your" at times appears incorrectly in place of "you're," a contraction of "you are." The contraction "who's" means "who is" or "who has" and does not serve as a possessive form. Some writers also confuse the possessive form "theirs" with the contraction "there's," a shortened form of "there is."

Do not add apostrophes to plurals that are not possessive, e.g., family names. Refer to the Johnson family as "the Johnsons," not "the Johnson's." Of course, if a noun follows the possessive, use the plural possessive, as in "the Johnsons' lease."

Singular words that end in "s" create problems for some lawyers. For example, when these words serve as adjectives before a noun, writers sometimes add apostrophes incorrectly, as in "the Paris' Agreement" and "the Brussel's memorandum." The names of the cities explain location, not ownership. Omit the apostrophes.

5.5.2   Marking Omissions with Apostrophes

Use an apostrophe to indicate missing letters or numbers. For example, in contractions such as "isn't" and "didn't," the apostrophe marks the deletion of "o." Most writers use the word "o'clock" without being aware of its original form, "of the clock." You can designate graduation classes with only the last two digits preceded by an apostrophe, as in "Class of '02."

Insert an apostrophe also when you omit the word "of" in duration-of-time phrases. You can shorten these phrases by making the noun that follows "of" possessive and placing it before the modified noun. With this revision, "a delay of thirty days" becomes "thirty days' delay."

5.5.3   Making Symbols Plural with Apostrophes

The apostrophe also can be added to make symbols plural, although some stylists argue against this function. For example, you can write "the 1990's" or "the 1990s."

Exercise

Convert each modifying phrase to a possessive noun that precedes the first noun.

A. 1. The claim of the Wilsons

2. The testimony by Evelyn Bates

3. The policies of the partner-in-charge

4. A document drafted by John Bradley and Barbara Reed

5. The business owned by Thomas Jones

6. The class action suit of the women

7. A wait of three years

8. The unemployment rate in Kansas

Identify and revise incorrect possessive forms and contractions in these sentences

B. 1. Mr. Fosse, whose a member of the D crew, complains that CIB discriminated against him under Title VII of the 1964 Civil Rights Act.

2. The Minneapoli's office received your fax on October 30.

3. Hampton exercised it's right to service FHA mortgages last year.

4. Apex's new marketing campaign targets teenager's.

5. If your able to attend this CLE program, please reply by September 15.

6. All partners should attend the Whites fiftieth anniversary party in the atrium of the Dalla's office at 8 P.M. on November 30.

Answers

A. 1. The Wilsons' claim

   2. a. Evelyn Bates' testimony

     b. Evelyn Bates's testimony

   3. The partner-in-charge's policies

   4. a. John Bradley and Barbara Reed's document

     b. John Bradley's and Barbara Reed's document

   5. a. Thomas Jones' business

     b. Thomas Jones's business

   6. The women's class action suit

   7. Three years' wait

   8. a. Kansas' unemployment rate

     b. Kansas's unemployment rate

B. 1. Incorrect form: "whose"

     <u>Revision</u>: "who's"

   2. Incorrect form: "Minneapoli's"

     <u>Revision</u>: "Minneapolis"

   3. Incorrect form: "it's"

     <u>Revision</u>: "its"

   4. Incorrect form: "teenager's"

     <u>Revision</u>: "teenagers"

   5. Incorrect form: "Your"

     <u>Revision</u>: "you're," "you are," or "you will be"

   6. Incorrect form: "Whites"

     <u>Revision</u>: "Whites' "

     Incorrect form: "Dalla's"

     <u>Revision</u>: "Dallas"

CHAPTER SIX

～ *The Writing Process* ～

Writing is a process, not an instantaneous act. Each written product should begin with random thoughts and evolve into a polished final product. Do not try to produce a perfect first draft. Instead, concentrate on one step of the process at a time. With this approach, you can eliminate writer's block and complete a document quickly.

The writing process consists of three stages: prewriting, drafting, and revising. This chapter explains these steps and effective techniques for each one. Excerpts from writing in an appellate case, *Noble Sales Agency, Inc. v. Fox Co.*, illustrate the process.

6.1 Prewriting

Begin with prewriting, the preparation before drafting. Lawyers' prewriting consists of three separate steps: legal research or taking notes, brainstorming, and outlining.

Before you take notes, assess the scope of the assignment. Estimate the time required in light of appropriate billing costs. As you plan, also consider your reader's expectations. If necessary, ask the assigning lawyer about the approximate preparation time for the project and the length of your final document. Litigators should check with the court about page or word limits for briefs. If other attorneys will write sections of the paper, allow time for revisions to create a unified style and approach.

With an imminent deadline, you may be tempted to skip the prewriting steps. Yet careful preparation can eliminate the need for extensive revisions and thus save you time overall.

6.1.1   Legal Research or Taking Notes

First, collect material for your assignment. If you are preparing a legal memorandum, make notes about the assignment, the facts, and legal research. For a brief, you also may be working from an earlier memorandum. Documents in the case will comprise your materials if you are planning an appellate brief. Before drafting a letter, review the client's file and other relevant papers.

6.1.2   Brainstorming

As you brainstorm, jot down your ideas. Let them flow without judging them. Do not try to classify or order them. Do not be concerned about grammar, style, or spelling. Record even your hunches. Important assertions may appear next to supporting detail. With this approach, you will be more creative than if you write in complete sentences and paragraphs. When you brainstorm, the creative right side of your brain can work without corrections from the left side. Because you separate these two functions, you perform both more effectively.

To brainstorm with voice recognition computer software, record ideas as they occur to you. These responses might come to you randomly or be observations about the assignment, facts, research, or an earlier document in the case. For example, in *Noble Sales Agency, Inc. v. Fox Co.*, the litigator brainstormed by reviewing the trial transcript and noting relevant points to use in the appellate brief.

First, he reviewed the case history. In *Noble v. Fox*, Noble Sales Agency Inc. ("Noble") had sued the writer's client, Fox Company ("Fox"), for breach of contract in common pleas court. Noble alleged that Fox breached a manufacturer's representative agreement with Noble and wrongfully terminated their agency relationship. Fox denied liability, arguing that the agreement was void for lack of consideration and that Noble was equitably estopped from enforcing the agreement. After five days of trial before a jury, the court entered a directed verdict in favor of Noble on its breach of contract claim. Fox appealed the trial court's judgment, arguing that the court committed reversible error in refusing to allow the jury to decide the validity and enforceability of the contract.

As the litigator brainstormed, he read the trial transcript and selected relevant points for his brief. His notes appear below, with parties identified in parentheses:

8/7
pg. 169

<u>Temple</u> (president and owner of Noble) <u>states</u> that Martin Fox's sales manager never told him that he intended to give Temple a long-term contract. <u>Temple then states</u> on page 170 that he wasn't surprised when he got the contract even though he'd already indicated that he asked for one for ten years without ever getting one. On page 171, <u>Temple also states</u> that it was Mr. Little (a former Fox employee who then worked for Noble as an independent salesman) who sent him the contract and negotiated basically for the contract with Martin and <u>then he indicates</u> that Little wasn't an officer of Noble. <u>This certainly seems like a point to raise in our statement of facts</u>. <u>So we can say that</u> based on the facts as presented at trial, after eleven years of being repeatedly turned down for a long-term contract, Mr. Temple gets in the mail a contract that was negotiated by a nonemployee and not sent by the Fox Company to him and he says that this didn't surprise him at all. <u>That would certainly seem to create an issue of fact on the question of whether</u> there was something unusual about the circumstances in which this contract was entered into. <u>And it would certainly suggest that</u> there was no meeting of minds as to the meaning of the termination clause. (Emphasis added.)

You can observe the attorney's thought process in this passage. The first three underlined clauses introduce Temple's statements. In the other underlined clauses, the litigator notes those statements' relevance in his argument. Hedging verbs, e.g., "seem" and "suggest," show his tentative thinking at this stage.

The passage also illustrates qualities of brainstorming with voice recognition software. Two long sentences ramble on and on. Pronouns such as "he," "this," and "that" lack clear antecedents. Some sentences begin casually with "so" or "and." Yet the purpose of brainstorming is to record ideas as they occur to the writer, not to create perfect prose. These notes will provide a basis for the litigator's outline, the next step in the prewriting process.

6.1.3   Outlining

For many lawyers, outlining is the most difficult part of the writing process. An outline serves as a transition between brainstorming notes and a first draft. As you outline, determine the logical relationships among your ideas. Develop each step of legal thought, i.e., draw a "road map" for the paper. Writers who do not outline before drafting sometimes discover problems in logical development later. Planning in advance can eliminate the need for extensive revisions.

Use these techniques to make an outline from brainstorming notes:

1. Order the elements as they will appear in your paper.

2. Establish a hierarchy, i.e., separate main ideas from supporting detail.

3. Study logical development.

4. Delete ideas that don't fit.

5. Reorder where necessary.

6. Add logical steps omitted in brainstorming.

Choose an outline form that will be practical for the assignment. For short papers, many writers prefer an informal outline. Long documents may require a traditional outline form with Roman numerals, uppercase letters, Arabic numerals, and lowercase letters to show the relationship of important ideas to supporting points.

Some lawyers write more effectively if they skip the outlining step. After brainstorming, these writers simply want to get something down on paper. They then revise extensively and create a polished final draft. If you prefer not to outline, be sure to allow extra time for revising.

In *Noble v. Fox*, the writer wanted to make an outline in complete sentences. Because the facts and the issues were complicated, he needed to state points precisely. The litigator's brainstorming consisted of notes taken as he reviewed the trial transcript. After quoting statements by Noble's president, the attorney noted their relevance in Fox's argument. Using these notes, he made an outline of trial errors. An excerpt from the outline follows:

III.   *The Trial Court Erred to Fox's Prejudice in Failing to Allow the Jury to Consider Whether Noble Was Equitably Estopped from Asserting Any Rights It Might Otherwise Have Possessed under the Second Agreement.*

* * * *

C.   *The record reflects that issues of fact existed on each of these points:*

CHAPTER SIX

* * * *

2.   *Testimony showed* Noble knew that Fox's general manager
     would not approve long-term sales contracts. *Thus, as noted,*
     Noble surreptitiously negotiated with Martin to obtain the
     Second Agreement and then remained silent concerning its
     existence. *From this evidence, the jury reasonably could
     conclude that* Noble's conduct was deliberately deceptive and
     geared toward inducing Fox to continue its business relationship
     with Noble under the misconception that the First Agreement
     still governed. (Emphasis added.)

The litigator created a carefully structured outline with a section heading and introductory statement. Section 2, which contains several sentences, will serve as the basis for a paragraph in the first draft. Complicated sentences in section 2 replace the "looser" and rambling sentences in the brainstorming. Qualities of spoken English in the lawyer's earlier notes, such as ambiguous pronouns and sentences that began with "so" or "and," have been revised.

The litigator's thought process is obvious in his outline. Underlined structures introduce statements about Noble's behavior. He also analyzes trial testimony, draws inferences, and explains the jury's logical conclusion.

6.2 The First Draft

To create a first draft, briefly analyze the overall development of the document. Review your outline, if you have one. Then determine where to start. Although many lawyers draft an entire document from beginning to end, others prefer to focus first on sections that seem easy to write.

Consider your first draft an attempt simply to get your ideas down on paper. Do not question whether each word, sentence, and paragraph is flawless. If you seek perfection at this stage, you will lose valuable time and interrupt your creative flow. You can revise more efficiently after completing the project and setting the paper aside for a few minutes.

In *Noble v. Fox*, the litigator's careful outline in complete sentences formed the basis for a first draft for Fox's argument. With this full outline, he made only a few changes to create a draft. Revisions are underlined in the excerpts of the outline and first draft:

231

LEGAL WRITING

OUTLINE

III. *The Trial Court Erred to Fox's Prejudice in Failing to Allow the Jury to Consider Whether Noble Was Equitably Estopped from Asserting Any Rights It Might Otherwise Have Possessed under the Second Agreement.*

* * * *

C. *The record reflects that the issues of fact existed on each of these points:*

* * * *

2. *Testimony showed Nobel <u>knew</u> that Fox's General Manager would not approve long-term sales contracts. Thus, as noted, Noble <u>surreptitiously negotiated with Martin</u> to obtain the Second Agreement and then remained silent concerning its existence. From this evidence, the jury reasonably could conclude that Noble's conduct <u>induced</u> Fox to continue its business relationship with Noble under the misconception that the First Agreement still governed. (Emphasis added.)*

FIRST DRAFT

III. *The Trial Court Erred to Fox's Prejudice in Failing to Allow the Jury to Consider Whether Noble Was Equitably Estopped from Asserting Any Rights It Might Otherwise Have Possessed under the Second Agreement.*

* * * *

<u>Finally, even if the Second Agreement was found to constitute a valid contract, Fox was still entitled to argue that the contract was unenforceable due to the affirmative defense of equitable estoppel.</u>

* * * *

The record reflects that issues of fact existed on each of these five points:

* * * *

2. *Testimony showed <u>that—based upon prior dealings—Noble was alerted to the fact</u> that Fox's General Manager would not approve long-term sales contracts. Thus, as noted, Noble <u>was forced</u> to obtain the Second Agreement <u>in a highly unorthodox</u>*

manner and then remained silent concerning its existence. From this evidence, the jury reasonably could conclude that Noble's conduct *was deliberately deceptive and geared toward inducing* Fox to continue its business relationship with Noble under the misconception that the First Agreement still governed. *(Emphasis added.)*

Most of the litigator's changes from the outline strengthen his argument in the first draft:

1. After the heading, the writer begins with a concession but then asserts the validity of Fox's argument.

2. In passage 2, the adverbial phrase "based upon prior dealings" provides evidence for the next clause.

3. The writer replaces "Noble knew" with "Noble was alerted to the fact." The litigator undoubtedly thought that the verb "alert" was stronger than "knew." By adding "the fact," he wanted to stress the truth of his statement. Yet he substitutes a passive verb and wordy phrase for an active verb.

4. In the draft, the attorney argues that Noble Sales Agency "was forced" to obtain an agreement "in a highly unorthodox manner." The passive verb places blame directly on Noble. But "highly unorthodox" may be less accusatory than "surreptitious."

5. "Noble's conduct induced Fox" has been changed to "Noble's conduct was deliberately deceptive and geared toward inducing Fox." With this revision, the litigator harshly condemns Noble's behavior.

6.3 Revising

Divide the revising process into steps. When you complete a first draft, you are too close to your writing to evaluate it objectively. Set the paper aside before you revise. In addition, allow time for several sets of revisions. With each review, you can make additional changes.

6.3.1 Checklist

As you revise, consider the questions below.

Content

1. Does this paper fulfill the assignment?

2. Have I developed ideas logically?

3. Have I fully explained the implications of statements?

4. Are applications (parallels between cases cited and the client's situation) clear?

5. Have I introduced cases by explaining their significance in the development of the argument or analysis?

Length

1. Is the length appropriate to meet firm expectations or court page limits?

2. Have I been selective about which points to include?

3. Could I shorten the paper by avoiding repetition and eliminating extra words?

Tone and Diction

1. What tone (e.g., objective, assertive, aggressive, conciliatory) will be most effective?

2. Should the tone change within the paper?

3. Is diction consistent with the intended tone?

4. Have I used each word correctly?

Sentence Structure

1. Is each sentence as concise and direct as possible?

2. Have I divided long sentences?

3. Do sentences vary in structure and type, e.g., simple, compound, complex, active, passive?

4. Have I begun sentences with contrasting structures such as introductory adverbs, phrases, and clauses?

Grammar and Punctuation

1. Are grammar and punctuation correct?

2. Have I looked for structures that I tend to use incorrectly?

Paragraph Structure

1. Does the first sentence state the goal of each paragraph?

2. Have I carefully developed each paragraph?

3. Does each paragraph end with a strong sentence?

4. Do transitions show relationships within paragraphs and between paragraphs?

Other Factors

1. Does the assignment require a unique focus (e.g., unusual facts, a need for hedging, or analysis or argument based on only one case)?

2. If so, have I changed the traditional format to accommodate the new focus?

6.3.2   Revising the First Draft

In many law firms, the writer and the assigning attorney revise each draft. The supervising lawyer brings a new perspective to the paper and thus should be able to review it objectively. When two or more attorneys revise a draft, aim for a consistent approach and style. Both attorneys should consider content, length, paragraph structure, sentence structure, tone, diction, grammar, punctuation, and any unique factors.

In the excerpt from the brief in *Noble Sales Agency Inc. v. Fox Co.*, below, the supervising attorney's revisions are underlined, and the original phrasing appears in parentheses:

E.   *The Trial Court Erred to Fox's Prejudice in Failing to Allow the Jury to Consider Whether Noble Was Equitably Estopped from Enforcing (Asserting Any Rights It Might Otherwise Have Possessed under) the Second Agreement.*

* * * *

Finally, even if the Second Agreement was found to constitute a valid contract, Fox was still entitled to argue that the contract was unenforceable <u>on the ground</u> (due to the affirmative defense) of equitable estoppel.

* * * *

The record reflects that issues of fact existed on each of these five points.

* * * *

<u>Second, the</u> (2.) testimony showed that—based upon prior dealings—Noble was alerted to the fact that Fox's General Manager would not approve long-term (sales) contracts <u>with its representatives</u>. Thus, as noted, Noble was forced to obtain the Second Agreement in a highly unorthodox manner and then remained silent concerning its existence. From this evidence, the jury reasonably could conclude that Noble's conduct was deliberately deceptive and geared toward inducing Fox to continue its business relationship with Noble under the misconception that the First Agreement still governed. (Emphasis added.)

These revisions strengthen the litigator's argument, and most are more concise than the original phrasing:

1. In the heading, the supervising attorney substituted one word, "enforcing," for the phrase "asserting any rights it might otherwise have possessed under." The revision is more persuasive because "enforcing" implies that the agreement was valid.

2. The next change, using "on the ground" instead of "due to the affirmative defense," is more direct.

3. By adding "Second, the" and deleting the number before "testimony" in point 2, the litigator creates a stronger transition from earlier material.

4. Finally, the lawyer changed "sales contracts" to "contracts with its representatives." This revision emphasizes the relationship between the two opposing parties.

6.3.3   Revising the Second Draft

As he revised the second draft of the appellate brief in *Noble v. Fox*, the partner had two goals: to strengthen the argument and to conform to the court's restrictions on length. The brief was much longer than the court's forty-page limit. After a petition to file twenty extra pages was denied, the assigning lawyer cut sections of argument and eliminated extra words. His changes in the excerpt appear below, with revisions underlined and the original phrasing in parentheses:

5.   *Assignment of Error No. 5: The Trial Court Erred to Fox's Prejudice in Failing to Allow the Jury to <u>Decide</u> (Consider) Whether Noble Was Equitably Estopped from Enforcing the Second Agreement.*

* * * *

   (Finally), even if the Second Agreement was (found to constitute) a valid contract, Fox was still entitled to argue that the contract was unenforceable on the ground of equitable estoppel.

* * * *

   The record reflects that <u>jury questions</u> (issues of fact) existed as to (on) each of these <u>issues</u> (five points).

* * * *

   Second, the <u>evidence</u> (testimony) showed that (—based upon prior dealings—) Noble <u>knew</u> (was alerted to the fact that) Fox('s General Manager) would not approve long-term (sales) <u>contracts with its representatives</u>. Thus, (as noted,) Noble was forced to obtain the Second Agreement in a <u>surreptitious</u> (highly unorthodox) manner and then remained silent concerning its existence. From this evidence, the jury reasonably could <u>have concluded</u> (conclude) that Noble's conduct <u>induced</u> (was deliberately deceptive and geared toward inducing) Fox to <u>believe</u> (continue its business relationship with Noble under the misconception) that the First Agreement still governed its business relationship with Noble. (Emphasis added.)

The revised argument was more persuasive after these changes:

1.   The assigning lawyer replaced "consider" with "decide" in the heading. "Decide," a stronger verb, emphasizes the jury's potential power and the trial court's error.

2.   The partner deleted an awkward adverb and a wordy passive verb in the first sentence. "Finally" does not express the logical relationship between the heading and sentence. By stating that the agreement "was a valid contract" instead of "was found to constitute a valid contract," the litigator eliminates extra words and stresses the contract's validity.

3.   In the second sentence, the partner wanted to emphasize that the trial court had erroneously and improperly refused to let the jury decide these issues. Focusing on the legal process, he substituted "jury questions" for "issues of fact," and "issues" for "five points."

4.   The partner made four revisions in the first sentence of the last paragraph:

a.   He changed "testimony" to "evidence." Because testimony is only one type of evidence, this revision strengthens the argument.

b.   To be more direct, the partner reversed two of the associate's revisions in the first draft:

i.   First, the assigning lawyer deleted "based upon prior dealings." The partner believed that it was not necessary to state a basis for Noble's knowledge.

ii.   Substituting "knew" for "was alerted to the fact that" eliminates a passive verb and a wordy phrase.

c.   By deleting the possessive and the title "General Manager," the partner emphasizes Fox's policy, not the behavior of one employee.

5.   Two revisions in the second sentence of that paragraph are consistent with his earlier ones:

a.   The litigator removed "as noted," the second introductory element, because it added little meaning.

b.   He reversed the associate's earlier revision by replacing "highly unorthodox" with "surreptitious." The partner wanted to stress the clandestine quality of Noble's behavior.

6.   Changes in the last sentence shorten it significantly:

a.   The partner first changed a verb in the present tense to "could have concluded," which matches earlier references to the judicial process.

b. He shorted the "that" clause to make it more persuasive. Contrast two versions of the excerpt:

   i. Noble's conduct was deliberately deceptive and geared toward inducing Fox to continue its business relationship with Noble under the misconception that the First Agreement still governed.

   ii. Noble's conduct induced Fox to believe that the First Agreement still governed its business relationship with Noble.

All of these changes reinforce the argument that Fox has been wronged.

6.4 Proofing

After you revise the style, content, and organization of a paper several times, proofread it carefully. Attention to detail is very important in legal writing. A paper should create a positive overall impression. Regardless of the audience, your professional competence will be judged partly on your writing.

Separate the review into two steps, revising and proofreading. With this approach, you can perform both more effectively. Each process calls for a different type of thinking. While you are concentrating on substance, it is difficult to notice typing and spelling errors. Similarly, you can proofread more efficiently when you are not evaluating content.

As you proof, do not rely solely on the spell-checking feature that may be part of your word processing software. Although computer spelling programs identify many typing errors and misspellings, checkers do not recognize words that are misspelled but match the proper spelling of other words. If you type "trail" instead of "trial," a computer program will not note the error.

To proof more accurately, use three techniques:

1. Review the paper carefully. Read it slowly several times, concentrating on the spelling of each word, on punctuation, and on spacing. Do not evaluate content.

2. Read each line of the paper aloud from right to left, noting spelling, spacing, and punctuation. This deliberate review of "cosmetic"

qualities will interrupt your focus on content. If possible, work with a colleague to proof by reading words, punctuation, and spacing to each other.

3. Ask secretaries or word processing operators to proofread a paper.

Regardless of the technique, proofing a draft for a long period of time is not effective. If possible, set the paper aside between readings so that you can review it objectively.

6.5 The Writing Process: Before and After

A before and after contrast in writing from *Noble v. Fox* shows a dramatic evolution in substance and form. Excerpts from the writer's brainstorming and final draft appear below:

<u>BRAINSTORMING</u>

(Notes recorded with voice recognition software as the litigator reviewed the trial transcript)

> *8/9*
> *pg.151*
>
> *Martin also confirms he told nobody at Fox about executing this document.*

> *8/9*
> *pg.151*
>
> *He also indicates that he does not remember whether he signed the copy of the agreement that he retained.*

> *8/9*
> *pg.152*
>
> *This is critical. Here Martin indicates quite clearly that he did not put the contract in the appropriate Noble file and he didn't do so because he was afraid that he would be fired if anybody found out about the contract.*

8/9
pg.152

Martin confirms that he never received anything back formally from Temple regarding the contract.

8/9
pg.153

Martin indicates that Temple said after receiving the contract that he hoped he never had to use it in a court of law. He said this in a telephone conversation where he thanked Martin for the contract.

8/9
pg.154

Martin confirms that he never wrote anything anywhere indicating that he had executed this contract so no one at Fox, once again, had any knowledge that it existed.

FINAL DRAFT

5. *Assignment of Error No. 5: The Trial Court Erred to Fox's Prejudice in Failing to Allow the Jury to Decide Whether Noble Was Equitably Estopped from Enforcing the Second Agreement.*

Even if the Second Agreement was a valid contract, Fox was still entitled to argue that the contract was unenforceable on the ground of equitable estoppel.

* * * *

The record reflects that jury questions existed as to each of these issues.

* * * *

Second, the evidence showed that Noble knew Fox would not approve long-term contracts with its representatives. Thus, Noble was forced to obtain the Second Agreement in a surreptitious manner and then remained silent concerning its existence. From this evidence, the jury reasonably could have concluded that Noble's conduct deliberately induced Fox to believe that the First Agreement still governed its business relationship with Noble.

The attorney began with a list of a sales manager's statements and ended with a powerful argument. Note differences between the fragmented effect of the brainstorming text and flowing prose in the final draft. Choppy sentences beginning with the name of the speaker have become smoother and more sophisticated. In the final draft, they contain introductory elements and subordinate clauses. After reviewing the brainstorming passage, the litigator chose actions described there and inserted them in conceptual statements concerning the legal process. Lead-ins such as "the evidence showed that" and "from this evidence, the jury could have reasonably concluded that" provide a context for the parties' behavior. Several sets of revisions by the writer and assigning lawyer led to the polished and forceful prose in the final draft.

CHAPTER SEVEN

∼ *Paragraph Structure* ∼

Craft your paragraphs carefully. Each paragraph is a building block of legal thought. As you draft and revise, shape each paragraph to advance logical development within your document. Begin with a clear topic sentence that states the paragraph's goal. Then develop logical steps within the paragraph. Conclude with a powerful sentence that reinforces or wraps up the central point. Finally, insert transitions to show relationships within the paragraph and to link it with others.

A litigator crafted paragraph 1 to argue against a gag order:

1.   *Moreover, the adverse and chilling effects of the gag order, though difficult to quantify, will without question be far-reaching. If the order is not invalidated, the* Daily Herald, *which already has some difficulty acquiring information from law enforcement agencies, will find that information even less accessible. Those who are already reluctant to talk to the press will feel justified in taking an even more secretive posture. The chilling effect that will undoubtedly occur will work to the detriment of not only the* Daily Herald, *but also the general public, who will find information regarding the criminal justice system increasingly scarce.*

The lawyer carefully structured this paragraph as a building block of her argument. First, "moreover" links the paragraph to the previous one. The topic sentence then characterizes the effects of the gag order. Examples follow in the next two sentences. Finally, the lawyer uses a powerful concluding sentence to extend the consequences of the gag order beyond the client to a broader audience, the general public. The "not only . . . but also" structure emphasizes the order's effects.

7.1 Topic Sentences

Your first sentence should state the paragraph's main point. A strong topic sentence creates a context for the reader and anchors the paragraph in the overall logical development of the document. Topic sentences may be simple or complex, short or long.

In legal memoranda, topic sentences usually explain the law or apply it in an objective fashion:

1. *The EPA found that Boston Power's project did not fall within the routine exception.*

2. *Section 105 grants the Bankruptcy Court broad equitable powers to issue injunctions against state courts.*

3. *The corporate veil has been pierced in only three reported cases under Delaware law.*

These topic sentences establish a clear sense of direction for each paragraph. Without seeing the paragraphs, you can predict their development. For example, sentence 1 introduces reasons why the project does not fall within the exception. After sentence 2, the writer describes the court's powers. An analysis of three reported cases follows sentence 3.

Use persuasive topic sentences in briefs to shape the reader's perception of the intended outcome. When topic sentences state a major point, they reinforce the argument. The conclusion is clear, even before the reader reaches its formal statement at the end. Note these topic sentences from briefs:

4. *Chemco erroneously contends that the case management order of September 5 will safeguard the privilege that Martin asserts.*

5. *The Seventh Circuit has stated repeatedly that former IPI 7.02 and 7.06, the instructions given at Ms. Ortega's trial, are unconstitutional.*

As you read these sentences, you can determine potential paragraph development. After sentence 4, the attorney explains why Chemco's contention is wrong, and sentence 5 leads to details of the Seventh Circuit's statements.

CHAPTER SEVEN

7.1.1 Changing Direction within a Paragraph

As you revise each paragraph, analyze the relationship between the first and second sentences. If the second sentence changes the paragraph's logical direction, draft a new topic sentence.

In paragraph 1(a), the second sentence introduces a new topic. According to the topic sentence, this paragraph is about *Diggers*:

> 1(a)   *In* Diggers, *a condemnation case, the court held that the trier of fact is "not required to accept as correct, even the uncontradicted opinions of expert witnesses as to value but may consider the nature of the property involved and any other facts or circumstances within their knowledge in arriving at a verdict, provided there are in evidence sufficient facts on which they may draw a legitimate conclusion."* Diggers *[cite] (quoting* Georgia Power Co. v. Harwell *[cite]). In* Hogan v. Olivera *[cite], the court held that the trier of fact may fix a value lower or higher than that of the uncontradicted opinion "provided that the verdict is not palpably unreasonable under all the evidence."*

After telling the reader about *Diggers*, the writer then turns to a different case, *Hogan v. Olivera*. The "addition" quality of the second sentence signals the need for a topic sentence that explains the connection between the two cases:

> 1(b)   <u>*In two other Georgia cases, courts granted a trier of fact more flexibility in fixing the value of property*</u>. *The court in* Diggers, *a condemnation case, held that the trier of fact is "not required to accept as correct, even the uncontradicted opinions of expert witnesses as to value but may consider the nature of the property involved and any other facts or circumstances within their knowledge in arriving at a verdict, provided there are in evidence sufficient facts on which they may draw a legitimate conclusion."* Diggers *[cite] (quoting* Georgia Power Co. v. Harwell *[cite]). Similarly, the* Hogan v. Olivera *[cite] court held that the trier of fact may fix a value lower or higher than that of the uncontradicted opinion "provided that the verdict is not palpably unreasonable under all the evidence."*

With this topic sentence, the writer provides a context for the details of the two cases and quotations.

When the second sentence reverses the logical direction of a paragraph, draft a new topic sentence. Look for transitions such as "yet," "but," "however," "instead," or "on the contrary." "However" changes the logical direction in paragraph 2(a):

> 2(a)   *In Tennessee no statute governs the enforceability of covenants not to compete. However, section 47-25-101 of the Tennessee Code states: "All arrangements, contracts, or agreements made with a view to lessen, or which tend to lessen, full and free competition are declared to be against public policy." Thus, under Tennessee law, covenants not to compete, although enforced in certain circumstances, are not favored.*

According to the topic sentence, the paragraph explains how no Tennessee statute governs the enforceability of covenants not to compete. The reader expects to hear more about the absence of relevant law. But the writer then quotes a code section and reaches a general conclusion. To improve the topic sentence, combine parts of the first two sentences:

> 2(b)   *Although no statute governs the enforceability of covenants not to compete, the Tennessee Code provides some guidance. Section 47-25-101 states: "All arrangements, contracts, or agreements made with a view to lessen, or which tend to lessen, full and free competition are declared to be against public policy." Thus, under Tennessee law, covenants not to compete, although enforced in certain circumstances, are not favored.*

Exercise

Analyze logical development in these paragraphs and create new topic sentences as needed.

A.   The initial inquiry for courts in determining whether a job function is essential is whether the individual who holds the position is required to perform the function. The second inquiry is whether removing the function would fundamentally alter that position. *See* 29 C.F.R. § 1630.2(n). This analysis includes consideration of six factors: the employer's judgment, written job descriptions, amount of time spent performing that function, consequences of not having the plaintiff perform the function, terms of a collective bargaining agreement, and work experience of past and current employees in the plaintiff's position.

B.   If an owner fails to correct a violation, the Department of Housing Preservation and Development ("HPD") may commence an action in the housing part of the Portland City Civil Court for the recovery of civil penalties with costs and disbursements. Additionally, HPD may institute an action in a court of competent jurisdiction for an injunction requiring an owner to abate or correct any violation of the Housing Maintenance Code.

Answers

A. The second sentence changes logical directions by introducing a second inquiry. Add a topic sentence that includes both steps:

   To determine whether a job function is essential, courts apply a two-pronged test. The initial inquiry is whether the individual who holds the position is required to perform the function. The second inquiry is whether removing the function would fundamentally alter that position. *See* 29 C.F.R. § 1630.2(n). This analysis includes consideration of six factors: the employer's judgment, written job descriptions, amount of time spent performing that function, consequences of not having the plaintiff perform the function, terms of a collective bargaining agreement, and work experience of past and current employees in the plaintiff's position.

B. The topic sentence tells the reader that this paragraph will deal with a potential suit in civil court, but the second sentence explains a second type of action. Begin with a strong topic sentence: "The Department of Housing Preservation and Development ("HPD") has two courses of action against an owner who fails to correct a violation."

7.1.2   Topic Sentences in Analytic Writing

Use strong topic sentences to establish a clear sense of direction in legal memoranda. These assertions should be objective and neutral in tone. As you draft the first sentence of each paragraph, consider your goal for that unit of thought.

A strong topic sentence introduces paragraph 1. The writer analyzes whether a boiler conversion will qualify as a "modification" under the Clean Air Act:

1.   *Given the scope of the work involved and the prior EPA decisions, it is unlikely that the Burton boiler conversion project will qualify for the routine maintenance, repair, and replacement exception.* *Resuming coal burning at the Indianapolis boiler will, at a minimum, require the replacement of the dismantled coal feeding system, the removal of the refractory brick, and a complete replacement of the bags at the baghouse. Such work is rarely performed in the industry and goes beyond what the EPA has considered "routine" in the past. While technically this change may be a maintenance and repair project with a low overall cost, the conversion will probably be deemed a physical change that does not qualify for a routine maintenance, repair, and replacement exemption.*

With the topic sentence, the writer announces the subject of the paragraph: that the conversion project probably will not qualify for a routine exception. This sentence sets the stage for the rest of the paragraph, which explains why the project does not fit into the routine category. In the conclusion, the lawyer predicts the EPA's response.

Note the strong topic sentence in paragraph 2, taken from a memo concerning federal preemption of state law:

2.   *The Supreme Court has identified three circumstances where federal statutes may preempt state law: express preemption, field preemption, and conflict preemption.* *In express preemption, Congress adopts express language that shows the intent to preempt state law, thus defining the existence and scope of the preemption. In field preemption, federal regulation supplants state law where the "scheme of federal regulation is so pervasive as to leave no room for supplementary regulation." Finally, conflict preemption can occur where state law "stands as an obstacle to the accomplishment and execution of the full purposes and objectives of Congress." Both express and conflict preemption principles apply in Tepco's situation. (Citations omitted.)*

The topic sentence names three types of preemption. To support this assertion, the lawyer explains each type. She then applies this law to the client's situation.

Both writers observed the principles of good paragraph structure. They begin with direct topic sentences that explain the main point. Subsequent sentences flow logically from the topic sentence and develops one idea in depth.

Exercise

Analyze the effectiveness of the topic sentence in this paragraph.

> In *Palmetto*, the court held that an assignor's failure to comply with the requirements of the Claims Act would not invalidate the creditor's security interest in the collateral. *Lazere Financial Corp. v. Palmetto Pump & Irrigation, Inc.*, 81 B.R. 109, 111-12 (M.D. Fla. 1987). Similarly, in *Altek*, the court applied the general principles of Article 9 to determine the priorities between competing claims to collateral that had been assigned without compliance with the Claims Act. *General Cable Co. v. Altek Systems, Inc.*, 14 B.R. 144, 149-50 (N.D. Ill. 1981); *see also Sterling Nat'l Bank & Trust Co. v. Borstein*, 20 B.R. 633, 637 (S.D.N.Y. 1981).

Answer

According to the topic sentence, this paragraph will discuss *Palmetto*, yet the second sentence introduces another case, *Altek*. The paragraph needs a topic sentence that explains the connection between the two cases.

7.1.3   Topic Sentences in Persuasive Writing

Craft strong topic sentences to advance your argument. Your first sentence should shape the reader's perception of the case and applicable law. Analyze your objectives and the most effective way to start each paragraph. The topic sentence serves as the first building block of that paragraph's argument. Choose the most effective tone, e.g., assertive, prescriptive, or aggressive. Within an argument, topic sentences should vary in length and structure.

In a reply brief, an attorney used a long topic sentence to introduce the paragraph below:

> *The Glenco accommodation contained one crucial condition precedent that LMB cannot demonstrate it fulfilled: LMB had to be among the three lowest bidders to receive the "preference treatment" or "special consideration."* The uncontroverted evidence demonstrates that LMB was not among the bottom three bidders. In fact, LMB was the highest of the seven bidders. Nevertheless, Central

went above and beyond its accommodation by permitting LMB to participate in the second round of bidding along with the three lowest bidders. When the new bids were tallied, LMB still remained the highest bidder The spreadsheets provide incontrovertible proof that LMB did not fulfill the condition precedent to the separate Glenco accommodation. Indeed, LMB has not proffered, and cannot proffer, any evidence to the contrary.

The litigator begins with a direct statement that establishes a clear direction for the paragraph. In this topic sentence, a long independent clause introduces an appositive. The appositive, which explains "condition precedent," is also an independent clause. Yet the sentence's length does not detract from its power. The topic sentence clarifies an essential condition that LMB cannot fulfill: it had to be among the three lowest bidders. The writer then provides evidence about LMB's high bids, Central's giving LMB a second chance to bid, and LMB's remaining the highest bidder. The conclusion reinforces the topic sentence by stressing LMB's inability to prove that it was a low bidder.

Strong topic sentences are essential in a brief's conclusion. Note the forceful topic sentence in the concluding paragraph below:

> *This entire lawsuit is merely Plaintiff's improper attempt to coerce Defendants to solve her landfill problems. In filing and pursuing the suit, both Plaintiff and her counsel blatantly violate Rule II. The City respectfully requests the imposition of sanctions against both Plaintiff and Plaintiff's counsel, for reasonable expenses and attorneys' fees as determined by the Court.*

By characterizing the suit as an "improper attempt to coerce Defendants into assisting her," the writer strongly condemns the plaintiff's actions. Diction such as "clear," "merely," "improper," and "coerce" creates a defensive tone. The topic sentence effectively sets the stage for the rest of the paragraph.

In these two excerpts, the litigators crafted topic sentences that serve different functions. In the first paragraph, the litigator develops the topic sentence in more detail throughout the paragraph. The topic sentence of the second excerpt characterizes the lawsuit. The writer then points to consequences. He names a rule that plaintiff violated, and asks the city for sanctions and attorneys' fees.

Exercise

Analyze the effectiveness of the topic sentence in these paragraphs.

A. In a motion for summary judgment, a litigator asserts that a warranty bars defendant's lost profit counterclaims.

> Each of LMB's counterclaims seeks damages to which LMB is not entitled under the terms of the Warranty. For example, in Count I (Counterclaim ¶ ¶ 9 and 10), LMB seeks consequential damages that the Warranty excludes. Similarly, in Count II, after alleging that Birch Company breached express warranties, LMB seeks $7,200,000 in consequential damages. (Counterclaim ¶ 15). Once again, the Warranty excludes these damages. In Counts III and IV, LMB seeks consequential damages (Counterclaim ¶ ¶ 20 and 25) and alleges that Birch Company breached implied warranties. Count III claims that Birch Company breached the implied warranty of merchantability, and Count IV alleges that Birch Company breached the implied warranty of fitness for an intended purpose. Birch's Warranty, however, expressly disclaimed those warranties by stating:
>
> > THE FOREGOING WARRANTIES ARE IN LIEU OF ALL OTHER WARRANTIES, EXPRESSED OR IMPLIED, INCLUDING BUT NOT LIMITED TO THE IMPLIED WARRANTIES OF MERCHANTABILITY AND FITNESS FOR A PARTICULAR PURPOSE.

B. In a memo of support of a protest of a reasonable compensation issue, an associate argues about the qualifications of a company's two officers.

> Mr. Simon and Mr. Reed have received the Minority Contractor of the Year and Administrators Award for Excellence from the Small Business Administration. SiReed, Inc. also has been recognized as the Minority Business of the Year by the Environmental Protection Agency and has earned the Governor's Minority Business of the Year Award. Moreover, in June Mr. Reed was inducted into the Aston High School Hall of Fame for outstanding achievement and professional excellence.

C. In a brief, a lawyer argues that because the Blake law firm has represented Appellant Ms. Rogers for most of her adult life, Blake should be disqualified from representing Respondents.

> The Blake law firm had long played a role in the affairs of Ms. Rogers and the Silverhood trust. The trust itself was set up with Blake's advice. (Ex. 1000, 4/29 Letter, App. at 2.) Blake advised both Third Trust and Ms. Rogers' father when he resigned as trustee. (Smith, Tr. 4330, App. at 3.) The firm stepped naturally into an advisory role for Ms. Rogers—so much so that Blake itself later said that it had "represented [Ms. Rogers] for most, if not all of her adult life with respect to trust, tax, and personal matters." (Ex. 1311, 7/3 Letter, App. at 1.)

Answers

A. This strong topic sentence asserts that LMB is not entitled to damages under each of its counterclaims. The writer then explains Counts I–IV and why the warranty excludes damages in each count.

B. This weak topic sentence lists two awards. Use a stronger topic sentence:

> Both Mr. Simon and Mr. Reed have been recognized by state and local organizations for their success in managing SiReed, Inc.

C. This strong topic sentence states that Blake has played an important role in Ms. Rogers' business affairs. The writer then describes ways that Blake has represented her during most of her adult life.

7.1.4   Topic Sentences in the Fact Section

Draft strong topic sentences to guide the reader through the fact section of a memo or brief. With this technique, you can move beyond telling the story from beginning to end. Instead, you introduce a framework for the details in each paragraph. Strong topic sentences also influence the reader's response to the story, an important factor in persuasive writing.

7.1.4.1   In Legal Memoranda

A lawyer used strong topic sentences in passage 1 below, taken from the fact section of a legal memorandum. The issue is whether Buxton's potential transfer of assets to a joint venture would constitute a transfer of "all or substantially all" of the corporate assets and thus require shareholder approval. Each topic sentence sets the stage for the details in the paragraph:

1.   *Buxton is an international producer and supplier of numerous high-performance engineered materials. Buxton operates two business segments, the Metals Group and the Electronics Group. The Metals Group produces alloy products in strip and bulk form, beryllium products, and combinations of precious and non-precious metals in continuous strip form. The Electronics Group manufactures precious metal alloys and specialty alloy products.*

As part of its corporate strategy, Buxton is considering whether to enter into a joint venture. The proposed joint venture would focus on selling high-performance alloys in strip form to customers in the telecommunications, computer, and automotive industries. Buxton would sell certain unfinished alloys, including copper beryllium alloys, to the joint venture. The joint venture would complete the pro-duction process.

If it enters into the joint venture, Buxton would retain significant assets but would transfer other assets to the joint venture. The pro-cessing plant for transforming the cake to strip products would be transferred to the joint venture. Buxton would continue to mine, pro-cess, and produce the alloys in cake form. Buxton would retain its ore mining operations, the facilities necessary to process ore and alloys to cake form, its finishing shapes, and its entire Electronics Group.

The writer drafted general topic sentences that guide the reader through details that follow. In the first paragraph, the topic sentence places Buxton in a category of manufacturers before the reader learns about divisions within the business. The second topic sentence introduces the joint venture to prepare the reader for specifics of the plan. In the third paragraph, the topic sentence explains generally about Buxton's retaining and transferring assets before the writer lists specific assets and their owners if Buxton enters into the joint venture.

In paragraph 2, a lawyer also crafted a strong topic sentence to begin the fact section of a legal memorandum:

2.   *The Securities and Exchange Commission has initiated an investi-gation of accounting regularities at Greco, a former subsidiary of Layton. The SEC's investigation focuses on, among other things, Greco's accounting for derivative transactions. Pursuant to that in-vestigation, the SEC has asked Layton to produce all materials in its possession that document its own accounting practices with regard to derivative transactions between January 1 and June 30. Taxco acted as Layton's auditors during this period and approved Layton's Financial Statements. In this role, Taxco contemporaneously created documents responsive to the SEC's request.*

This topic sentence introduces the SEC's investigation of Greco's ac-count practices. The overview prepares the reader for technical informa-tion about the investigation.

7.1.4.2   In Persuasive Writing

Topic sentences in persuasive writing should not only guide the reader, but also anticipate the argument. For example, in paragraph 3, a lawyer crafted a strong topic sentence to "sow the seeds" of her argu-ment. In an appellate brief, she asserts that a judgment against Chemco, manufacturer of Zappo insecticide, should be reversed. Before she argues that the owner's negligence caused the death of a prize bull, she tells the story of spraying the bull with Zappo:

> 3. *Foreman Mason instructed two illegal aliens, neither of whom read or spoke English, to do the spraying.* These men had been employed by Red Ranch for only three or four weeks, and neither Smith, Red Ranch's owner, nor Mason knew their names. Smith testified that he had hired them without inquiring into their backgrounds or previous work history, asserting: "I don't think I really cared, at the time." Neither had ever before sprayed for flies. Mason instructed these two totally unqualified employees to mix the Zappo in a hand sprayer and testified that he directed them to spray the pens, but not the bulls. (Citations omitted.)

Although the topic sentence above is objective in tone, it subtly anticipates the litigator's argument. By referring to the workers as "illegal aliens," the writer states that they and the ranch's owner acted surreptitiously and in blatant disregard of immigration laws. Moreover, the phrase "neither of whom read or spoke English" implies that the workers would not fully understand their boss's instructions. In addition, the writer casts doubt on the foreman's judgment. He knew, or should have known, that his workers did not speak English. Yet he gave them oral instructions in English about how to apply a poisonous product near valuable animals.

Later in the same fact section, the writer crafted another strong topic sentence to anticipate the negligence argument:

> 4. *Smith's witness Dr. Roberts and Chemco's witness Dr. Colt agreed that Plaintiff's bull died as a result of being overdosed with Zappo, an overdose that may have exceeded fifty-eight times the maximum recommended dose, assuming it was diluted at all.* There is no evidence that Chemco would have had any adverse effect on the bull if Red Ranch's employees had followed their instructions to spray only the pens and not the bull itself, or if any application to the bull had been limited to a fine mist spray of one to two fluid ounces of a 1 percent solution, as instructed by the label for direct application to cattle.

Repetition in "overdose" and "overdosed," and the phrase "fifty-eight times the maximum recommended dose" point to negligence of the Red Ranch's owner, not Chemco, as proximate cause of the bull's death.

Exercise

Analyze the effectiveness of the topic sentence in the paragraph below.

In the defendants' motion for summary judgment based on the plaintiff's deposition testimony, a lawyer argues that the plaintiff was fired because he failed to perform in a competent manner. The paragraph below appears in the middle of the fact section.

> Mr. Smith went on vacation for two weeks on June 15. Smith Dep. at 245. During that time, Ms. Collins learned that Smith had been calling people such as Brown, complaining about Elwood and seeking assurances about his job. Interrogatory Response 3. Smith, in short, had become a disruptive influence. Ms. Collins, who believed that Smith should have been terminated earlier, planned to terminate him when he returned to the factory on July 1. Interrogatory Response 3.

Answer

This weak topic sentence focuses on Smith's vacation. Use a stronger topic sentence:

> Ms. Collins decided to terminate Smith when she learned that he had become a disruptive influence.

7.1.5 The Topic Sentence Test

As you revise, test your topic sentences. First, create a new last page of the document. Next, copy the first sentence in each paragraph, in order, onto the last page. Add more pages if necessary. Then trace the overall logical development of your analysis or argument. Revise the topic sentences as needed so that each one creates a conceptual link in logical development.

While editing a motion for summary judgment, the writer applied the topic sentence test, as shown in 1(a):

1(a)   *Plaintiff's Harassment Claims under Title VII and Ohio Rev. Code § 4112.01 Fail as a Matter of Law.*

- *Carroll Enterprises cannot be held vicariously liable under Title VII for any alleged harassment of Jones by Mr. Roberts.*

- *When an employer is not given notice, or when an employer has an adequate and effective harassment policy, the employer is not liable under Title VII.*

- *Ohio's discrimination law, Ohio Rev. Code § 4112, follows federal Title VII law.*

- *In this case, Carroll did have a strong anti-harassment policy.*

- *It is doubtful that an employer could do more than Carroll Enterprises has done.*

- *Carroll Enterprises is entitled to judgment on both state and federal harassment claims as a matter of law.*

Without additional context, you can follow each step of the argument in these strong topic sentences.

Furthermore, each point corresponds to part of the law school writing formula IRAC, which stands for "Issue, Rule, Application, Conclusion":

1(a)　*Plaintiff's Harassment Claims under Title VII and Ohio Rev. Code § 4112.01 Fail as a Matter of Law.*

- *Carroll Enterprises cannot be held vicariously liable under Title VII for any alleged harassment of Jones by Mr. Roberts.* **(Issue converted to conclusion)**

- *When an employer is not given notice, or when an employer has an adequate and effective harassment policy, the employer is not liable under Title VII.* **(Rule—Federal)**

- *Ohio's discrimination law, Ohio Rev. Code § 4112, follows federal Title VII law.* **(Rule—Relation of state law to federal law)**

- *In this case, Carroll did have a strong anti-harassment policy.* **(Application)**

- *It is doubtful that an employer could do more than Carroll Enterprises has done.* **(Application and conclusion)**

- *Carroll Enterprises is entitled to judgment on both state and federal harassment claims as a matter of law.* **(Conclusion)**

The topic sentences in passage 2, also from a motion for summary judgment, do not create conceptual links between paragraphs:

2.　*Plaintiff Alleges No Facts That Would Establish an Improper Relationship between Axco and the Arbitrator.*

- *Plaintiff suggests that he would have objected to the arbitrator had he known that Thomas Fox, an officer of Axco Corporation, is Chairman of BAB's Large, Complex Case Council.*

- *Plaintiff does not allege that the arbitrator, Mr. White, has any relationship with Axco or the committee in question.*

- *In essence, Plaintiff claims that this case should have been considered large and complex, and if it were treated as such, Mr. Fox's council chairmanship would disqualify Mr. White.*

Readers will have difficulty understanding the argument's development from these topic sentences. Create conceptual links between them to strengthen the argument.

7.1.6   Topic Sentence Length

Use short topic sentences to launch each paragraph. If you cram too much information into the first sentence, it may trip up the reader:

1(a)   *In fact, in light of the purpose of the Alternative Mortgage Transaction Parity Act of 1982, which was to eliminate discriminatory impacts on nonfederally chartered institutions due to existing state and federal regulation of alternative mortgage transactions, applying the Illinois Interest Act to the Hunter line of credit would be an obstacle to fully implementing the AMTPA.*

This complicated sentence contains two introductory phrases, a long "which" clause, and an independent clause. To create a stronger beginning for the paragraph, divide the topic sentence:

1(b)   *In fact, applying the Illinois Interest Act to the Hunter line of credit would be an obstacle to fully implementing the Alternative Mortgage Transaction Parity Act of 1982 ("AMTPA"). The purpose of the AMPTA was to eliminate discriminatory impacts on nonfederally chartered institutions due to existing state and federal regulation of alternative mortgage transactions.*

Short topic sentences are more persuasive than long ones. Note the topic sentence below from a post-hearing memorandum:

2(a)   *As acknowledged by Thomas Princeton, Acting Director of the NHTSA's Office of Defects Investigation and overall supervision of the survey (Princeton Hng. Tr., p. 321), the agency action sought to be reviewed here, the NHTSA's conduct of this survey in alleged violation of the Federal Reports Act and governing OMB directives, is final and complete (Princeton Dep., p. 127):*

Q: Is the survey now complete?

A: Yes.

This topic sentence is convoluted and extremely long. The litigator skill-fully uses deposition material but buries it at the end of the sentence. For a more forceful beginning, draft a shorter topic sentence:

> 2(b)   *Even an NHTSA Director admits that the agency's survey is complete.*

Then continue with the details of the deposition:

> 2(c)   *Thomas Princeton, Acting Director of the NHTSA's Office of Defects Investigation and overall supervision of the survey (Princeton Hng. Tr., p. 321), stated that the agency action sought to be received here, the NHTSA's conduct of this survey in alleged violation of the Federal Reports Act and governing OMB directors, is final and complete (Princeton Dep., p. 127):*
>
> *Q: Is the survey now complete?*
>
> *A: Yes.*

Use short topic sentences to begin an argument. In a lawsuit concerning the time of release of retained monies, an attorney began a reply brief in this way:

> 3.   *This case arises out of a construction contract. On October 15, Plaintiff Blackstone Ventures contracted with Defendant Bowen County, Kansas to construct an expanded wastewater treatment plant at the site of the existing plant. The construction contract identified Park as the engineer on the project.*

This chatty topic sentence simply states the dispute's origin. The lawyer establishes a context before presenting the numerous details of parties' names, dates, locations, and actions.

In the summary of argument in the same brief, the writer used an even shorter, more direct topic sentence:

> 4.   *Plaintiff is wrong. Section 13-10-2(b)(2)(C), upon which Plaintiff relies, specifically provides for release of retainage "at substantial completion of the work or such other standard of completion as may be provided in the contract documents. . . ." The Construction Contract provides for release of all retainage at final completion of all work. But Plaintiff fails to quote the above highlighted statutory language. When Bowen County brought this omission to the*

Court's attention, Plaintiff simply ignored it. Nevertheless, when the two statutes and the Construction Contract are quoted in full, § 13-10-2 is consistent with § 13-10-20, and the Construction Contract accords with each. Finally, Plaintiff attempts to fashion a question of fact where none exists by ignoring plain language again. Plaintiff argues that the parties somehow intended to release retainage at substantial completion of Phase I and Phase II. The Construction Contract belies this argument; the contract clearly provides for the release of retainage upon final completion of all "the work."

The terse topic sentence, "Plaintiff is wrong," focuses the reader's attention on the lawyer's most important point. Before presenting more information, the writer shapes the reader's perception of the plaintiff's argument. No modifiers complement the subject-verb-complement structure. The litigator characterizes the plaintiff's argument in an aggressive, straightforward way.

7.2 One-Sentence Paragraphs

By definition, a paragraph is a group of sentences that develop one idea in depth. Most paragraphs should begin with a topic sentence, develop one unit of thought, and end with a strong concluding sentence. Although a one-sentence concluding paragraph can be effective in persuasive writing, use this structure sparingly and only after careful consideration of context.

Divide long sentences that look like paragraphs. For example, in a memo about the Illinois statute of limitations' application in latent injury tort actions, an attorney wrote paragraph 1(a):

1(a)   *The difficulty that split the court in* Ravin *also arises in our case; in the procedural posture of a summary judgment motion, all material facts underlying the conclusion that the plaintiff possesses sufficient information must be uncontested, and the only reasonable conclusion that may be drawn from those uncontested material facts is that plaintiff knew or should have known about her injury and its wrongful cause.*

The content of this paragraph is coherent and logical. The writer begins with a general topic, states the rule, and applies it to the client's situation. But the paragraph is compressed into one rambling sentence. As it runs on and on, each point blends with others. This structure undercuts the power of the lawyer's strong language. Divide paragraph 1(a) into three sentences:

> 1(b)   *The difficulty that split the court in* Ravin *also arises in our case. In the procedural posture of a summary judgment motion, all material facts underlying the conclusion that the plaintiff possesses sufficient information must be uncontested. The only reasonable conclusion that may be drawn from those uncontested material facts is that plaintiff knew or should have known about her injury and its wrongful cause.*

If a paragraph consists of only one short sentence, analyze whether it belongs in the previous paragraph or in the next one. Note the second paragraph in passage 2 from a memo concerning jurisdiction over trademark and unfair competition claims brought under the Lanham Act:

> 2.   Steel v. Bulova Watch Co. *establishes a strong precedent regarding the claims we brought under § 1125(a) and (b) of the Lanham Act.*
>
> > *[Cite and long discussion about facts and the court's reasoning; discussion continues in a second long paragraph.]*
>
> > Bulova *held that "the Lanham Act revealed a Congressional intent to exercise its power to the fullest."*
>
> > *In fact,* Bulova *was recently cited in our particular court.*
> > *[Discussion of case that cited* Bulova.*]*

As you revise a one-sentence paragraph, analyze logical development in the section. In passage 2, the writer first introduces *Steel v. Bulova Watch Co.*, an important case for the consideration of claims brought under the Lanham Act. A long discussion of the facts and the court's reasoning follows. In the next paragraph, the lawyer included only one sentence, which quotes *Bulova's* analysis of the Lanham Act. The next paragraph begins a new topic concerning *Bulova*, i.e., its use in a recent case.

Next, determine where the one-sentence paragraph belongs. The quotation in the second paragraph in passage 2 characterizes the Lanham Act, linking the sentence with material in the first paragraph. Integrate this statement from the court's holding into the discussion of *Bulova*. Don't present the quotation alone as an afterthought.

7.3 Persuasive Concluding Sentences

As you draft each paragraph of an argument, plan a strong concluding sentence. Do not let your paragraphs trail off. Instead, shape their endings to reinforce your point.

A short summary sentence can be effective to conclude a brief's final paragraph. Begin with assertions and build a dramatic argument. Then draft a concise final sentence. Show the reader how to interpret that argument. End quietly, but firmly, as you persuade the reader that there is only one viable outcome in the case.

A litigator used this technique to defend the manufacturer of a drain cleaner that appealed a judgment of $1.62 million. The plaintiffs were a minor who suffered burns, allegedly from contact with the drain cleaner, and her mother.

In one section of the brief, the attorney argues that the father was a responsible adult who was aware of the danger and whose subsequent negligence was the sole proximate cause of the child's injury. The writer (1) establishes that the father read the warnings on the drain cleaner's label, (2) states the warnings, and (3) describes the father's negligent actions. Note the section's final paragraph below:

1.   *When the actions of the father are compared to the standard of law set out by the Ohio courts, it is apparent that the negligence of the father was the sole proximate cause of any injury suffered by the child. The Ohio Supreme Court articulated the following standard in* Thrash v. U-Drive-It Co., *158 Ohio St. 465, 110 N.E.D. 419 (1953):*

> *Where there intervenes between an agency creating a hazard another conscious and responsible agency that could or should have eliminated the hazard, the original agency is relieved from liability. A break in the chain of causation thereby takes place which operates to absolve the original agency.*

It is beyond question that the father was such a responsible agency. He could have totally eliminated the hazard by:

1.   *Leaving the child on the first floor in the care of another of the adults present, including the mother; or by*

2.   *Closing the bathroom door; or by*

3.   *Replacing the cap on the product after using it; or by*

4.   *Observing the entry of the child into the bathroom and removing her; or by*

5.   *Placing the container in a secure position and by conducting himself in such a manner that he would not knock the container to the floor.*

His failure to do any of these things was the sole proximate cause of any injury suffered by the child.

The litigator carefully crafted this paragraph to conclude the section. The topic sentence states that a comparison of the father's actions and the Ohio standard points to the father's negligence. Next, the lawyer sets forth the standard. After asserting that the father was a responsible agency, the writer lists simple actions that the father could have performed to prevent the accident. Each obvious task is followed by "or by," a phrase that creates a sense of the father's many options. As the alternative actions accumulate, the reader wonders why the father did not perform any of these simple tasks. After convincing the reader how easily the father could have prevented the accident, the litigator concludes with a short sentence:

His failure to do any of these things was the sole proximate cause of any injury suffered by the child.

The direct final sentence contrasts with the long, dramatic list of actions the father could have performed to prevent the injury. This writer does not use complicated diction, metaphor, or strong language to conclude. Instead, he demonstrates a fine sense of the argument's rhythm by using a short, simple assertion to end the paragraph.

In a bitter case, a litigator also concluded a brief with short summary sentences:

2.   *Against this factual recitation, the true frivolity of Battle's fraud charge can be appreciated. It was a cynical move, born of desperation, with no foundation in fact. The charge has taken on color only because of Battle's remarkable persistence, which has produced a mass of testimony, notes, memoranda, and other documents that, when assembled, inevitably (human nature being what it is) show unreconciled differences, a hiatus or two, a few ambiguous phrases, etc. With these paltry reeds, by use of innuendos, half-truths, and irresponsible charges, Battle has woven an airy basket argued to contain fraud. In fact, it contains nothing. There is no fraud.*

The concluding statements contrast sharply with other sentences in the paragraph. The litigator begins with two short, accusatory sentences that characterize the fraud charge. Then sentences become longer, more complicated, and more dramatic. The argument reaches its most powerful point in the image of the airy basket representing Battle's fraud charge. After that metaphor, the litigator changes the tone. Two concluding sentences are short and direct:

> *In fact, it contains nothing. There is no fraud.*

Earlier flowery diction gives way to short, simple words. The writer judges and dismisses Battle's argument in these final sentences.

The next paragraph is unorthodox in structure, yet effective. Maintaining the tone established earlier, the litigator concludes:

> *There is no merit in Battle's motion. It should be denied.*

Like the previous paragraph, the brief ends with short sentences that summarize the argument.

Glossary

active voice   The verb form used when the actor precedes a transitive verb and performs its action.

adjective   A part of speech that describes a noun or pronoun.

adverb   A part of speech that modifies a verb, an adjective, or another adverb. Adverbs explain where, when, or how.

adverbial clause   A clause that functions as an adverb.

antecedent   The intended noun referent for a pronoun. The antecedent should be the noun that directly precedes the pronoun that agrees with it in gender and number.

antithesis   A contrast expressed in two elements.

appositive   A noun that stands next to another noun to identify it, explain it, or supplement its meaning.

clause   A group of related words that contains both a subject and a predicate.

collective noun   A noun that refers to a group but is grammatically singular.

colloquial adverb   An adverb that takes on a new, informal usage.

comma splice   Two independent clauses linked with only a comma.

complement   A noun or adjective that completes the subject.

complementary infinitive   An infinitive phrase that completes the action of the main verb.

complex sentence   A sentence that consists of one independent clause and one or more dependent clauses.

compound predicate   Two or more predicates with the same subject.

compound sentence   Two independent clauses linked with a coordinating conjunction.

conjunctive adverb   A word that serves as an adverb and a connective.

coordinating conjunction   A connective such as "and," "but," "or," "nor," "for," "so," or "yet."

dangling modifier   A phrase or clause that does not refer to its intended subject.

demonstrative pronoun   A pronoun such as "this," "that," "these," or "those."

diction   Word choice.

direct object A noun or pronoun that receives the action of a verb in the active voice.

extra stepping An unnecessary description of a writer's perceptual processes.

fragment An incomplete sentence.

gerund A verbal that functions as a noun. To form a gerund, add "-ing" to the present tense of a verb.

hidden verb A verb contained in a multisyllabic noun.

impersonal expression A wordy structure consisting of (1) "it" followed by "to be" and an adjective, or (2) "there" followed by "to be."

indefinite pronoun A pronoun such as "each," "either," "neither," "one," "everybody," or "anyone."

independent clause A clause that can stand alone as a complete sentence.

indicative mood Verb forms used to express statements and questions.

indirect object A noun or pronoun indicating to whom or for whom something is done.

infinitive A verbal that functions as a noun. To form an infinitive, insert "to" before the present tense of a verb.

intensive pronoun A pronoun that follows and emphasizes the noun to which it refers.

introductory element An adverb, phrase, or clause that precedes a main clause.

Latinate diction Multisyllabic, abstract words derived from Latin and Greek.

litotes An understatement for effect, in which something is expressed by negating its opposite.

main clause An independent clause modified by a dependent clause.

metaphorical language Language comparing two unlike things that have a common connection.

modifier A word or group of words that explains, describes, or qualifies another.

nonrestrictive adverbial clause An adverbial clause that adds extra information in a by-the-way fashion about a precisely identified term.

nonrestrictive appositive An appositive that adds extra information in a by-the-way fashion about a precisely identified noun.

nonrestrictive clause A relative clause that adds extra information in a by-the-way fashion about a precisely identified noun.

GLOSSARY

nonrestrictive phrase A phrase that adds extra information in a by-the-way fashion about a precisely identified noun.

noun A part of speech that names a person, place, or thing.

noun phrase A phrase that consists of a noun and its modifiers.

objective pronoun A pronoun that functions as direct object, indirect object, or object of a preposition.

overblown rhetoric Language that is shrill and exaggerated.

parallel structure Use of the same grammatical structure in elements of a comparison, contrast, or series.

participial phrase A phrase consisting of a participle and its modifiers.

participle A verbal that serves as part of a verb phrase or as an adjective.

passive voice The verb form used when the receiver precedes a transitive verb and receives its action. A passive verb consists of a form of "to be" followed by the past participle.

past participle A participle that indicates a past state. To form the past participle for a regular verb, add "-ed" to the present tense.

phrase A sequence of grammatically related words without a subject and a predicate.

predicate A verb or verb phrase, including any modifiers or complements.

preposition A part of speech that links and relates its object to another word in a sentence.

prepositional phrase A phrase that contains a preposition and its object.

present participle A participle that indicates a present state. To form a present participle, add "-ing" to the present tense of the verb.

reflexive pronoun A pronoun that appears in the predicate and refers to the sentence's subject.

relative clause A dependent clause that serves as an adjective and begins with "who," "whom," "whose," "which," or "that."

restrictive adverbial clause An adverbial clause that establishes an essential condition for the action or state of being expressed by the modified term.

restrictive appositive An appositive that creates a subcategory of a general noun.

restrictive clause A relative clause that creates a subcategory of a general noun.

restrictive phrase A phrase that creates a subcategory of a general noun.

sentence modifier An adverbial phrase that modifies or explains the rest of the sentence.

simple sentence A sentence consisting of one independent clause.

state-of-being verb A verb, such as "to be," "to seem," or "to appear," that expresses a state of being.

subject A noun, pronoun, or verbal about which something is asserted in the predicate.

subjective pronoun A pronoun that functions as subject or complement.

subjunctive mood Verb forms used in contrary-to-fact clauses, clauses after "urge-demand" verbs, and other specialized usages.

subordinate (dependent) clause A clause that cannot stand alone as a sentence.

subordinating conjunction A connective that introduces an adverbial clause.

syntax Word order or arrangement in a sentence.

throat clearing A wordy introduction.

transition A word or phrase that relates ideas by linking sentences or paragraphs.

transitive verb A verb that can take an object.

verb phrase A phrase that consists of a main verb and any helping verb.

verb A part of speech that expresses an action or a state of being.

verbal A verb form used as a noun or an adjective. Verbals include infinitives, participles, and gerunds.

Index

INDEX

Conjunctive adverbs, 66, 80, 84, 148, 199, 203–6, 214, 220

Connectives
  causal
    See Causal connectives
  See Conjunctions

Context, 46–47, 130
  accuracy and, 131–32
  topic sentences and, 110

Contractions and apostrophes, 223

Contrary-to-fact clauses, 192

Contrasting
  elements, 67–68
  structures, 12–13, 234
  terms, 62–64
  tone, 95

Convoluted subject-complement match, 27

Coordinating conjunctions, 14, 72, 144, 195, 197–98

D

"Danglers," 46
  adverbial clauses, 190–91
  gerund phrases, 188–89, 157–60
  infinitive phrases, 160, 189–90
  modifiers as, 183–91, 198
  participles, 184

Dashes
  See Punctuation

Definitions, structure of, 28

Demonstrative pronouns, 168–69

Dense prose, 53, 89

Dependent (subordinate) clauses, causal, 149

Diction, 89
  word choice and tone, 46–48, 89, 122–23

Dividing long sentences
  See Sentences

Drafts
  final, 240–42
  first, 231, 235–36
  second, 237–39
  See also Writing Process

E

Elements, contrasting, 67–68

Eliminating
  actor/agent, 102
  impersonal expressions, 34–35
  monotony, 13–14, 103, 128
  redundancy, 33–34, 39, 37
  repetition, 13, 29, 31, 128–30, 254
  wordiness, 30–33, 42, 44
  writer's block, 227

Expressions, shortening without changing meaning, 34–36

"Extra stepping," 44–45

F

Fact sections.
  See Stating facts

Final draft, crafting, 240–42

First draft, 231, 235–36
  revising, 235–36
  See also Prewriting

Flair, writing with, 117–41

"For," 80–81

Fragments, sentence, 72, 76, 79–80

G

Gerund phrases, 157–58
  dangling, 188–89
  possessive form for subject, 157–59

Good legal writing defined, 1

Grammar, 143–94, 235

Grammatical structure, 57–58

INDEX

Y

Advance Praise for *Legal Writing*: *Form and Function*

"Jane Richmond's book is the best cure around for lawyers' tendency to tie themselves—and their readers—into linguistic knots when they write about complex legal topics. It proves that we can write clean, crisp sentences about even the most complicated subjects, and shows us how, step by step. For those who care about the craft of legal writing, this book is indispensable."

> ～ Stephen Armstrong
> Director of Career Development
> Wilmer, Cutler & Pickering

"This book is a gem. It is lucid, concrete, and comprehensive. It should be of value to both experienced as well as novice lawyers."

> ～ Robert P. Lawry
> Professor of Law
> Director, Center for Professional Ethics
> Case Western Reserve University
> School of Law

"I now have seven reference works on my desk: *The Chicago Manual of Style*, Fowler's *Modern English Usage*, *The Elements of Style*, *The Compact Oxford English Dictionary*, *Webster's New Dictionary of Synonyms*, *Roget's Thesarus*, and Jane Richmond's *Legal Writing: Form and Function*. After perusing the last, I predict that it too, will soon be missing its cover."

> ～ Gary Kinder
> Kinder Legal
> CLE Writing Instructor and
> best-selling investigative journalist